freebie.robloxiakid.com/r

DIARY OF A ROBLOX NOOB
The Complete Series

ROBLOXIA KID

Contents

3 BONUS STORIES

My dearest fans
and reviewers:

YTAHA
Coolalto940
Diamondminer168
Dragonfire
Tobi Salami
Ellen Henry
Natalija F.
JV

THANK YOU!!!

UNOFFICIAL

GRANNY

BOOK 1
ROBLOXIA KID

Prologue

A Bear Trap in More Ways Than One.

When faced with your imminent end, a lot of things can run through your mind. Good thoughts, bad thoughts, crazy thoughts... a lot of random thoughts can pop up. I guess that's just the way it is. I mean, when you're at the edge and about to die, what else can you do?

So, there I was, the strong bear trap clamped firmly onto my leg. Its large metal claws had popped up out of nowhere. Let me tell you now, it felt beyond painful; I can't describe just how agonizing it was. Imagine the feeling of falling down a flight of stairs that's full of Lego bricks, then landing on a trampoline with even more Lego bricks, all while it's raining Lego bricks. That seems about right.

Anyway, the metal clamps bit into these short and blocky

legs of mine, and I was going nowhere.

"Argh! I can't move! Help! Help!"

I called out for help, but none of my friends answered. I tried to move my leg, but the bear trap just bit more firmly into it. The room was so dark that I had walked right into Granny's infamous bear trap without realizing. I had heard stories of how players sucked into Granny's home ran into one of these things and got stuck, eventually meeting their end. Despite such tales, I never could have imagined just how dreadful this actually was. I was now experiencing the trap first-hand, and believe me, it was not fun.

There was no way I was moving from that spot. Just when I thought things couldn't get any worse I suddenly heard a low growl from a short distance in front of me. The growl didn't sound welcoming at all.

The room I had entered had been dimly-lit, its darkness concealing the bear trap. Now, I was starting to realize that there was more than just the bear trap to worry about. I looked straight ahead, and saw two red eyes staring back at me from the darkness. I didn't think things could get worse after getting stuck in a bear trap *and* desperately needing to use the toilet.

"Uh oh."

Slowly, the animal emerged from the darkness. I could see it a lot clearer now, and I realized what it was. It was a large bear. The bear was huge in stature, but it was actually pretty thin. It reminded me of my older sister a little. I could see its ribs sticking out from its fur. Its mouth was frothing, dripping with saliva, and it was staring right at me. This animal had not eaten for a long time, and I was its next meal.

The bear was looking right at me now and I could hear its stomach growl with anticipation. My leg was still held painfully in place by the bear trap. Yup, this was not good. In fact, it was probably one of the scariest situations I had ever found myself in. Scarier than the time I forgot to buy my mother a gift on Mother's Day.

"Nice bear. Nice bear. You wouldn't want to eat me. There are a lot of high-level Roblox players out there. They're fatter, have a lot more meat, and would taste a lot better too. And..."

The bear cut me short as it snarled and growled at me. It flashed its claws towards me, and I could see just how sharp they were. Images of being cut up and chewed up by that thing ran quickly through my head, and I screamed out desperately for help.

"No, no! Help! Decks! Dan! Tina! Anyone! Help me!"

That was when the bear rushed towards me, its claws and teeth exposed. I heard its deafening growl and I closed my eyes. I knew that I was done for now.

Suddenly, everything seemed to be happening in slow motion. The bear was still rushing right at me, but it seemed to be slowing to a crawl. My thoughts all played out in front of me, and the one thing that I kept repeating in my head was:

"How did I get into this mess?"

Entry #1

The Mysterious House

Okay, where do I start? Well, first of all, this was definitely one of the wackiest and most off-the-wall games I had ever played in Roblox. And that's saying a lot. I've played more than my fair share of games and I've seen all kinds of stuff, from the weird to the wild to everything in between. That being said, I'd never played anything like Granny, which was, without a doubt, the creepiest and nuttiest game in Roblox. Oh, and did I mention the scariest? Well, what can I say? I didn't even want to play it. The game just sucked me and a bunch of other players into it, and that's where our story and my scariest ever diary begins. Welcome to Noob's diary in Granny!

So how did I end up playing Granny? Well, that's the thing: I didn't really want to play Granny at all. I had heard scary stories about this game in Roblox, a server that was unlike any other. While other servers were cities or even worlds that were larger than life, I'd heard that Granny was nothing more than a house.

Yeah, it was a big house all right, but I'd heard that the size only made it scarier. That's because the house was so big that players regularly got lost and never returned once they were inside the huge, creepy place. I'd also heard about players getting sucked into the house for no reason. Apparently, the house was drawing players into itself like some kind of vacuum cleaner or black hole. No one really knew what type of force was at fault, but it was there, and it was doing its dirty work.

Like all bad news you hear, I didn't really pay much attention to any of it. I certainly never thought it would happen to me. No way! I just kept on living my life and chilling, not knowing that Granny would eventually suck me in, and I would find myself right in the middle of all of it. Then again, isn't that always the story of my little Roblox life?

I was in the middle of playing Mad City when it happened. Yeah, Mad City was another pretty crazy server at Roblox. I had heard about how there were a lot of gangs in Mad City that were always at odds with the cops. Shootouts, robberies, all of that was pretty common stuff for Mad City. So why would I even think of playing in that server, you ask? Well, that's just me. I am a rebel at heart. I once forgot to do my homework and told my teacher that the dog ate it. I don't even own a dog. But for games, I just love to play anything dangerous. That's just the Noobster for you. I live for action and adventure! Aaaand, I often get what I want. In spades.

"All right, rookie. So, it's your first day at Mad City! What do you expect?"

I enlisted at the Mad City police department to get some action going. Yeah, I know it was a pretty crazy idea trying to be a cop, especially in Mad City of all places! My partner, Kenny, liked to chat a lot, and he always had two things with him: his pistol and a doughnut. He often had both in each hand, which meant that he was an awful driver.

It was my first routine patrol and Kenny was driving the squad car while I sat beside him. I had no idea how the car could support both of us: Kenny was a heavyweight of sorts, and it showed with his round belly. His belly was so big that you could serve Christmas dinner on it.

"It's Noob, not rookie."

Kenny laughed.

"Same thing to me. Want some doughnut?"

Kenny offered me a bite of his half-bitten doughnut. I could see the grease, chocolate and custard filling dripping down the sides. Kenny was getting a lot of grease on his hand as he held that half-eaten thing. He was the expert on doughnuts, maybe in a past life he was one. It was anything but appetizing. Of course, I declined.

"Uh, no thanks! I'll pass on that."

Kenny shrugged his shoulders. He probably didn't even want to share the doughnut.

"Hey, food is food. You're going to need a lot of food to get through Mad City, believe me."

I thought that was an odd thing to say. I guess Kenny ate to pass the time when there wasn't a crime. The man was practically a human bin.

That was when we heard a shot ring out.

"There you go! Just what I was talking about. There's never a dull moment in this town, kid!"

"That sounded pretty close by."

"I think it came from the hardware store at the corner of

the block."

Kenny had an unusual radar-type sense for these things. We turned the corner and saw two perps holding up the hardware store, just like Kenny had said.

"Whoa! How did you know it was here?"

"You get used to these things when you've worked here as long as I have. And a doughnut helps. A lot."

I would have to take Kenny's advice a little more seriously. We stepped out of the car and packed our guns; it was time to get to work. Kenny quickly shoved the rest of the doughnut into his mouth like a starved pelican.

"Mad City police! Drop your weapons! Come out the store with your hands up!"

I shouted at the perps with as much authority and intimidation as I could muster. I sounded confident, but I was shaking in my boots. I was so nervous that I even farted.

"We ain't coming outside for no coppers!"

Well, so much for negotiations. The perps were crouching behind the front desk of the hardware store. I wasn't sure if the owner had been shot or not.

Kenny and I stood outside the store. Using the corner wall for cover, we waited, ready for anything.

"This looks bad. Stay sharp," Kenny ordered.

The perps started firing first. Safe behind our cover, the bullets flew right past us, but we couldn't stay there forever. We had to make a move.

I stepped out from behind the wall and fired a few shots back. Their bullets came a lot closer to me than I wanted them to.

"Are you trying to get yourself killed? Those perps are playing for keeps! Stay covered. Those perps look real serious. I'll dash back to the car and radio for some backup. I think we'll need it."

I heard Kenny, but I couldn't just stand there and do nothing while they pinned us down. Well, actually I probably could have but I was just too cocky. A veteran cop in one of the most notorious cities in Roblox, Kenny gave great advice. Advice that I definitely should have listened to, but I didn't. Maybe I should have tried that doughnut after all...

I stepped out from my cover, and tried to fire again. I figured I could take on these perps, and get some kind of citation. Just imagine! A new cop at Mad City stopping a robbery. I would be a hero! I would be famous! I would get a million girlfriends! Or a million Robux. Either one would suit me fine.

Yeah, keep dreaming, Noob. This time, I paid for my brashness. I felt the shot hit me, knocking me backwards.

I lost consciousness and everything went black. The last thing I heard was Kenny. I heard him talking to me, but it was too late.

"What did you do, Noob? I told you to stay in cover!"

Yeah, those were the last things I heard before the darkness closed in on me, like a pair of dark hands covering my eyes. I didn't expect to wake up after that. I figured I was done for, and I had no one to blame but myself...

I woke up with a major headache. My head felt like someone had played several games of soccer with it and I could barely get up. This was like taking a bath with Lego bricks. Somehow, I managed to open my eyes and take a look around me.

"Ouch! My head! What happened? Wait, I remember! I just got shot! I'm supposed to be outside the hardware store. Where am I?"

I looked around at my surroundings. I definitely wasn't outside the hardware store anymore. Instead, I was inside what appeared to be an old, rotting house. The paint on the walls was peeling off, and the floorboards looked so unstable and creaky that I was reluctant to stand on them. There were cobwebs everywhere and I thought I would choke with all the dust in the air. On the opposite wall, a pair of shattered windows were boarded up, and the bulb above us flickered on and off, barely giving out any light. What kind of place was this?

There were several other players in the room too. Like me, they were all just waking up. One of them was even pretty famous. I had seen him play in several servers and he often liked to post vids about his game experiences.

"Danny SN? Is that you? What are you doing here?"

"Hey, aren't you Noob?"

It was Danny. He actually recognized me! Despite meeting in such a scary situation, I found that very cool. I was really surprised that a famous Roblox-er like Danny SN knew me. For a moment, all my confusion and tension vanished.

"Whoa! You recognize me? I mean, you're Danny SN!"

"And you're Noob! I mean, I played a few servers you were in. I actually bumped into you before and I've got to say I liked what I saw back then."

I was happy to see that Danny was a cool and nice guy. It was wonderful that he knew and remembered me. This was better than Christmas and my birthday combined.

"Gee, thanks, Danny! I'm surprised you even remember me."

"I try to make a point of remembering every player I play with. After all, we're all really just trying to have fun, right?"

"Sorry to disappoint you, guys, but I don't think we're going to have fun here. I'm pretty sure this is Granny's house!

One of the other players in the house spoke up. She sounded really scared, and I couldn't blame her. After all, this was Granny; none of us wanted to be here or to face her. Granny was more terrifying than a bear with five shark heads.

"Casey's right! We were sucked into this place by Granny! Man, I've heard about players getting sucked into this game and never coming back. I heard she just sucks players from their servers at random and brings them over to her place here. I never thought that I would actually become one of those victims. I'm Decks, by the way."

"Nice to meet you guys. I'm Noob. I'm a cop at Mad City. I was actually trying to stop a hardware store robbery when I got shot and ended up here. Hang on a minute! I was shot! I was shot! Why am I not shot anymore?"

"I hear Granny has all sorts of crazy powers. Your wound must have healed when you got sucked in here. Unfortunately, Granny's crazy, and she's going to do a lot more than just shoot you."

Do more than shoot me? Oh no, I don't know what could be worse than that. Maybe Granny will hug me to death or insult my ability to play computer games (which is much worse than death). That was when we saw a huge figure dart out from the corner of the room. The figure was dark, and I couldn't make out who, or what, it was. I instinctively reached for my gun on my hip. My hand fumbled around but found nothing.

"What is that thing?"

"I don't know! But someone's got to do something! You're a cop, Noob! Shoot it!" Danny ordered.

"I would if I had my gun! It's gone!"

We all thought that it was Granny, and that she was going to cut us up, or worse. Nothing of the sort happened.

"Will you guys get a grip? It's nothing! Just a spider," Decks said.

Decks was right. It was just a spider darting from one cobweb to another. The dim and flickering light cast it with a huge shadow, making it look massive for a moment. I mean Granny could possibly swing from cobwebs too, it seemed like anything was possible with her.

Decks sounded really calm and level-headed. With an attitude like that, he would have made a better cop than I did in Mad City.

"No need to scare the cop, Casey. We were all minding our own business until Granny came and dragged us here. We have to find a way out!" Decks said.

"That's going to be a lot easier said than done, Decks. I've heard that this house may seem small on the outside, but it's a lot larger than it looks on the inside. A lot of players have found themselves lost in Granny's place, never to return again."

"Don't remind us all, Dan. We all know that this is a pretty bad situation. We just have to stay positive and try to find a way to get out of here," Casey replied.

Casey was right. It was bad. What we didn't know at that point though was that it was about to get a whole lot worse.

"Well, we all agree that we have to get out of this house. The question is, how are we going to do that when we can't get out of this room?"

Dan was right. We were locked in. Just as we were discussing the problem, however, we heard a clicking sound and the door slowly opened. We looked at each other with confusion and suspicion.

"That door was locked! Why is it suddenly open now?" Decks exclaimed.

"Something's definitely not right about the door opening just like that. It's almost as if Granny wants to get us out of this room."

"She wants to hunt us down like some kind of sport," Casey agreed.

Dan shrugged his shoulders.

"Probably so, but we really don't have much of a choice. We can't stay in this room forever."

Dan had a point. If we went outside, we were definitely taking a big risk of running into Granny, who was almost certainly lurking in the house somewhere. However, staying in the room was not an option either. If only we had some kind of Granny radar gun.

"I guess we really don't have a choice. We have to try to get out of here," Casey reasoned.

"Yeah. I better go out first. I'm the biggest dude around here."

Decks was right. He was pretty big, but I also could tell that he was scared out of his mind at being the first to step outside. Since he was so big though, he was probably the one who could best handle himself should things get out of hand. I would love to see him wrestle Granny to the floor, much like you'd fight over the Xbox controller with one of your younger siblings.

"We're right behind you, Decks," Dan said.

The four of us slowly moved towards the door. Just as he had promised, Decks was the first in line. He slowly pulled on the handle of the door and opened it fully. The door squeaked and creaked and really needed some oiling.

"The coast is clear, guys. There's no sign of creepy Granny anywhere," Decks confirmed.

"Well, let's get moving then while we can," Dan

responded.

We were surprised to walk out of the room without anything happening. We had expected Granny to come out of nowhere, but she didn't. I guess she was biding time before she made her first move. Possibly still sitting on a rocking chair, plotting her next move like evil grannies normally do.

The room opened onto a long hallway with several other doors. Suddenly, we heard several voices coming from another room.

"Is somebody out there? Help!"

The voices came from behind one of the closed doors.

"There are other players here too!" I said.

"We better open that door."

I pulled on the door but it was locked. Of course it was going to be locked though, Granny didn't want us to escape.

"Please, you have to help me! I don't want to be locked in this room forever!"

"Take it easy! We're going to get you out of there," I shouted back.

"The door's locked. I'm going to have to kick it down."

None of us doubted that Decks could do just that. After all, he was pretty big and strong-looking. Decks could probably fight a herd of elephants with his little finger. He raised his foot and pulled it back. Taking a deep breath, he kicked down the door with one powerful push, sending it flying.

"It's open! Come on!"

Decks rushed into the room, and we followed. There were other Roblox players inside. They all looked pretty relieved to see us and seemed just as frightened as we were.

"Thank goodness! I knew there were other people aside from us in here!"

"How long have you guys been here?" Decks asked.

"I don't know. If you guys are like us, then you would have just been minding your own business, then suddenly you woke up here in this place. We were all locked up in this room together. I'm assuming you guys had a similar experience? I'm Shelby, by the way, and these are my friends: Carlos, Pitt, Dickie and Tina.

Shelby looked like a real smart guy, while his friends all

looked like your average Roblox player. They were all pretty afraid and in shock at what had happened. Yeah, they were much like us. They were all just chilling and playing, doing their own thing, until the mysterious force that was Granny whisked them away and brought them here. Yeah, we were all pretty unlucky all right.

"Well, I'm Decks, this is Danny SN, that's Casey and this is Noob. It looks like we were all brought together by Granny somehow."

"I've heard a lot of bad stuff about Granny," Carlos admitted.

"We all have. We've all heard about the mysterious force taking Roblox players and sending them to this old and dingy house. I never expected to end up a victim myself though."

"None of us did. We'll all just have to work together to get out of here," I replied.

"Exactly. We better stay together and keep moving. Maybe we'll find a way out of this place."

"Sorry, but that doesn't sound like much of a plan," Pitt said snidely.

Dan looked at him with annoyance for a moment before

answering.

"All right. Maybe it isn't much, but do you have any better ideas?"

Pitt didn't answer, and neither did his friends. I guess that was their answer. They really didn't have much of a choice; we would all have to stick together if we wanted to have a chance of getting out of this crazy place in one piece. It was like awkwardly meeting all of your relatives during Christmas time.

"Come on. We better get moving," Decks insisted.

So, there we were. Several players all stumbling around in one group, trying to find a way out of the crazy, maze-like house. It wouldn't be easy to find the exit, especially knowing that Granny was sure to strike at any moment.

Entry #2

Exploring Granny's Creepy House.

We wandered around the house for what seemed like forever. Each door seemed to look just like the one before it. The whole wall was like a giant snake that slithered around in a long and endless loop.

"Where are we going? Each door seems to be the same, and the walls seem to go around in circles. This whole dingy house feels like a cramped maze!" Shelby exclaimed.

"I know! We've been at this forever! And Granny hasn't even made her move yet," Tina whined.

"This is getting crazy. We have to do something other than wander around the house like this," Dan agreed.

He was right. If we kept at this, we would never find the way out. We were like little mice going around in circles, and I couldn't shake the feeling that this was exactly how Granny wanted it to be. DARN YOU EVIL GRANNY!

"How about we open each door we see?" I sheepishly volunteered. I was really hoping someone else would speak up, but since I already told everyone that I was a cop, I felt I had to prove myself.

"Good thinking, Noob! Let's do that! It's better than wandering around in circles like this," Dan replied.

It was the only logical solution. After all, we couldn't keep going around like this. We had to do something to help us find the way out. I mean, what else was there to do, stay in the room and play charades? I don't think so.

"No way! We don't even know what's behind those doors. One of those rooms is bound to contain a trap... maybe more than one. Who knows what's lurking behind those doors?" Casey argued.

"No, I agree with Dan and Noob. We're never going to find the way out or discover anything useful if we don't open more doors," Decks said.

No one really liked the idea of opening doors or breaking down locked ones to see what was behind them. The whole house was just plain creepy. Still, no one said anything after Decks spoke. Everyone knew that we didn't really have any choice. It was either explore and risk getting hurt, or just wander around in circles indefinitely.

"You guys are right. We should start opening doors, even if it's scary," Dicky agreed.

"It seems like we're all kind of in agreement then," Tina said.

"Alright, so we open doors. Who's going to stay in front and take the biggest risk?"

"I will. I am the biggest anyway, and I already kicked your door down," Decks said.

No one tried to say otherwise. I was glad that Decks was willing to take the risk. If he wasn't, I really wasn't sure who would go up front.

"Well, we might as well start with this door here," Pitt said, pointing at the door right in front of us. It was closed, like all the other doors in that creepy place. Decks stepped forward with no sign of fear or hesitation. Decks was a big guy, the only problem he had was fitting through the actual door.

"All right, I'm opening it. You guys had better step back or something."

"I'll come with you. It's better that you go in with some

help," Shelby offered.

Decks nodded and gripped the doorknob.

"On three. One, two..."

Decks turned the doorknob. It wasn't locked. The door opened easily, and the two of them stepped into the room. The room was pitch black, and we all had no idea who, or what, was inside. It could have been Granny in that room for all we knew. I have to admit, Decks and Shelby really had a lot of guts stepping into the room like that. It was like stepping into the unknown, literally.

"All right, turn on the light!" Decks ordered.

I fumbled for the light switch just inside the door and flicked it on. A bright light came over the room that turned out to be the kitchen. Immediately my eyes caught the stove under an old chimney. The countertop had not been used or cleaned in a while, and it was grimy and covered in dust. There were shelves and cupboards that looked very old. It also smelled quite bad.

It really should have been cleaned a long time ago, but I was sure that Granny wasn't one for cleaning around the house. By now, we were all sure that Granny was not one to care much about keeping her house in order. Though it's not like Granny was unable to clean the house. Supposedly, she had the speed and stamina of an Olympic athlete.

"That's one awfully dirty kitchen! I sure wouldn't want to let my kitchen get like that!" Tina exclaimed.

"I have to confess that my kitchen kind of ended up this dirty once," Casey said.

"Hey, guys, you can compare home-making notes later. Maybe we should all just focus on finding something useful in here," Dan said.

He was right. It was time to get serious and start looking for items that could really be of use against Granny. After all, from the stories we'd heard about her, she was very dangerous, and we had to be ready for anything.

"I've got a rolling pin. This might come in handy," I said.

The rolling pin was large and made of wood. It was good for rolling dough, but it would also make a good weapon if needs be. Just thinking about it made me squirm a little. I didn't want to use a cooking utensil for such a purpose, but I really didn't have much of a choice. None of us did.

"This might come in handy too," Dick said.

He grabbed a frying pan. I figured he had the same idea as I did with the rolling pin. If not, then at least he can make an omelet.

"I guess this kettle ought to do," Casey said.

"What's that supposed to do if Granny attacks?" Dan asked.

"The kettle is full of boiling water. You wouldn't want any of this splashed on your face, right? I figure Granny won't want any of it on her face either."

"Ouch. Well you could also make her a nice cup of tea?"

"This oven mitt might be... well, it might be a good boxing glove for fighting Granny," Pitt said. The last thing granny would expect is getting attacked with an oven mitt.

"Were you ever good at any kind of fighting?" Carlos asked.

"Not really, but I'm sure this mitten will be good enough for an old woman like her. I mean, it's sure to hurt if I punch her with it!"

"Yeah, maybe so, but I wouldn't need a glove like that to get an old lady like Granny. If you ask me, I could take on anyone with my bare fists!"

Despite just meeting these people, I could tell that Carlos was the cocky type. He did not bother even trying to look for anything to help him against Granny. Instead, while we searched, he did some shadow boxing in a corner; it appeared that he really did believe that his fighting skills alone would be up to the task. Maybe he had experience in fighting evil grannies before?

"Uhm, no offense Carlos, but are you sure that you can handle Granny? I mean, I haven't seen you fight before or anything, and I don't mean to judge, but Granny's got a pretty fearsome reputation and all," I questioned.

"Yeah, I've heard about her reputation. I've heard all sorts of crazy stories about her. I'm sure all of those stories are nothing but crazy tales to scare kids!"

"I don't know about that, Carlos. I mean..."

I was cut short as the lights suddenly went off. Casey and Tina wailed loudly and we all started shouting. It was worse than any jump scare you could imagine.

"Hey, what's going on?"

"Who turned out the lights?"

"Hey!"

I stumbled around in the dark, just like everyone else. I had no idea what was going on, and we were all pretty much terrified. I took a step forward and felt my foot land in something wet and sticky. I could suddenly smell something horrid.

"Somebody turn on the lights!"

I heard a lot of moving and stumbling but I couldn't tell what was going on. It was like someone had tossed a giant blanket over us all, and we were just moving in the dark.

I heard Decks moving around the room. I could tell it was him because his large frame made heavy footsteps on the ground. It was like hearing a bull moving around in a china shop. I heard the flick of a switch and, finally, the lights came back on.

Everyone squinted and rubbed their eyes as light flooded the entire room again. We looked at each other; something was definitely wrong. I took the opportunity to glance down to see what I stepped on and it appeared to be dog poop. There was no dog in the room from what I could see. I think maybe Granny put it there to mess with us. I didn't want to tell the others out of sheer embarrassment.

"Is everybody okay?" Decks asked.

"I-I think so..." Pitt said, checking himself out as if convinced there was a wound somewhere on his body.

"Oh my gosh! Where's Carlos?" Casey questioned.

Everyone stood silent and looked around. There were no signs of Carlos anywhere.

"Carlos! Where are you?" Dan shouted.

There was no reply except the echo of Dan's own voice bouncing around the entire house. There was an uneasy tension in the room. Everyone knew that something had happened to Carlos... something bad.

"Oh my gosh... Granny has made her first move... what are we going to do?! Who's going to be next? I knew this was going to end badly for me--"

"Whoa, hold up there! We're not about to leave anyone behind, you got that? We got here as a group and we're going to leave this stinking house as one!" Decks shouted, interrupting Tina's panic.

Decks was definitely the commanding presence in the group, and everyone silently acknowledged him as the leader of our little pack. We all silently nodded our heads in agreement.

"Decks is right. We just need to calm down. I'm sure Carlos is around here somewhere; we've just got to know where to look for him," I said calmly.

Shelby had seemed awfully quiet this whole time and I caught him shaking his head.

"Shelby, what's wrong?" I asked him.

"I don't know, dude. I think I've seen this before in a video... Granny strikes when everyone least expects it... Carlos is a goner, I'm sure of it. And in time... everyone else here will be too," Shelby said grimly.

Shelby was probably one of the smarter guys in the room, and those words coming from him didn't make any of us feel any better. Maybe I was safe from Granny since I had dog poop on my shoe and I wouldn't seem like much of a player. Though if she appeared in front of me, I knew that kicking her with my dog poop shoe could be fairly effective.

"Hey, if you're going to be so negative the whole time, then you can stay here in the kitchen and mope all day while you wait for that old hag to get you! Otherwise, gather up all the stuff you might need from here and follow me!" Decks commanded.

Before anyone else had time to say anything, we heard the sudden sound of heavy footsteps in the distance. All our heads turned in the direction of the sound. There was no mistaking it; it was definitely Granny. I mean, who else could it have been? Unless some random dude had decided to take a relaxing stroll around this creepy house, it could only mean one thing…. Granny was nearby.

"W-who was that?!" Tina shouted.

I could tell that she was starting to get really scared by everything that was happening. I mean, we were all scared, no doubt about it. Who wouldn't be, right? But Tina was the worst of us all. It's almost as if I could smell the fear coming from her body! I bet she didn't like watching scary movies and stuff like that.

"Granny! Who else could it be? We'd better go check it out!" Decks said.

"Wait! What if that was Carlos?" Pitt replied.

"Impossible! We called for Carlos earlier and he didn't say a thing! That can't have been him!"

"Look, guys, I don't think it matters right now who that was. We'd better get out of this kitchen. The longer we stay here, the slimmer our chances are of breaking out of this creepy place! Let's move!" Dan ordered.

We quickly moved around the kitchen, collecting together anything we might need. I even saw Pitt snatch an oven mitt from one of the drawers before leaving the place.

What on earth are you supposed to do with an oven mitt in a fight exactly?! Offer your opponent a poisonous pie? Bake them to death? It was a really weird weapon of choice if you ask me; Pitt would have been better off taking a fork, or even a small glass. But that was his choice, and I guess it was still better than what Carlos did: arrogantly not picking anything at all because he thought he was tough enough to fight Granny with his bare fists.

We began to exit the kitchen slowly, each of us following the person in front like a train made up of frightened people. We scanned the corridor and turned in the direction of the sound of footsteps from earlier.

Entry #3

The Secret Door.

We were back in the same hallway again with the doors that all looked the same. Dan and Decks seemed to know where the footsteps had come from though, so they took the lead and the rest of us followed them. After passing by several identical wooden doors, we finally stopped at the end of the hallway in front of the last wooden door in the whole place.

"This is where the footsteps came from, guys," Dan said.

"You sure about that? How can you be absolutely sure that the footsteps came from behind that door?" Pitt asked.

"It's a good guess. It sounded pretty far away when we heard it in the kitchen," Decks explained.

"I don't know, guys... what if Granny is behind that door? What if she's going to take us all down as soon as we open it?! I'm scared. I don't want to go in!" Tina said, clearly panicking at the thought of what was to come.

None of us wanted to admit it, but we all agreed with Tina. Nobody wanted to face Granny. There was a long, silent moment in which no one said a word. You could almost have cut the tension in the air with a knife or an oven mitt! It was Decks who eventually broke the silence.

"Look, guys, there's no other choice. We've got to go in there. We can't just stay here forever."

Everyone knew that Decks was right, but nobody wanted to admit it. Everyone felt safer in the hallway, but we couldn't stay here forever, right? It was a crazy idea. We had to go in, whether we liked it or not.

Everyone silently nodded their heads and gave Decks the go signal to kick the door down. We readied the kitchen utensils that we had grabbed from the kitchen earlier and prepared for the worst. We looked like a bunch of grumpy chefs who wanted to fight a customer who insulted our cooking. Decks took a deep breath one last time and kicked the door down with so much force that it flew across the entire room.

"Freeze!" Decks shouted.

Freeze? I'm thinking this dude must have been a cop before he got into this mess with the rest of us! Maybe he

was a cop from another server or something. Someone who was so calm and commanding in a crisis had to have had some kind of training. I suddenly felt embarrassed. I was a new cop at Mad City, and I hadn't done anything great so far; I'd just ended up in this mess.

We followed Decks into the room and looked around anxiously. There was nothing here. It was completely empty, and there was no proof that Granny or Carlos had ever even been here. The only thing inside the small room was a really strange-looking, dirty, patterned carpet hung on one of the walls. This could make a great present for my sister.

"There's no one here," Pitt remarked.

"Thank you, Captain Obvious," Shelby said with a sarcastic tone in his voice.

Pitt glared at Shelby but didn't reply. Everyone was busy investigating the small room and looking for clues, hoping to find any sort of sign that could lead them to Carlos, and hopefully the exit. I still can't believe we lost Carlos. I was really looking forward to seeing him go head to head with Granny. It would have been hilarious as well as entertaining.

"There's nothing here. How could the footsteps have come from this room? They must have come from one of those other rooms we just passed," Casey said.

"Keep looking, guys. There's got to be something in here... like maybe a hidden drawer or door somewhere," Decks insisted.

I stared at the strange, dusty old carpet that hung on the wall and placed my finger on my chin. It was literally the only thing in the room, and I wondered if it were some kind of clue or something. I touched the carpet with my hand; it felt really old and ragged, obviously, but I could also feel something else. Something strange. I really hope there wasn't more dog poop.

"Guys... I think... I think there's something beyond this carpet," I shouted.

The others quickly turned their attention to the carpet in question. Decks closely inspected the carpet like it were some kind of criminal and grabbed one of its ends.

"Only one way to find out," he said.

Decks quickly pulled the carpet with all of his strength,

revealing the wall underneath... and a hidden door. It was a really narrow door, so small in fact that I couldn't imagine someone as big as Decks being able to fit through it. Maybe we should have brought some butter from the kitchen so that we could cover him in it and squeeze him through.

"A hidden door!" Pitt exclaimed triumphantly.

"Again, thank you, Captain Obvious," Shelby replied.

"What's your problem, man? Why are you always cutting me out like that?" Pitt said angrily. I could tell that the tension between these two was increasing at an alarming rate. I could anticipate the kitchen utensils being flung around like a chef who had a make a cake in under 30 minutes.

"Ohh... I don't know. Maybe it's because you keep telling us things we already know?"

"Well, Mister Genius Pants, how come I haven't heard you share with us a magical solution that'll get us out of this place?!" Pitt fired back.

"I've got one for you--"

"That's enough!" Decks shouted.

Decks' voice echoed throughout the entire room, quickly

stopping Pitt and Shelby in their tracks. Decks was a big dude, and one you probably didn't want to make angry. He could probably eat you.

"Fighting each other is not going to get us out of this house! We need to work together to get out of this mess! Now if you two want to throw down and get into a fist fight, then be my guests! But you're both going to be left here if you do, so good luck dealing with that nutcase Granny on your own!" Decks cried.

"He started it!" Pitt responded childishly.

Decks gave Pitt a glare that could have sent a lion shaking in its boots. Pitt got the message and pretty much zipped his mouth from that point on.

The silence was soon broken once again though as all of us suddenly heard the faint sound of a person crying for help. It was coming from beyond the small door, and we all knew that we had to get in there whether we wanted to or not.

"That sounded like Carlos!" Casey said.

Decks let out a deep sigh and prepared his leg for another kick. He thrust his foot forward and the small white door immediately caved in. It tumbled down the staircase for what seemed like forever until we finally heard it land deep down in the basement.

I've got a lot of horrible memories of that crazy staircase. It was narrow and small, just like the door, and the damp and cold gave it a weird smell. The old and awful-smelling walls were made of stone and it felt like they were about to eat you up and collapse in on each other at the same time.

Everyone in the room gulped and nodded their heads. We all knew that there was a difficult task ahead of us.

"I guess we've got to go down there now," Tina said nervously. I felt like holding her hand, not because she was scared but because I was.

Entry #4

Into the Depths of the Stone Dungeon.

Decks nodded and headed through the door first, although that probably wasn't such a good idea. As the largest one of our group, I noticed that he had a hard time squeezing through the door to the narrow staircase, and an even harder time going down the stairs. We wouldn't dare say anything about his wide bodyframe in case he ate us. Everyone took Decks's lead and began to descend down the stairs into the cold depths of Granny's creepy house. The air seemed to get thicker and colder with every step that we took.

After climbing down the stairs for what seemed like an eternity, we finally reached the bottom and saw a large hallway that looked remarkably similar to the one above, although the walls were made of stone. There were some torches placed on the walls and there were a number of identical wooden doors all placed next to one another. It was another maze, and it was all part of Granny's creepy and evil plan. I swear if I see another maze right after this maze, then it will be too soon and I will just cry.

"Well, this honestly doesn't look very different from the house upstairs," Shelby said.

"Yeah, you want to stay up there? Be my guest, dumb-dumb!" Pitt sneered.

"Why you--"

Before Pitt could say anything further, Shelby lunged himself through the air and a fist fight broke out between the two of them. Pitt and Shelby were both throwing their fists wildly at each other, although I noticed that neither of them was landing any good shots. Clearly, neither of the men were fighters but were just really angry with one another. They were slapping each other as though they were clowns in a circus. They had almost zero fighting skill and everyone in the room could tell. It was like watching two puppies fight over a toy.

Before things got any more out of hand, Decks plunged into the fight and quickly broke the two apart. Decks grabbed them both by their shirt collars and carried them like a sack of potatoes. Decks was very different to Pitt and Shelby; I could definitely tell that this dude knew what he was doing. Not only was he big, but he also knew how to use his size to his advantage. He probably fought in some martial arts training camp or something before he got into this mess. I could imagine Decks fighting with a bear on the edge of a mountain. If there was anyone in the group that could stand a chance against Granny, it was him.

"All right, that's enough! Back it up, you two! I've had just about enough of this nonsense!" Decks said loudly. His voice echoed throughout the entire stone hallway in a really creepy way.

"He keeps messing with me, dude!" Shelby fired back.

"He's the one who started it! He said I was dumb and that I kept mentioning the obvious!" Pitt retorted.

"Look, I don't care what your reasons are for fighting--"

"Uhh, guys..?"

All of us turned our attention to Danny SN who was literally trembling in his shoes. His outstretched finger pointed towards something dark in the hallway, and we immediately realized why Dan was so scared. Standing right there in the distance was Granny. She didn't say anything, but just stood there like some sort of creepy statue with her glowing red eyes. Pretty much everyone in the hallway was frozen with fear - even Decks. No one expected to see Granny like this, but then again, who were we kidding? Granny was going show up sooner or later, and it's not like she was going to tell us before she made her move.

"I-i-it's... G-Granny!" Tina said. She could barely finish her sentence and she sounded like she was about to break down with fear.

Decks quickly snapped out of his trance and dropped both Pitt and Shelby onto the cold, hard, stone ground. He set off running after Granny like a cheetah who had just spotted its next meal. Decks could easily eat Granny like the big bad wolf.

"Come here, you!" Decks shouted as he ran towards his target.

Just as Decks reached Granny and was about to give her a giant knuckle sandwich with his fist, Granny disappeared into thin air like some kind of weird and mystical ninja. Decks looked around confused - there was no trace of Granny anywhere now.

"H-how did she..? But I thought..."

"It's obviously a trick, Decks. She wants to confuse us into thinking that she's everywhere. She's probably using some kind of magic spell on us. We've got to keep going," Dan explained.

"But how? These doors all look the same, just like upstairs. And there might be traps beyond these doors," Decks replied.

"I have an idea," Dickie said.

Dickie had remained pretty quiet the entire time that we'd been here, so we were all surprised to finally hear him talk.

"Shoot."

"I counted all of the doors while you guys were fighting and all that... and I think I have a plan. There's eight of us here right now, yes? Tina, Decks, Noob, Dan, Casey, Shelby, Pitt and me. That's eight people and there are eight doors," Dickie explained.

"Ohh, I see where you're going with this... so if all of us open one door each, we can cover more distance and hopefully find some kind of exit out of this place. Smart!" Shelby told Dickie.

Dickie smiled and nodded. I had to admit, it was a pretty

good plan alright. While the rest of us had been busy panicking, Dickie had actually hatched a well-thought-out plan.

"N-no way! I'm not opening any of those doors! What if Granny's waiting on the other side of the door that I open?!" Tina said nervously.

"You have to, Tina. It's the only way we can cover more ground and get out of here," Pitt replied calmly.

"He's right. And besides, if she does show up when you open your door, just call for help. I'll come crashing in and I'll beat her up for all that she's done to us!" Decks said angrily.

Decks' last remark seemed to give Tina a little bit of confidence. She took a deep breath and picked out one out of the eight wooden doors in the hallway. The rest of us picked our own, and soon we were all standing in front of our respective doors, waiting to open them at the same time.

"Everyone ready?" Decks called.

"Yeah."

"Ready."

"I'm good."

"Let's do this!"

"O-okay."

"Let's go."

"Yes."

We pushed open our individual doors slowly. The doors all creaked at the same time, and the creaking sounds echoed throughout the entire hallway. Nobody said a word for a few minutes until Dan finally broke the silence.

"My room is... empty. And it's got another door ahead."

"Mine too," Pitt said.

"Same here."

"My room's empty too!" Tina added.

Unfortunately, my room wasn't empty, and it didn't seem to lead to nowhere like the others. Inside the room was a long and narrow hall. The hall was dimly-lit and I could barely see anything, but it seemed to lead to somewhere. It probably had a line of dog poop for me to step on. I just felt Granny wanted to torment me with it.

I guess this is the part where you can squarely blame me for my own misfortune. Rather than calling out to Decks and the others for assistance, I decided to explore the place for myself. Call it a cop's intuition or maybe his pride; whatever it was, I figured I could handle whatever I bumped into. Of course, I was very wrong.

I hadn't walked far when I felt something large and metallic clamp down on my leg. It all happened so fast that it wasn't even painful. At least, not at first.

"What's happened...?"

I looked down and saw the large bear trap. It had sunk its metal teeth into my legs, and there was no way it was letting go. My leg was getting numb now and it was starting to really hurt. And that was when I saw the bear in front of me.

Yeah, everything had led to this terrible moment. I figured that I was going to die right here. I was going to die, not outside in the crazy streets of Mad City, chasing robbers or anything like that. No, I was going to die being eaten alive by a bear, a victim of one of Granny's most infamous traps. My life flashed before my eyes, and it was mostly of me playing video games. Well, playing video games and eating. I lived a good life.

But, fate, and Decks, had other ideas.

The bear was running towards me at full speed, but Decks moved even faster. Yep, Decks. He came out of nowhere and slammed into the bear, the two of them colliding like two trains running right into each other. I guess I was wrong earlier. Someone actually did hear me call out for help, and that person was Decks.

Decks and the bear were locked together in a rolling death grip. Neither of them were about to let go. I felt helpless as I watched the two of them fighting for my life, but what could I do? The bear trap was locked firmly on my leg.

After what seemed like an eternity, the two of them stopped struggling. The bear went limp, and Decks stood up. He looked terrible, but at least he was alive.

"Decks! You did it!"

"Yeah, and I don't want to do anything like that again."

"No argument here, but how did you defeat that bear?"

Just a lucky coincidence, I guess. I've been carrying around a tranquilizer dart ever since I visited Pet Simulator back in the day. I had a hunch it would in handy sooner or later. Apparently, I was right."

"No argument here again. But I guess I'm done for, anyway."

"What do you mean?"

I pointed at my bloody leg and the bear trap.

"I'm trapped in this bear trap. Unless you've got a sledgehammer or something like it, I'm not going anywhere. "

Decks shook his head.

"There ain't no way I'm leaving anyone here behind. I may not have a sledgehammer, but I might have something just as good."

"What do you mean?"

Decks whipped out a rusty key from his person.

"Where did you get that?" I asked.

"Remember when I saw Granny earlier and I tried to punch her and I missed and she disappeared? Well, Dan said that it was all a trick, but it wasn't. Not in the way we thought. She was no illusion. That was the real Granny. I managed to get close enough to her to pick her dress."

I couldn't believe what I was hearing! To do something like that, Decks must have experience as a minor thief or something like that.

"Pick her dress? You used to be a pickpocket or something?"

Decks smiled at me.

"Guilty as charged. You learn a lot of things growing up in the mean streets of Mad City."

I smiled at Decks. I couldn't believe someone as big as Decks could be so diligent as a pickpocket. I guess he had a lot to distract someone with.

"You sure you should be telling all of this to a cop?"

Decks smiled back at me, and shook his head.

"No, but I'm not going to let anyone die in a place like this. I was a petty thief back in the day, not a killer. Now, let's just hope this key is the right fit for that bear trap. It could be the key to anything."

Decks bent down and used the small, rusty key on the trap. I heard it squeak as it turned. Decks fiddled with the key a little longer and soon I was free! I howled in pain.

Attracted to my cry of pain, everyone came rushing through the door.

"Whoa! That looks real bad!" Dan said.

"Move over. I used to be a doctor before all of this craziness."

It was Tina. She moved towards me and examined my

wound.

"It's not that bad. Decks take off your shirt. I'll need you to tear it up. I can tie up the wound with it and minimize the bleeding."

Decks took off his shirt and ripped it up, just as Tina had said... Tina wrapped the cloth around my bleeding leg, fashioning a crude bandage to stop the bleeding.

"There, that should stop the bleeding. You're lucky, Noob. Although that bear trap looked menacing, it wasn't meant to kill. The real killer would have been that bear lying in front of you. A little real medication in some hospital, and you'll be fine- assuming you get out of here alive, of course."

"Of course. And Tina, Decks, thanks. I owe you both."

Decks shook his head.

"Forget it. Now, let's get moving. I want to get out of here."

We went back to investigating each door. Pretty soon, everyone realized that the room behind their door simply led to another room... and another... and another... and another. It was like a never-ending maze of doors and rooms that simply didn't end. A true labyrinth. This Granny person was crazy indeed! She wanted to drive us crazier than trying to play chess with a free-range chicken.

"How are we going to get out now? This is endless!" Pitt cried.

Before anyone could reply, the sound of Decks' loud voice crackling inside the weird maze filled the air.

Entry #5

Two Down, Seven More to Go...

"Guys! Guys! Come here! Carlos! He's here!"

Everyone quickly retraced their steps and made their way to Decks's location. It wasn't easy- the maze was really confusing and every room looked the same- but the sound of Decks's voice eventually led us to our destination.

"Carlos! Carlos! Wake up, man!" Decks shouted.

Stepping inside the room, we quickly noticed one thing that made this room stand out from the rest: there was a boiling pit of lava that separated us from Carlos! The pit was the entire width of the room, and the only way to get across was to jump over it. I suddenly felt a wave of nervousness overcome me; I wasn't good at jumping! One mistake and I'd fall to my death in the lava pit! Oh man, this was bad news!

We all kept calling Carlos' name, but he didn't respond. It looked as if he had a big red lump on his head; clearly Granny had whacked him pretty hard with something.

Carlos eventually regained consciousness and awoke slowly, looking really confused and dazed. I doubt he even had any idea where he was.

"H-huh... w-where am I..? Arghh! My head hurts!" Carlos said as he sat up and began rubbing his temples.

"Carlos! Thank goodness you're awake! Can you hear me?" Decks shouted.

"Yeah, man... I can hear you loud and clear. What's going on?"

"You're in Granny's house, remember? I'm Decks, and you were trapped with everyone else in the group! Then the lights went out and Granny kidnapped you!" Decks reminded him.

"Y-yeah... I think I can remember now... I don't remember how I get here in this room though. And what's that boiling pit of lava doing there?" Carlos said. I wanted to make a sarcastic joke about the lava actually being soup to help lighten the mood but didn't.

"I don't know. We're at the very bottom of Granny's house right now, probably the basement level. Do you think you can jump across here? We'll try to find an exit together," Decks said.

"Oh yeah, for sure. Pffft. Look at that lava pit. This will be easy. You guys do know that I'm a successful basketball player, right?" Carlos said arrogantly. Clearly, the knock to his head hadn't got rid of his overinflated ego. What was the point of him mentioning basketball? Was he going to dribble his way out of the situation?

We all looked at each other and shook our heads.

"Aww, come on! Don't tell me you guys don't play Basketblox! I'm the biggest star there! I'm totally the best basketball player ever! Everyone is always talking about my slick basketball skills. Ever see the time when I scored a huge slam dunk--?"

"Would you just shut up and jump already?!" Dan cried.

Carlos shrugged his shoulders and stood up. He squatted down low, preparing himself for the big jump across the lava pit. All of us were pretty sure that he'd make it across after his boasts about being a good basketball player.

But Carlos made one very big mistake.

He forgot to tie his shoelaces!

Rather than jumping across the pool, Carlos instead slipped forward into the boiling lava. It all happened so quickly. Everyone in the group shouted and stared in amazement as Carlos was disappearing from view.

"Carlos! Nooooo!" Decks shouted desperately.

Decks reached out his hand in order to pull Carlos from the pit, but it was too late. In just seconds, Carlos' body disappeared faster than toilet paper down the, well, toilet.

"Oh my gosh! Nooo! This is getting crazy! I've got to get out of here!" Tina screamed as sweat trickled down her forehead. She was freaking out so much that it was scaring the rest of us, I let out a little fart during the commotion. I was holding it in since we entered the room.

Tina turned back towards the door and started to make a run for it. She hadn't noticed though the small pebble in front of her. In her panic, she slipped on the stone and quickly slid backward into the boiling lava pit, just like Carlos before her.

"Arghhh! Help me!" Tina screamed desperately.

Tina slid into the lava pit so quickly that Decks didn't have time to save her. First Carlos and now Tina?!

Let me tell you now: games get pretty violent these days. But this? This was way beyond the scope of what I was prepared to see.

"Noooo! Darn it!" Decks cried.

Well, this was really getting out of hand. Granny was probably laughing somewhere in the dark about this. This was not good. Not good at all. Granny knew that lava pits were a Roblox players biggest nightmare after spiders with wings or penguins with rocket launchers.

"That's two down... seven more to go," Dickie said grimly.

"Why are you being so negative about this, man?! We'll get out of this alive, you'll see!" Shelby said.

I could tell that Shelby was also really scared but was doing his best to stay strong for the rest of the group. I had to admit though, Dickie was right. We were two people down and Granny probably didn't intend on letting any of us out of her madhouse. The big question was: who was going to be next? I gulped at the thought of being burned by Granny. I had to stay alive somehow... I had to get out of this place in one piece!

"Look, guys, everyone calm down! Look what happened

to Tina when she started to panic! There's a way out of this place, but we just have to stay calm!" Decks shouted.

"Calm?! Are you serious, man? We just saw two people get burned alive because of Granny's traps! Who's to say we're not next?!" Pitt shouted desperately.

"You want to go jump in the lava pit? Then be my guest! But our best chance of surviving is by staying calm!" Decks fired back.

"Decks is right. Let's exit this room calmly and slowly. There must be another room that leads to some sort of exit somewhere..." Dan insisted.

But there wasn't.

Once out of the boiling lava pit room, we thoroughly searched the other rooms in the hopes that we would find a door that would lead us out of Granny's house. But there was no such door. All the rooms simply led on to other rooms, and finally, after what felt like hours of searching and opening doors, everyone gave up and realized that there was only one way out of the dungeon: through the lava pit.

"We've been searching these rooms for hours! They just lead to more rooms and even more rooms! This is crazy! We're going to starve to death down here if we don't do something soon!" Pitt said.

"For once, I've got to agree with you, Pitt. We can't keep doing this forever. These rooms are just leading us nowhere. The only logical place to go now is across the lava pit. It's the only place we haven't explored yet," Shelby agreed.

Decks, strangely enough, was the only person who didn't seem to like the idea. I was surprised; he was the one in the group who seemed the bravest, despite all of the challenges we had faced so far.

"No, no, no! We're not going back there! There has to be a way out of this place in one of these rooms! Probably some kind of secret entrance just like that time where the carpet was hiding the door," Decks insisted.

"Look, Decks, we can't do this forever. We've been at this for hours now. There's clearly no trap door or secret entrance anywhere in these rooms; just concrete and even more concrete! We have to jump over the lava pit! It's the only way!"

Decks sneered and shook his head. He started to sway from side to side as though he was starting a dance routine.

"What are you doing?" I asked.

"I dance when I am scared!"

"I think Shelby's right, Decks. We've already lost Carlos and Tina. We'll all lose each other here if we don't make our move!" I told him.

Decks stopped dancing and reluctantly nodded his head. He obviously didn't like the idea, but what could he do? He was outnumbered six to one. None of us wanted to jump over the lava pit, but there was no other choice – it was either that or wait and starve to death. I'd sooner take my chances with the lava pit.

Danny SN was the first one to make the jump. His legs propelled him forward and up towards the other side. To be honest, I didn't think Dan would be able to make it, but he sure proved me wrong. I didn't think that someone who did mostly Youtube in his spare time would have the athletic skill to jump across a boiling pit of lava, but who was I to say? He did it, and he did it pretty well! He was like an elegant horse that escaped a farm for the first time.

Decks went next. Jumping to the other side was nothing for Decks. His huge, muscular legs easily propelled him into the air and he landed with a loud thud on the concrete on the other side of the boiling lava pit. Decks had legs like the Incredible Hulk; it was no surprise that he was able to make the jump.

One by one, with a little bit of help from Decks and Dan, the others in the group also successfully made the jump. I was the last to attempt it and I was really scared. I mean, who wouldn't be? One wrong move and I would easily end up like Carlos or Tina.

"Come on, Noob, you can do it!" Casey called out.

"Yeah, don't worry about it. Everyone else made it. We've got your back," Decks shouted.

I looked down at the boiling pit of lava one last time and took a deep breath.

"Here goes nothing," I thought to myself.

I squatted down and pushed off from the ground as hard as I could. It was a pretty good attempt, and I would have easily made it past the pit. There was one problem though...

I slipped!

I was just as clumsy as Tina and Carlos. I quickly found myself falling fast towards the pit of lava. I knew that it was the end so I simply closed my eyes and prepared for the worst.

Entry #6

Don't Slip, Don't Fall!

Just when I thought that I was about to get burned alive, I felt someone's hands grip my shoulders. It was Decks. His grip on me was really, really tight as he attempted to save me from my fiery fate. Think of a giant, eight-foot crab that just grabbed you with its giant iron claws or something.

"Oh no you don't! I've already lost two people; I'm not about to lose another one!" Decks cried.

With his great strength, Decks lifted me up from the pit of lava as if I was as light as a feather and tossed me into the concrete wall. I felt the hard stone wall slam against my shoulder, but hey, it was a lot better than getting burned alive.

"Ouch!"

"Sorry about that, Noob. I had to make sure you were as far away from the lava pit as possible."

"Great! We've all made it. We'd better keep going... we just might make it out of this alive!" Dan said happily.

Little did we know that the lava pit was just the first of many traps that Granny had in store for us...

We looked around for an exit and noticed a small door behind us. It creaked as the others had earlier as we opened it cautiously. But what we saw beyond the door definitely surprised us. This one wasn't like the others where the rooms simply led to other rooms... no, this one was very different.

It was a really, really, really big room... or should I say, pit. Where the floor should have been, there was only a gigantic hole, so deep that it appeared endless. The only way we could get across was to walk over a narrow wooden beam. There were no rails to hold on to; we simply had to balance ourselves and hope that we wouldn't fall into the deep pit below.

We all gulped and hesitated at the sight of the small walkway. It was so narrow that you had to place one foot on the beam at a time or else you'd fall below.

"What is this?!" Shelby cried out.

"It looks like some kind of really, really narrow bridge... I think I can see a door at the end of it though," Pitt shouted.

"This is insane! That walkway is way too narrow! We'll never get across!" Casey panicked.

"Not if we do it really, really, really slowly," Decks said reassuringly.

Decks was probably going to have the hardest time getting across the bridge since he was the biggest. He would have to balance his weight on the walkway and that wouldn't be easy.

After a few minutes of silence, Decks broke the tension in the air.

"Look, we've got this far, right? I mean, we found the secret dungeon in the house, we found Carlos, we made it across the lava pit and now we're here. There's no turning back. We have to move," Decks said grimly.

"This is all part of Granny's evil plan... we've got to make her pay somehow, guys!" I said.

"Don't worry, dude. I'm sure we'll get out of this place, one way or another," Dan told me reassuringly.

Dan smiled at me and that was all the encouragement I needed to get across. I mean, hey, if a big Youtube star believed in me and in the rest of us, then why shouldn't we believe in ourselves?

Decks took his first steps on the narrow walkway and the rest of us quickly followed him. Each of us cautiously took one step at a time, making our way across the walkway very slowly. One wrong step and we could all fall to our doom.

Our strategy seemed to be working; I was surprised to see that we were all making pretty good progress despite the narrowness of the walkway. In fact, I could clearly see the door on the other side which meant that we were already halfway across. Everything was going great...

Until Decks slipped.

His foot was just too big. It caught the edge of the narrow walkway and the rest happened so fast that I can't remember much of it to be honest with you guys.

As Decks fell, I saw Pitt, Shelby and even Casey grab a hold of him to try and pull him back up onto the walkway... but Decks was just too heavy. Dickie, Dan and I watched in horror as four of our new friends fell to their doom in the deep, black pit. We heard their cries as they fell deeper and deeper into the endless cavern of darkness.

"Noooooo!"

"Heeeeeeelp!"

"Ahhhhh!"

I tried to reach out for their hands but it was too late. Dan instinctively pulled me back and gripped my shoulders.

"No! Don't even try, dude! You'll just fall down as well! It's too late for them! We've got to keep going! We're almost across, man!" Dan said.

"But those guys were our friends!" I protested.

"So were Carlos and Tina. It's just the three of us now. And the only way to help them now is by making that evil, crazy old coot pay," Dickie said angrily.

He was right. There was no way we could save our friends now. It was much too late for them. Granny had to pay for all of this, one way or another. I was ready to dropkick her in the face.

After a few more tense moments, Dickie, Dan and I successfully crossed the narrow walkway and made it over to the wooden door. All three of us breathed a sigh of relief, and boy was I thankful that I was one of the lucky ones who had made it this far.

Entry #7

The Final Fight.

"This is it, guys. This is the moment when we put an end to all of this", I said to Dickie and Dan.

"Wait, what? How can you be sure that this is the last room? We walked through countless rooms earlier; how can you be so sure that this is the one?" Dan asked.

"Well, uhh... I don't know, really. I've just got this gut feeling that this is it. Yeah, maybe I'm wrong, but whatever. Just get ready, guys," I told them both.

Dickie and Danny took out the kitchen materials they had chosen earlier and readied themselves for a fight. Dickie took out the frying pan and Dan took out a large, wooden spoon. I hadn't noticed Dan taking the spoon earlier; he must've snuck it out just as we were about to leave.

I took out my own weapon of choice... the rolling pin. A frying pan, a wooden spoon and a rolling pin... not exactly destructive weapons of war, but better than trying to fight with just our bare hands, I guess.

All three of us took a few deep breaths before opening the door and stepping inside.

Through the door was a stone room, just like all the others, although this time it was much bigger. Much, much, much bigger. There were no narrow walkways, boiling lava pits or extra doors inside. Nope, it was just a really large stone room with four torches attached to the walls on each side of us. And who was in the middle of it? Yes, you guessed it. The villain of the night: Granny herself.

"Well now, boys... I'm surprised you made it this far. I didn't think that anyone would actually get past all my traps and make it here...," she said menacingly. There was something weird about the way in which she spoke; her high-pitched voice made her sound a lot like a bird talking.

"You're going to pay for all the people you've taken down, Granny!" Danny SN shouted.

"We'll see about that. See, now that you're here, you can

freely exit the house through a final door that's hidden within this room... but it will only show itself if you can beat me!" Granny said, letting out an evil laugh.

Danny SN and Dickie had heard enough. They'd suffered enough and they'd had enough. They weren't about to talk to this crazy old coot any longer. Both of them charged towards her with their kitchen utensils in their hands, ready to fight.

And then the most incredible thing happened. Right before our eyes Granny *self-multiplied*. I mean literally! Suddenly, there were three Grannies to take care of, and each looked more evil than the other...

I saw the shock on Dan and Dickie's faces, but I had to admit, they reacted fast. They separated and went for the two Grannies on the sides, leaving me to fight the one in the middle.

I took a deep breath and ran ahead, hoping to end things with one swift blow. But Granny was a lot faster than I had expected. She moved like a ghost and immediately knocked me down. I hadn't even done any damage yet, and I was literally shaking in my boots. I could feel that the end was near, much like when I forgot to bring my homework to school.

"W-wait, p-please! Have mercy! I used to have a totally awesome life in Roblox! I should never have become a cop! Never! I just can't do this kind of stuff! I'm too young to get whacked in the head with a baseball bat by some creepy old woman!" I pleaded.

Yeah, I know how that came out. I looked and sounded like a total wuss. A coward. A yellowbelly. The list of awful names could go on and on. But I was terrified, and I just couldn't help myself. Being in that situation was just too horrifying; no amount of training could have prepared me to face the monster that was Granny.

But Granny didn't care. She didn't care if I, or any of her victims, were scared stiff. In fact, she enjoyed all of this. If she was once human, she certainly was not anymore; she was something else entirely now. And I would have to face this monster with nothing but my rolling pin.

She dived straight at me like an eagle that had spotted its target. Without thinking, I quickly reached for the rolling pin that I had taken earlier and used it as a shield against Granny's attacks. I know what you're thinking: what good could a rolling pin do against a baseball bat? I know, it was a silly idea... but it actually worked. Granny was about to nail me, but she stopped dead in her tracks when she caught a glimpse of the rolling pin.

"Nooo! What are you doing with my rolling pin?! That's the same rolling pin I've used to make cookies for Slendrina! Give it back!" Granny ordered.

Granny grabbed the end of the rolling pin and began to pull. I pulled back, and a small tug of war ensued between the two of us. While we were both fighting for the rolling pin, the other two Grannies suddenly evaporated. It was clear that mine was the real Granny now, so Dan and Dickie had to come help me. That is unless they had bigger things to do...

Thankfully, I watched them both lunge themselves straight at Granny. She never saw it coming. Dickie began whacking her with the frying pan and Dan used his wooden spoon.

It was a really strange sight, seeing two guys beating up a crazy old lady with kitchen utensils, but I can't say she didn't deserve it... not after what she had done to our friends earlier. Though it didn't seem like the guys were doing much damage anyway.

Granny was still fighting me for the rolling pin when suddenly her teeth fell out. That's when I thought that we'd hit her with a devastating blow, but then I realized that Granny had false teeth.

Still, there was no escape for Granny now and she knew it. Unable to let go of the rolling pin, at some point Granny fell to the floor and collapsed. She had taken a pounding from Dan and Dickie, and she was done.

"W-what happened?! Is it over?" Dan said as he looked around, still partially concussed and confused about what had happened.

"I think we beat her," Dickie said.

"Yeah, guys! You totally did it! You beat that crazy old coot!" I said.

You could hear the joy and excitement in my voice. I was so relieved and thankful that this was all over. I had just about had it with this terrible place and the many death traps inside. The dark corners, the rotting floors, the traps, the overgrown spiders, the large holes... all that was done. We were all going to survive our encounter with Granny!

Or were we?

It was a little early for us to celebrate, but we all realized this too late. It turned out that Granny wasn't done with us. Not by a long shot.

Dickie didn't even see it coming. None of us did. That old

windbag moved so fast, it seemed unnatural for, well, an old windbag. Out of nowhere, she kicked Dickie from behind. I knew that Dickie was not getting up from this hit. Another one of us down, and in the most unexpected manner.

"Dickie, no!"

Dickie wasn't answering, and he wasn't moving on the ground. Granny had taken another victim.

I raised my rolling pin to try and smash her the way she had smashed Dickie, but it was no use. Granny moved fast and swung hard. Her baseball bat struck my rolling pin and she snapped it in two. Dan and I couldn't believe it. How could an old woman do something like that? Granny had unbelievable strength.

Then again, she had a lot of unbelievable stuff going for her. Like I said before, she was like some kind of inhuman creature that was anything but normal. I mean this was way beyond the scope of your regular granny being cranky because she missed a nap.

I rushed towards Granny but she was too fast. She struck me in the gut with her baseball bat and I instantly felt the wind knocked out of me. I couldn't breathe, and I doubled up in pain, collapsing on the ground and clutching my stomach.

"You crazy old monster! You're going to pay for all of this! You're going to pay!"

It was Dan. He was enraged and frustrated now. He couldn't believe that Granny was still somehow standing; he had to do something. So Dan rushed at Granny, which really wasn't the smartest thing to do. In fact, it was just about the worst thing he could have done.

And here's why. Granny was standing next to the wall, and right before Dan was about to tackle her, she used her unnatural speed to move out of the way. So Dan crushed right into the wall.

Ouch.

"Dan! Stop! No!"

In the meantime, I was still lying on the floor, in too much pain to even try and stop Granny. The pain in my stomach was too intense to even try to move.

After what seemed like an eternity, Granny turned towards me.

"Both your friends are done for, fool. Now, it is your turn."

Granny walked towards me. I was in too much pain to get up from the floor and she knew it. She wasn't even rushing towards me. I realized that she was going to take her time with me. What was she about to do with me?

One thing is certain: she wasn't about to make me an apple pie and let me go.

"You're all going to pay. All of you," Granny said.

Her voice sounded like something between broken glass and a crow cawing. It was hoarse and could barely be heard.

"Why are you doing this? What did we ever do to you?"

Granny shook her head. She was in no mood to give me answers.

Once again, I pretty much thought that I was done for. But that was when the unexpected happened.

"Hey, ugly! I'm not through with you yet!"

I heard the familiar voice from behind Granny. It couldn't be? How was this possible? Granny turned around, her face a picture of shock. Behind her stood Decks.

"You? You fell into the bottomless pit! How are you even still alive?"

Granny couldn't believe it, and neither could I. I had seen Decks fall into that bottomless pit with our other friends with my own eyes. Decks should have been done for, but he wasn't. Somehow, he had managed to climb out, and he now stood in front of Granny, face-to-face.

I could see that there was something different about Decks. He looked a lot more haggard and beaten up than last time I'd seen him, as if he had gone through a meat grinder and survived. But there was also something more. There was something different about the way Decks stared at Granny.

It seemed like Decks was no longer afraid. There was no fear in his eyes. He stared down Granny, as if his eyes could burn holes through her. Decks wasn't backing down; he was now fearless.

"No one's ever survived falling down the bottomless pit. No one!"

Decks grinned and laughed softly at Granny. It seemed as if he were laughing at death itself. Hearing Decks, I actually felt more afraid of him at that moment than of Granny.

"Yeah, well, I guess I'm no one then."

Decks whipped out a deck of cards from his body. He

hadn't had them on his person before. At the sight of them, Granny seemed genuinely terrified.

"The cards of fate! How did you get a hold of them?"

Decks shook his head.

"I don't need to answer any of your questions."

Decks pulled out a card from the deck and tossed it at Granny. He tossed the card so fast, I barely managed to follow it with my eyes. The card struck Granny's hand. It cut her a bit, but she drew back in great pain. She then dropped her baseball bat, and clutched her wounded hand.

Yaaah! You cut me!"

"I'm going to do a lot more than just cut you, Granny. You're done for!"

Decks whipped out another card and tossed it Granny's way. The second card was more powerful than the first. It struck Granny right in the chest and something unbelievable happened. Granny exploded. It was as if Decks had tossed a bomb her way.

It was a small, controlled explosion that had just enough power to take Granny out. The entire house remained untouched, and I was also unharmed. When the smoke cleared, there was nothing left of Granny. She just evaporated.

"Whoa! Decks! You're... you're alive," I said.

Decks shrugged his shoulders. He still had the deck of fate held firmly in one hand.

"Yeah, I am."

"That's incredible! You're alive and you defeated Granny! That's... I just can't believe it!"

I was at a loss for words. I couldn't believe what I had just seen. I had really thought that I would never see Decks again.

"Hey, maybe I'm just a lot tougher to kill than I look."

Decks was being coy, but I had to know how he managed to survive such a fall.

"How did you do it, Decks? How did you survive that fall? And what are those cards you picked up?"

Decks was reluctant to provide answers. He just shook his head and stared at me. There was no hate in his eyes, but his gaze was as firm as it was with Granny earlier. So I decided to just leave it at that.

After all, it was hard to argue with a man who had cards

like that. Decks had just taken out Granny with those things. He had the cards stacked in his favor, literally.

"All right, I guess I'll leave it at that."

"Granny's done. We should be able to get out of here now."

We both suddenly caught a glimpse of a door that seemed to have magically appeared out of nowhere. This door was different from the others. Through its transparent windows we could see the most awesome thing ever. I immediately recognized the buildings and structures outside; this was the skyline of Mad City.

I don't know how it had happened, but somehow the house was just outside of Mad City now. I'll never fully understand that house, or Granny; it was as if both were magical things that existed out of pure evil. We had achieved freedom at last, and it was waiting for us just beyond the wooden door. We did it! We beat Granny and put her in her place!

"It's over. It's really over then. We can finally walk out of here," I said.

"Yeah, I guess it is. We were the only ones to make it out alive."

We stepped outside and saw Mad City up ahead. It would be a bit of a walk to get there, but Decks and I didn't mind. We were just relieved to still be alive.

"Is she really gone for good? Granny I mean," I asked.

Decks shrugged his shoulders.

"Granny and that house were like evil spirits or a virus or something. They can appear anywhere, and you can't really kill something like that."

We turned around and saw that the house had vanished. It had just been standing there moments ago, and now it was gone. Decks' words were already making sense.

"What are you going to do now?" I asked Decks.

Decks smiled at me and nodded towards the pack of cards he still carried in his hand.

"I think I'll put these things to good use. After all, I did almost die back there to get them. A cop and a petty thief, the only survivors of Granny's house of horrors. Kind of ironic, isn't it?"

I couldn't argue with Decks. It was pretty strange that the two of us would be the only survivors. Strange, but it had to just be a coincidence, right? I mean, it wasn't like I would ever see Decks again.

"You're not going to go after me after all of this, are you?" Decks asked.

I smiled and shook my head.

"No way. You saved my life back there. Besides, I've probably got a lot more pressing things to do now."

Decks held up the deck of fate with pride.

"Pressing stuff? Like what?"

"I'm going to try and find my partner, and eat as many donuts as Robloxy possible."

And that's how the crazy adventure with Granny ended.

Sure, we may have lost a lot of friends in the process, but hey, they probably just respawned somewhere else and are living their best lives right now.

The important thing was that we did something that so many other players had failed to do: we defeated Granny, escaped her house and lived to tell the tale.

Follow Noob's adventures in Diary of a Roblox Noob: Bee Swarm Simulator.

DIARY OF A ROBLOX NOOB

BEE SWARM SIMULATOR

BOOK 1
ROBLOXIA KID

Prologue

The giant rogue vicious bee was hovering right in front of me. I looked straight into its beady red eyes and saw nothing but pure fury and rage. Maybe it was upset because it had a butt for a weapon? Bees are weird like that.

Anyway, it had a large, bloated body that was black and shiny. The bee was a lot larger than a normal bee, and nearly bigger than me. So large that no amount of bugspray could stop it. If anything, the bee would probably use it as deodorant. It also snarled like an angry, rabid dog just as it flew in front of me.

"That's one angry bee..." I said.

The words tumbled out of my mouth as if I was about to be sick. My body was trembling in fear, and I froze on the spot like a snowman who had nowhere to go. There was a cold sweat running down my forehead, and my panic was starting to overwhelm me.

"Take it easy, Noob. That's a rogue, vicious bee. I've dealt with these creatures before."

The know-it-all speaking was Mario. He was a round and

pudgy dude, with a big nose and thick moustache. He also dressed pretty goofy in his blue suspenders and red overalls. Kind of like some sort of cheesy video game superhero that had no business being in Bee Simulator. Then again, I couldn't really judge the guy. After all, he was just about the best player in the whole darned game. And I was the one who was always getting my butt kicked.

Now, I was about to get my butt kicked really bad, but this time not by Mario. The rogue vicious bee was right in front of us and I was the closest to it. It had me in my sights, and I knew that wasn't good.

"Rogue vicious bees react to movement and noise, Noob. Don't do anything that will startle it!" Mario instructed.

"Great, I really need to scratch my nose though," I replied. Mario looked at me sternly and yet he could see I was in agony.

"Just a quick scratch then, like you would with your butt in public," whispered Mario.

Mario spoke as if he were reading from a handbook on surviving a rogue vicious bee attack. Actually, if a handbook existed, he probably wrote it. I had never really seen one of these things before; I had read about them though and I knew how dangerous they were. I never realized that I would end up bumping into one of them.

"I'm trying to stay still here, Mario!" I said.

"I'll save you, boss!"

Suddenly, a small bee flew right at the much larger rogue vicious bee. It slammed into the giant black thing like a pancake flying into a brick wall, only the result was a lot worse. The small bee's attack was useless, he didn't even manage to shake the rogue vicious bee; instead, he managed to anger it further.

"Kaz! What did you do that for?"

I knew the answer to my own question. Kaz was one of my bees and was always trying to prove himself. Well, the only thing he had proved this time was how good he was at getting us all in trouble. I guess he wasn't the "bee's knees" after all.

"You've done it now! You've angered him!"

"Oops. Sorry?"

Kaz's apology was way too late. The rouge vicious bee was going to retaliate, and I was terrified that he would use his butt to do so. Suddenly, giant spikes started rising from the ground.

They shot up so fast that we didn't have time to think and somehow dodged them better than brussels sprouts at Christmas dinner.

But more and more kept surfacing. "Where are all these spikes coming from?" I asked.

"Don't ask! Just try to keep dodging them! That's what these things do! They summon those spikes from the ground!"

I should have listened to Mario's advice. It was impossible to keep dodging every one, even though I was jumping around like a bunny that had too much coffee. Eventually one of them found its mark.

"Ouch!"

The spike didn't get me completely. If it had, I wouldn't have been able to make another cool Noob-diary! No, I managed to roll away just in time and it missed my body, but it did slash my arm. Believe me, it hurt a lot.

"Yow! That spike smarts!"

The rogue vicious bee was now fluttering right in front of me. Up close, it looked huge. Like a big black asteroid that came from space.

It glared at me and smiled. I didn't think bees could smile

but here we are. What next, it would sing to me? The terrible creature was eager to take me down, and with a bad arm now, it sure seemed like I was done for.

"Shoo shoo, evil bee thing," I whelped out, "I don't have any honey and if I did, you definitely wouldn't get any!"

I wasn't sure if the rogue vicious bee even liked honey, this wasn't your typical bee. It probably wanted money or candy instead.

I couldn't get up from the ground. I knew that the rogue vicious bee was about to summon a spike from the ground to hit me where I lay, but I couldn't move. The pain in my arm was just too much. I figured I was done for.

I lay there on the ground as all sorts of thoughts started to run through my head. How did I end up here? What were the other challenges I faced in Bee Simulator? Was I a great player in the game? I guess all those questions didn't really matter now. After all, I was about to get spiked from the ground up by a rogue vicious bee.

Entry #1

It's Tough Being a Noob.

"Boy, this new game is something else!"

Yeah, that was me whining and complaining. I'm not usually one to complain or whine about any game I play in Roblox. After all, I've played just about every Roblox game there is to play, and then some!

So, what was this really tough game I was complaining about? It was Bee Simulator, of course. Basically, it's about growing your hive and getting the best bees to make you a lot of honey. Basically, it's all about getting the best bee for your buck. Haha, okay, I know, I know, that joke was just way off.

Anyway, I *was* complaining, but don't get me wrong here. Bee Simulator is not a bad game, not by a long shot. If anything, it's probably the opposite of a bad game. It's amazing. The payoff of building a large hive and having all those cool bees work with you is something else. It's something I would love to get. It's just so tough; I mean, I just don't know where to begin.

After all, Bee Swarm Simulator was supposed to be my vacation. You see, I've been working as a cop in Roblox Mad City for a while now, and as the server name suggests, the job is hardly a picnic. In fact, it's the toughest job there is. Trust me to go from fighting bad guys to being attacked by things that fly. And I was a pretty good cop too, how many cops do you know that can shoot with one hand and eat doughnuts on the other? I would even sometimes shoot through the doughnut hole to give me better accuracy.

But that's not all. I was recently abducted by the evil Granny to play insane games in her trap house. I somehow managed to survive, but the stress was just too much. It was a really scary game and many of my friends perished in unimaginable ways. The only good thing was that we successfully beat Granny, so bad that she needed a new walking cane. Still, I couldn't get back to Mad City immediately, so I asked for some time off and came here to relax.

I always thought bees were relaxing, I mean who doesn't love bees?

Only problem is, Bee Swarm Simulator turned out to be anything but relaxing.

"Come on, let's get moving to make that honey!" I shouted.

I was moving around the field and gathering more stuff for my bees to make honey. Yeah, I wasn't really doing a good job of it, but neither were my bees. I guess we were all just really off. There was no unity in our actions.

"Cut us a little slack here, boss! The boys are trying their best!"

The big yellow bee I was speaking to? That was my only rare bee. It was a bumblebee and his name was Nate. He was the only rare bee in my hive that was full of plain, old common bees. Not only did I not have any rare bees aside from Nate, but I also didn't have any epic or legendary bees to my name. Let's not even talk about event bees which were probably the rarest, strongest and coolest bee type. If you had bees like this, you were basically a legendary bee master. Well, I guess it really was no surprise why my hive wasn't producing as much honey as I wanted.

"Come on, Nate! You guys can make a lot more honey if you just put your backs into it!"

Nate shook his head.

"You think it's easy making all that honey? You try being a bee like us!"

I guess Nate had a point there. I needed to get more powerful bees if I wanted my hive to go anywhere.

I was really just getting mad at Nate and the boys out of sheer frustration. I guess I was becoming something of a bad boss to my poor bees. Yeah, I know, it wasn't right and it wasn't one of my best moments. Still, I couldn't help myself. Despite my best efforts, the hive wasn't producing as much honey as I wanted, and I was really looking like, well, a Noob in all of this. It was beyond embarrassing.

"Nate, can you buzz a little less? You sound like a chainsaw right now."

Nate was unimpressed with my remark, and he started making honey aggressively. As he flew over me, he accidently spilled some all over. At least I think it was by accident. He was flying above me for a good 5 seconds.

"Put that on your porridge!" said Nate.

I thought that was strange, I didn't have any porridge.

To make matters worse, I was sharing the same pollen field with another, much more experienced player. Mario. Mario was the complete opposite of myself in Bee Simulator. Where I was, well, a Noob, Mario was a real pro. He had amassed the biggest and most productive hive in all of Bee Simulator. His hive was so big, you could see it several miles away from the field. The hive was also full of the best and most productive bees ever seen anywhere. I only had one rare bee to handle all of the common bees in my hive, but Mario had several. His rare bees were the ones who did the bulk of the work in the hive, but he also had several epic and legendary bees as well. What he didn't have was an event bee, but that didn't really seem to matter. After all, event bees were pretty rare already, and his hive was already killing it, even without one.

"'Ey! Good morning neighbor! Am I interrupting some serious work there?"

Mario had a strange Italian accent, along with a thick moustache and a large belly, which could be because he has the most honey and scoffs most of it. He also always dressed in red and blue. I could have sworn that I had seen him in another game, but maybe that was just me.

"We're fine Mario."

I was definitely more than a little annoyed. I didn't like Mario dropping in like this and butting into my business. The guy always seemed to be butting in when I didn't really want him to be around. His annoying nature only made me even more jealous of his success at the server.

"You sure, neighbor? You seemed to be getting on poor Nate's case. I mean, take it from me. If you really want your bees to perform well, you can't go treating them badly. Not that it's any of my business."

"You're right, Mario. It's none of your business."

I just couldn't help myself. Mario was really getting on my nerves, even if he didn't mean to. I was also covered in honey, which may be why he came over in the first place, to maybe try and eat me.

"Whoa! Isn't that a bit harsh?"

Maybe it was, but I was just so frustrated. I mean, if it wasn't bad enough that my bees were all performing way below expected, I just had to be sharing the same field with one of the top players of the game! That was like rubbing salt on an open wound.

"You probably think you're some really cool master player

of the game, Mario! Well, let me tell you now, you're not! You're not as cool as you think! You should go crawl down a pipe and face a turtle or something!"

Mario seemed to smile under his thick moustache. I couldn't really tell because his moustache was so thick. In fact, it was often hard to tell his facial expressions. I only knew that if he was happy then he would jump up and down. Oh, also if he was laughing, the ground would shake.

"Been there, done that."

"Yeah, what do you mean by that?"

Before Mario could even answer, something came up that made my day even worse than it already was.

"Everybody run! It's a giant ladybug!"

Nate yelled the warning as my bees flew away in all directions. They all knew the ladybug was trouble, and so did I.

Entry #2

Trouble in the Fields and a Magic Tool.

"Run! Save yourselves! There's a giant ladybug coming!"

Being a bee wasn't sweets and honey all the time in Bee Simulator. There was always the chance that your poppy field would be invaded by several giant mobs that were pretty dangerous to bees, and even beekeepers like myself. Yep, the giant ladybug was just another example of that kind of mob.

I turned around and saw the giant ladybug coming our way. It was a huge, all right. She was big, red and very nasty looking, like a horrible wart on the bottom of your foot. She looked as if she could eat a bee just by looking at it.

"A giant ladybug! Come on, Mario!"

I motioned for Mario to move away, but he didn't budge an inch. He remained standing right where he was and stared the giant ladybug down. I couldn't see any kind of fear in Mario's eyes. I'm ashamed to admit that I was the complete opposite; there was just a whole lot of fear in my eyes and I wanted to get out of there as fast as I could.

"What are you standing around for, Mario? Come on! That giant ladybug isn't messing around. If we stay here, she could trample on us, or even eat us!"

Mario didn't say anything and just remained standing there. I was shaking in my boots already, but he wouldn't move. He wasn't afraid at all. Mario looked directly at the ladybug.

"I'm not going anywhere. You take another step and I'm going to trample on you real good!" he said to the Ladybug. I couldn't move, not because I was scared, but because I was so sticky from all the honey. I wished Winnie the Pooh could magically appear and lick me clean.

The giant ladybug smiled at Mario. She wasn't afraid of his threat. In fact, she seemed amused that this small and plump man would dare to challenge her.

Without thinking twice, the ladybug took another step

towards us.

"All right! That's it! You asked for it!" Mario said.

Mario ran right towards the giant ladybug without any hesitation.

"Mario! What are you doing?"

Mario didn't answer. His eyes were completely focused on the ladybug as he moved straight towards her. As he ran towards the giant bug, the giant bug ran towards him. It was kind of like two lightning bolts colliding with each other, or two giant trains driving straight at each other. Or two... well, you get the picture.

"Mamma Mia! I'm coming right at you, you dumb bug!"

At the last moment, Mario jumped over the bug's head and landed right on top of it. He landed with so much force that the giant bug was squished. It was actually kind of awesome seeing Mario do that. Well, he was a big guy, he could probably crush a baby elephant by sitting on it.

"Well, that takes care of that giant pest!" he said.

He squished the giant ladybug and a huge roar erupted from the bees. They were all buzzing in praise, it sounded like a giant electric razor. His bees and even my bees were cheering Mario. This was beyond embarrassing now. I just felt completely useless. What was the point of even trying to get better? How could I beat someone who could flatten ladybugs?

"What are you guys cheering about? Get back to work!" I barked.

Nate and the others were stunned silent and the buzzing promptly stopped. I had never been that harsh to my bees. This was a first even for me. Looking back, I admit that I'm really ashamed of my behavior, but back then I didn't feel any kind of shame at all. I was simply angry, frustrated, and jealous. I didn't have a clue how I could get better at Bee Simulator and get my hive to become more productive.

"Take it easy, Noob! Bees don't like to be treated that way. Nobody does!"

"What do you care? You're the dude with the best hive! I can't possibly measure up to you."

Mario shook his head.

"You don't have to be angry like this, Noob. You can get better. I can show you how to get as good as me. There's a magic tool that can increase bee production. Your bees will be making honey like hotcakes with it and..."

I raised my hand and shook my head.

"I think you've already done enough, Mario," I said.

Yep, that was the end of that conversation. I wouldn't hear any of it from Mario. Was I jealous of him? Absolutely. Was I insecure and way out of line? You bet. Was I full of pride, and full of myself? Yep. There was no excuse for my behavior. I wasn't myself. My frustration was really getting the better of me.

Things were bad then, but they were about to get a whole lot worse.

Entry #3

From Bad to Worse.

Later, I fell asleep pretty quickly. I'd had a tough day at the field, dealing with my jealousy towards Mario, and my own bees' growing frustration towards me. One thing that I've realized is that nothing gets anyone to sleep faster than exhaustion and frustration. You feel that and you pretty quickly go out like a light.

That night, I had the most wonderful dream ever. I dreamed of something completely different from my life at the server. Yeah, I was a total loser in real life, but in my dream, I had the biggest and most productive hive of all. I could see it glowing yellow in all its glory. It was a honey-making machine! The bees were all producing truckloads of honey and, most importantly, they were all happy. None of them were angry or frustrated with me. Better than that, I even had some legendary and epic bees to my name as well.

The best part? I had an event bee! I had a real honest-to-goodness event bee! Not even Mario had that. I would love to brag to Mario that I had an event bee, it would really wipe the smirk off his face, if I could see his smirk behind his thick mustache.

You can imagine just how happy I was. I'd have been happy to stay asleep forever! After playing Roblox, sleeping was my favorite hobby. It's the easiest hobby really, you just lie in bed and close your eyes. I don't know why adults complain about it so much.

"How's everything at the hive, Nate?"

Nate was smiling proudly at me. His smile stretched from ear-to-ear, and he looked way more than just pleased. He was really proud and beaming.

"Everything's running smoothly, boss! The hive has reached, well, epic proportions, no pun intended. Our epic and legendary bees are just pumping out that honey like crazy."

"Wonderful, wonderful! I'm so glad to hear that."

"Well, I also admit that we've been doing great work

because of the hive's new event bee. We've got a gummy bee!"

"Wow! That's amazing!"

It was really wonderful news. An event bee hatching from one of the eggs was already rare in itself, but a gummy bee? Wow, this was awesome! It was wonderful to have this rare event bee on my side. Take that, Mario! The only thing cooler than having an event bee was if it stung Mario.

"Everything's looking up, boss!"

"Great! You know something, Nate? I'm really sorry if I was a bit too hard on you and the boys before."

In my dream, I really felt the need to apologize to my bees. After all, they were working very hard at this, and I had been pretty cruel to them. They clearly didn't deserve that kind of treatment, and yeah, I was sorry for it.

Nate shook his head and smiled at me. He was really very understanding.

"That's quite all right, boss. I mean, that's all in the past now. Besides, everyone gets a little angry now and then and loses it, right? Me and the boys don't hold a grudge against you if that's what you think."

"Thanks, Nate. I really appreciate the hard work and understanding. A guy like me doesn't deserve it."

Nate shook his head.

"Nonsense, boss. We're here for you and we'll always make you proud."

"Wow. You guys are the best ever."

"Boss, wake up!"

"What? What's going on?"

I was shaken out of my dream rather rudely. I opened my eyes, still a little sleepy and confused. Awake now, I realized that it had all been a dream. I wish it could have lasted a little longer.

"Sorry to wake you up boss, but we've got some real problems here!"

I looked up and saw the yellow figure of Kaz. Kaz was one of the many common bees in my hive. Kaz was the typical kind of bee that you see in the movies, lots of energy and always excited. Because of his personality, I really didn't take him seriously. After all, Kaz had spilled and wasted a lot of honey more than once simply because he was so clumsy and energetic. Kaz was also nervous a lot of the time, as if he drank too much coffee.

"What's the big deal waking me up like that, Kaz? I was having the best dream ever, and you just interrupted it!"

"I know, boss! You were smiling, and I could tell you were having a good night's rest, but this simply couldn't wait! It's Nate! He's gone!"

"He's what?"

I sat up on the bed, now wide awake. I was so shocked at the news that I had to get up and start moving. I heard it but I couldn't believe it. Nate was gone! When it rains, it really pours. My hive simply couldn't afford for anything like this to be happening. I mean, nothing was working out for me already, and now this had happened. My only fairly good bee was gone. I simply couldn't let this happen.

"What are you talking about, Kaz?"

"I'm serious, boss! We looked everywhere in the hive. Nate's gone! It's like he just vanished or something!"

I stood up from my bed and ran around the hive looking for Nate like a headless chicken. Kaz was right behind me. I looked around desperately and asked every single bee if they'd seen him. Unfortunately, Kaz wasn't just having some kind of nervous breakdown here. After searching the hive and asking everyone thoroughly, I had to admit the terrible truth: Nate was gone.

"Where could he have gone, boss?"

"I don't know, Kaz. I just don't know."

I felt terrible. At the back of my mind, I couldn't help but think that I kind of deserved this. It was pretty obvious why Nate would do something like this. Kaz didn't want to tell me to my face, but we all knew the real score here. Nate ran away because I was yelling at him and treating him like garbage. The poor bee had simply gotten fed up with me. Honestly, I couldn't even blame him.

"This is just awful. Nate was our best bee."

"He was a rare bumblebee, boss. He wasn't just a common bee like the rest of us" Kaz said.

"Don't say that, Kaz. You and your fellow bees are important to this hive."

Kaz gave me a kind of pained look. It was almost as if he had slipped and sprained his ankle or something. That is, if he could even sprain his ankle in the first place. Did bees even have ankles at all? I don't know. Well, the point is, he looked really hurt.

"Really? Can you really say that we're important to you, boss? You were just, well, a Noob in this game, and we all still joined with you. We all did our best to make the hive great, even if you were still new to all of this. Everyone tried their best, especially Nate. But you always got on our case, including his. Can you really believe what you just said?"

Ouch. Everything that Kaz said was true. Considering how I treated them all, I was lucky that they didn't all run away like Nate.

"I.. I don't know what to say, Kaz. I, I.. guess you're right. I have been treating you all really badly. I'm sorry."

There really wasn't anything else to say. It was pretty tense and awkward at the same time. I felt terrible for how I had been treating them, and now Nate was gone too. This was really getting bad.

Entry #4

The Journey Begins

When Kaz told me that Nate had run off like that, I knew what I had to do. I wasn't really looking forward to doing it, but Nate was gone and I had no choice but to take ownership for my own mistakes.

"Mario, Nate's gone. I need your help."

Yeah, you guessed it. I went to Mario for help. I didn't want to, but what choice did I have? Mario was the best player in the entire server, so if anyone could help me, it had to be him. If he didn't want to help me, well, I guess I really couldn't blame anyone but myself.

"Yeah, I thought you would come to me soon. Actually, Nate approached me, before he ran away."

"He what?"

"Yeah. He approached me all right. He was asking how to find that legendary tool that I was mentioning to you. That tool that could really increase hive productivity. He said that he wanted to get it to please you, Noob."

I couldn't believe what I was hearing. Nate had approached Mario before he ran off and Mario hadn't even told me! Now I was really furious!

"He approached you? Why didn't you tell me?"

Mario shrugged his shoulders.

"I thought he wouldn't go through with it. I already told him how far away the tool was and how dangerous the quest to get it could be."

"Where is this legendary tool, and what is it anyway?"

"The tool itself is located in the Pine Tree Forest."

Kaz decides to speak up. He had spent the last fifteen minutes dying to say something. He just loved to talk.

"The Pine Tree Forest? That field is far from here, and is guarded by..."

Kaz couldn't even complete his sentence. His voice was trembling now. A first for Kaz. It must be good news.

"It's defended by Mantises and Werewolves. Yes, I know"

Mario said.

I had heard about the infamous Pine Tree Forest. Unlike most fields in the server, it was full of, well, pine trees. It was really dark in that field and it was hard to navigate around it. And the worst part? Well, Kaz was right. The forest was home to werewolves and mantises. It was way too dangerous for Nate to be going there. I had to get him back before anything happened to him.

"And the tool?"

"It's the Super Jelly generator. It's supposed to be an ancient machine that generates Super Jelly."

Super Jelly. It was supposed to be some kind of legendary item that was ten times stronger than Royal Jelly. No one had discovered it yet, but a lot of players whispered that it could actually be made. If Super Jelly could be made, that would really be a game changer. That was because bees loved Royal Jelly. It was also the key to generating a lot of rare, epic or legendary bees. If Super Jelly existed and was even stronger than Royal Jelly, who knows what it could do? Well, it was all a legend, and now Nate had run away because of it. That, and my own harsh and mean ways.

"This is all my fault. If I hadn't been so mean to my bees in the first place, Nate would never have run away. I have to get him back. I'm going to the Pine Forest" I said.

"You're not going alone. I'm going with you."

It was Kaz. This was a really big step for someone like him. Kaz was a nervous wreck all the time. He had a real reputation in the hive as a bee who would easily lose it. Honestly, he was the least likely bee to go on a dangerous mission like this. I guess he was really that much of a friend to Nate. And Kaz wasn't the only one who wanted to accompany me to the Pine Forest.

"I'm coming along too, Noob."

"You too, Mario? Why would you accompany us? This has nothing to do with you. If anything, it's my fault that Nate got into this mess."

"Not really, Noob. If I hadn't told him in detail about the Super Jelly generator, Nate wouldn't have run away. I should have already known that he would be only too eager to please you. I guess you were right, Noob. I guess in a way, I just decided to mind my own business because I was the top player around here. I kinda got insensitive too."

I didn't want to drag Mario into my own mess, but he was really insistent. Maybe he wasn't so bad after all. I would still let him go first when walking through dangerous fields though.

"Mario, you don't have to go with us..."

Mario shook his head.

"I do, and you're not stopping me, Noob. However, I do need to get a change of duds. I'm not going in there with my red and blue suit and my big belly. They might mistake me for some kind of a silly plumber or something."

Kaz and I looked at each other and chuckled. After all, it was a simple enough thing for Mario to get a change of clothes, but his belly, well, let's just say that no one loses weight in less than a day. It was so big that you might think he was having triplets.

"Just give me a moment to prepare..."

"Take all the time you want, Mario. This is going to be a pretty dangerous quest."

Mario was a big guy, so I imagine it would take him a while to get ready. Not so much on deciding what to wear but rather what could actually fit him. I don't think anyone cared what he wore, I know I didn't.

"It will probably be dangerous, but it will be worth it, Noob! Who knows? We may even find that Super Jelly generator in the forest. If we do, I'm giving it to you!"

Mario ducked behind his hive as he spoke. He disappeared from our view, and Kaz and I could only assume that he was changing clothes. We could hear a lot of panting and screeching from Mario. He must have been struggling with putting on a new outfit.

"You don't have to do that, Mario. The important thing is that we get Nate back safely."

"No, I insist. After all, I'm a little responsible for his disappearing like this too. You were right, Noob. I think I should have tried to help you get better in the game. After all, what are neighbors for?"

"Mario, I don't know... thanks, but let's just make sure Nate is safe first, alright?"

After a few moments, Mario reappeared. He looked completely different. His red and blue trousers were gone, and his moustache was completely shaved off! He now wore a yellow suit, complete with some wings on his back. They were just decorations of course; Mario couldn't really fly, and he wasn't a bee, but he definitely looked a lot different now. The best part? His belly was gone!

"Whoa! Mario, you're..."

Mario smiled at me and Kaz. He was savoring our looks of amazement. It was the first time we could actually see his smile since he removed his mustache. He had a gap in his teeth so big that you could fit a chocolate bar through, sideways.

"I lost weight? Yeah! What do you think of the new look?"

"You look completely different! You really look like a Roblox man now!" Kaz said.

"How did you do it? I mean, how did you...?"

"Lose the belly? It's okay, Noob. You can say it. I don't mind."

"Yeah, that. How did you do it, Mario?"

"Simple! I just took a good swallow of my hive's honey. My bees produce really great honey with amazing effects. Swallowing my hive's honey is a lot better than eating some magic flower!"

"What? What do you mean?"

"Never mind. Let's just go find Nate!"

"Wait! You guys are going on a quest? Maybe you could squeeze my quest in, too? I'll make it worth your while!"

The three of us turned around and saw a giant panda

walking towards us. The panda bear was huge; he would have been scary if he was any other animal than a panda bear. It was amazing how he could sneak up on us like that considering his size. That's the thing about pandas, they were the masters of disguise in the animal kingdom. Ever seen a panda in real life? Didn't think so.

"Whoa! Who are you?" Kaz asked.

"A wandering quest bear. I'm sure you're familiar with my type, Noob."

"They give quests and offer a pretty big reward for them. Yeah, I know your type," I replied.

The panda bear smiled and was clearly pleased. He started shaking his hips in excitement. I couldn't help but wonder if he was a honey bear in disguise. I would carefully monitor him during our journey.

"Great! I'm glad to see that you are all familiar with a bear like me. So, you all know that I don't just give out quests for free; you'll be rewarded handsomely if you accept. I just overheard you guys talking about going out into the world to find your bee, and I just remembered that I need to get this huge honey jar. It's located right before the dandelion field - you can't miss it."

"You want us to get a honey jar? A jar that we can't miss

it?" I questioned. It seemed too easy to be true.

The panda bear nodded. If I was as big as the panda bear, I would probably refrain from consuming honey for a while.

"Yep! It's that simple. Get me the huge honey jar and I'll reward you and your hives with all the honey you could desire. Believe me, you can't miss it! Simple, right?"

"I think we should accept the quest, Noob. After all, panda bears are known for their honesty and good word. I think we would really be rewarded for this," Mario said. Maybe he was just a regular panda after all.

I shrugged my shoulders. I guess it couldn't hurt to accept a little side quest, right? What I didn't know then, but would find out later, was that was the kind of attitude that got a lot of dudes killed.

"Okay, sure. We'll do it."

"Great!"

It was settled right then and there. The three of us would look for Nate. Maybe we would find the Super Jelly generator, maybe not. Maybe we would even find that huge honey jar the panda was ranting about. That wasn't really important to me. What was important was the safety of my rare bee. I realized that I had been really mean to him and all my other bees. I was aware now that getting better at the game wasn't worth becoming such a mean dude, and I didn't want Nate to pay for my attitude problem. I just hoped that we could find him in time.

Entry #5

The Attack of the Ants.

Getting to the Pine Forest wouldn't be easy. The three of us knew this and we prepared ourselves as best as we could. To get there, we would have to get past the Cactus field, and then the Pumpkin field. These two fields were guarded by werewolves, so we were already sure to encounter the things before we even got to the Pine Forest. Yeah, that was a very comforting thought.

We hurried out of our field and left right away. The three of us knew that we couldn't wait. Time wasn't on our side here. The sooner we found Nate, the better. There were just too many dangers everywhere, and we had to make sure that Nate was safe. I didn't even want to think about the possibility that something had already happened to him. I had to believe that we would find him. If we were too late, I would never forgive myself.

It would be a long way to the Pine Forest. We traveled along the long and wide Dandelion field first. It was the first of a few fields we would have to go through before reaching the Pine Forest. This was a field that was full of dandelions, just as the name suggests. The field was littered with the flowers and it was really easy to wander around and enjoy yourself if you were a bee.

"This is definitely the first field that Nate would have passed through. I'm sure of it, simply because I'm a bee too, and I would have done the same thing" Kaz said. Kaz was right. I could imagine him having a field day here. It seemed like the kind of place where bees would go on dates.

"I know what you mean. The smell alone is so wonderful; I'm sure it would be irresistible for him" I said.

It was so relaxing walking through that field full of dandelions. The smell was so easy on the nose, and having all those pretty flowers all around you was really very comforting.

"I could just stay here and collect pollen all day if we weren't looking for Nate."

"I know what you mean, Kaz. This dandelion field is really

easy on the senses. Nate definitely passed through here. It's simply in your bees' nature."

It didn't take us long to find something large in that dandelion field. The object stuck out like a sore thumb. Literally.

"Look!" Kaz said.

He flew over a huge jar. I approached it and saw that it was full of honey. It was even marked as "the large honey jar." This must be the honey jar that the panda had been asking for.

"So, this is what that big panda was looking for," I said.

Mario nodded. He looked like he wanted to taste the contents because he was licking his lips and rubbing his tummy.

"He was right. This was easy."

But Mario was about to eat his words. We all should have realized that nothing comes easy in Bee Simulator. As we stared at the jar, a massive rogue vicious bee popped out of nowhere right in front of us. I was the one closest to the honey jar and it flew right in front of me.

"A rogue vicious bee! It must have been guarding that honey jar!" Kaz said, clearly startled at the size of it. Kaz fled faster than a cheetah desperately needing to use the toilet.

"Sorry guys, you are on your own!"

Thanks, Kaz. I knew you were nervous about everything, but I didn't think you would bail on us. I then remembered something.

"Wait Kaz, there is a candy store in the next field after this!"

Kaz did a u-turn and came back. He *loved* candy. Didn't your mom ever pretend there was a candy store nearby when you went out shopping? Everyone falls for that.

I started to think twice now about accepting the panda's quest. He never mentioned anything about a rogue vicious bee guarding his honey jar!

That was when complete chaos erupted, and the rogue vicious bee summoned his spikes from the ground. One of them managed to nick me, and I was lying on the ground, totally exposed. Yeah, this was how I ended up in that sticky situation I talked about in the real first entry. My life flashed before my eyes, it was mostly of playing videogames and sleeping. I was done for, for sure.

Or maybe not.

The bee buzzed around, and it was clear that I had enraged it. I expected it to summon another spike from the ground, but it did not. It seemed I wasn't destined to die. Not just yet.

"Hold it right there! No one's taking down Noob on my watch!"

It was Mario. He zipped towards that rogue vicious bee with the speed of a bullet. He sure moved a lot faster than a man his size should. Before it could summon another one of those nasty spikes from the ground, Mario jumped on top of the rogue vicious bee with tremendous force, flattening him like a pancake. I guess I had distracted that rotten bee long enough for Mario to make his move.

"Mario! You saved me!"

"Forget it, Noob! I'm sure you would have done the same for me. Anyway, we've got the huge honey jar that the panda wanted so let's keep going. We've still got a long way to go, and a lot of danger to overcome."

Mario couldn't have said it better. As you might have noticed, I had a newfound respect for my neighbor. But my appreciation for Mario was cut short when we all suddenly felt the ground shaking beneath our feet.

"Whoa! What's going on? It feels like an earthquake!" I

said.

The ground was shaking so badly that we could both barely stay standing. It was so scary that I screamed like a little girl.

"I'm really glad I don't have any legs or feet to walk on the ground with!" Kaz said.

"Yeah? That won't really matter if you get squashed with that thing!"

I was the one who noticed the giant ant first. It was so massive that every step it took made the ground shake and tremble. For something so huge, it was quite strange, because we never saw it coming. It was almost as if that big bug came out of nowhere.

A giant ant was the worst thing that we could have stumbled upon. It was the rarest of ants in the whole server. Despite this, it was clearly the most dangerous. One stomp of its several huge feet and we would be squished like bugs.

"Where did that thing come from?" Kaz said.

"Does it matter? Let's just get out before it steps on us!"

We made a break for it, but it was too late. The giant ant saw us and, well, it wanted to stomp on us right then and there. Still, that wasn't the end of our troubles. Along with a giant ant came the inevitable swarm of ants. We could all end up with ants in our pants!

"The ants are swarming behind him! This is bad! This is really bad!" Kaz said.

"What are we going to do now, Mario? I doubt even you could jump over that giant ant and trample him! Even if you did, there are so many other ants there that you couldn't possibly stop all of them at once!"

"I think I have just the thing!"

Mario whipped out a giant jar from his person. I really don't know how he managed to carry it with him during the journey. Who knew what he had brought along with him and what he could do with it? This was Mario we were talking about here after all...

Mario tossed the giant jar away from us. The jar shattered, revealing what appeared to be a lot of Royal Jelly. It wasn't just Royal Jelly, however.

"How did you manage to place all that Royal Jelly inside a single jar like that?" I asked.

"It's not just Royal Jelly; it's Royal Jelly mixed with my own hive's honey. The resulting mix is a lot denser than you can imagine, and you can stuff a lot of it into the jar. It's also super sweet, and ants of any size love anything that's sweet."

Kaz got really excited on seeing the royal jelly, more excited than ever. He was flying around in circles like a drunk helicopter.

"Don't even think about it!"

Kaz started to buzz aggressively, "I want just a little taste!"

"If you eat that royal jelly then we won't be going to the candy store later!"

Kaz immediately behaved himself.

The moment Mario shattered his jar, all the ants ignored us and swarmed around it. They simply couldn't get enough of the stuff. The giant ant trampled upon several of the smaller ants just to get at the sweet puddle that Mario had tossed their way. A lot of the small ants were squished, but there were more than enough to take their place. I couldn't believe it, but the ants were all fighting for that small puddle of sweet goodness.

"Amazing! They're all fighting for it! You're really something else, Mario!"

"You can praise me later. Let's just keep running now that their attention is off of us!"

It was a brilliant move by Mario who had managed to throw the ants off our trail. If Mario wasn't here, I probably would have cried and quit the game entirely.

"Boy, you really can do anything, can't you, Mario?"

Yeah, that was me there, gushing like a teenage girl with a crush. I just couldn't help myself. I know I was really hard on Mario's case at first, but things were different now. They had to be; I mean this was the second time that Mario saved my skin from a monstrous mob. I was so glad that he was on our side.

"Thanks for the compliment, Noob, but I'm not immortal, perfect, or anything like that at all. I'm really just here to find Nate, like you and Kaz."

"And we'll do that. We've got to find him!" I said.

"I sure hope so."

The three of us looked back after we had put a considerable distance between ourselves and the ants. We heard in the distance the sounds of munching and trampling. The ground underneath us shook really badly, but as we gained ground, the tremors got weaker and weaker. Soon enough, we were way past the ants and they had completely forgotten about us. They were too busy eating up that mixture that Mario had prepared. Well, that was one obstacle we had overcome. I just hoped that we would be strong enough to overcome anything else that came our way and still find Nate.

Entry #6

The Werewolf.

After we got past the ants and the dandelion field, we approached a field that was vastly different from the previous one. While the dandelion field was full of attractive flowers and wonderful smells, this one was noticeably different. There weren't any flowers in this field at all, and it looked pretty barren. The field looked hot, dry and parched. There was nothing that grew here except for several cactuses that were spread all over the field.

"Whoa! What is this place?" I asked.

"This is the cactus field. This is the field that's closest to the Pine Tree Forest. We're getting close," Mario said.

Well, that was definitely a relief. After the experience

with the giant ant and the other ants, I really just wanted to get back home and tend to my bees. I could see that Kaz was also getting nervous and going back to his old, jittery self.

"I sure can't wait to find Nate and get back home," Kaz said.

"Same here. I just can't wait to get back home. I don't want to face any more hostile mobs than we have to."

"Well, in that case, I really hate to disappoint you both, but there's probably a hostile mob guarding this field. I heard reports that a werewolf guards the cactus field," Mario said.

"Yeah, it's really reassuring," I said.

Despite our fears, we all advanced towards the cactus field.

The cactus field was, well, full of cacti everywhere we looked. You would have thought that we would have gotten pricked or nipped by all those spikes. Well, we didn't, not with Mario around. He surprisingly knew his way around this sharp field.

"You seem to know your way around here," I said.

"Yeah. I tried harvesting pollen here with my bees once,

but I gave up after several tries."

"You giving up? Somehow, I can't seem to imagine that," Kaz said.

"I agree with Kaz. You seem to know how to take down just about every mob, Mario. Why did you give up harvesting this field?"

"Well, as you can both see, the field isn't really ideal. It's full of cacti, and it's also incredibly hot here. I probably could have made a go of it, but it wouldn't have been worth the effort, even if I did manage to get a good amount of pollen with my bees."

I wiped my forehead. The sweat was dripping from my head in buckets. Mario was right. It was pretty hot here, all right.

"I can see what you mean about the heat," I said.

"I guess it would have been pretty tough harvesting this field."

"Believe me, Noob. If you want your hive to grow, it's best that you make the most of the common fields all over the server, just like the one we have. Just stick to it, and your hive will grow and produce a lot of honey in time."

I guess there was a lot of merit to what Mario said. I just couldn't really completely go for it because, I admit it, I was still pretty envious of all his achievements in the game. Well, I tried to set my jealousy aside. After all, it was that jealousy that got Nate in trouble in the first place. It was best to just let it go completely. Kaz looked around anxiously.

"Where is this candy store boss?"

"Oh, did I say candy store? I meant sandy floor, you like sand, don't you?

"Well yes, yes I do but we have no time to play in the sand."

Mario looked over at me. He knew there was no candy store (probably), but it was a little white lie I had to tell Kaz to keep us going. Besides, Kaz has definitely earned some candy, so I'll reward him once we are home.

In any case, I think he knew I had enough to worry about so didn't say anything.

"I guess you know your stuff, Mario. After all, you do have a lot of experience tending to a hive."

"You'll get there, Noob. Trust me."

The three of us approached the end of the field and came

across a single cave. It looked really dark inside.

"This is where the field ends. What's inside that cave?" I asked.

"Well, uhm, this is the end of the field. The cave leads out of the field and towards the pumpkin field."

"And one step closer to the Pine Forest and Nate!" I said.

"Yeah. But we'll all have to get through that cave."

Mario turned towards it, and I could detect some fear in his voice. That was new. Mario seemed like the fearless type, and I wasn't used to seeing him show even a little fear and hesitation.

"Something wrong, Mario?" I asked.

"Nothing. It's just that, that cave is where the werewolf in this place lives. Or so they say."

"Yep. That doesn't sound very reassuring at all," I said.

"Come on, guys. We all have to keep going. We can't stop now. Nate's depending on us."

Mario was right. We had to enter that cave and keep going, even if we were more than a little afraid of what we might find inside.

"Well, bees first!" I said.

I motioned for Kaz to enter, and he just fluttered around us. Yeah, he wasn't going in there first all right.

"I am sure there is candy in there Kaz, caves are always full of candy!"

"You are thinking of treasure Boss!"

"Candy IS treasure!"

"I'll go in first. You guys watch my back."

It was Mario. He went right in that dark cave, and Kaz and I followed. He carried this really big torch to light the way. It gave us a lot of light, and we could see right in front of us now. The light from the torch made entering the cave a little more bearable. We were all afraid but being able to see in front of us made a big difference.

We kept walking for some time through that cave. It seemed to be quite long and wound around like some large snake. It was really spooky too.

"Are you holding my hand?" said Mario.

I laughed, "no, it's probably Kaz!"

"But I don't have hands, I am a bee."

"OK, I am holding your hand, I am scared!"

"This cave seems to stretch to forever!" Kaz said.

"Don't worry. It will end. It's got to. And when it does, we'll reach the pumpkin field."

"Wait a minute, Mario. You did say that you tried to start a hive here at the cactus field, right?"

Mario nodded.

"Yeah. What about it?"

"I don't get it. I thought you had already been there. Didn't you go inside this cave?"

Mario shook his head.

"Why do you think I am letting you hold my hand?!"

Mario took a deep breath to try and relax.

"I said that I went to the cactus field. I didn't say that I explored the cave here. This cave is completely new territory, even for me."

"So, you've never been here? How did you even know about the werewolf?" Kaz asked.

Mario shrugged his shoulders.

"Stories from other Bee Simulator players. They all talked

about this really scary werewolf that guarded the cactus field. They mentioned that he lived in this cave. I never really stayed long enough to find out if there was any truth to the stories."

"I see. So you've never seen or encountered the werewolf yourself?"

"Exactly, and I would really hope to keep it that way."

Kaz smiled and fluttered about with some excitement.

"Well, we've been walking through this cave for some time, and we haven't caught a glimpse of any werewolf so far. Maybe it's all one big story. I mean, you know how it is? Maybe the werewolf is just a story to keep everyone away from the cactus field. Maybe we won't encounter him at all!" he said.

"I really hope so, but we've already encountered a ladybug and a giant ant and his fellow smaller ants. I wouldn't bet on the werewolf being nothing but a myth."

"Come on, Mario! Don't say that. Let's think positive here," I said.

"Let's just be ready for anything."

Sound advice coming from a true beekeeper like Mario, for sure. However, there was no way we would be ready for what would come at us right then and there.

It was the werewolf. He came at us from out of nowhere. Even with the torch in front of us, we still never saw him coming. His speed was amazing.

Suddenly, it was right in front of us. It was large and had a fearsome growl.

"Good doggy, good doggy!"

I desperately checked my pockets for anything I could use to distract him but all I found was a mint. Unless he had bad breath then I was in deep trouble.

We all did the most logical thing. It was really the only thing anyone could have done. We ran out of there. More accurately, we ran away in the opposite direction of the werewolf.

We ran as fast as we could, and we could hear the werewolf howling from behind us. We were all scared, even Mario. This was the first time I had really seen Mario scared. For the longest time, I had seen him as some kind of amazing player who could do anything. I guess it turned out that he was a lot more similar to me, or anyone else for that matter, than I had first thought.

"That's the scariest werewolf I've ever seen!" Kaz said.

"Is there really such a thing as a werewolf that isn't scary?" I said.

Kaz and Mario didn't answer. That was my point, exactly.

We kept running but, right at that moment, the werewolf suddenly appeared in front of us. I don't know how he did it, but it always seemed as if he were one step ahead of us and could pop up from out of nowhere. Did he have some kind of magical powers? I would later learn that there was a much simpler explanation for this than I thought.

The werewolf in front of us gave out a loud roar. This roar was even scarier than the last one and echoed throughout the whole cave. I covered my ears and shook in terror. This dangerous mob was right in front of us, and there seemed to be no way out.

"Don't eat us, please!" Kaz said.

And that was when it happened. I closed my eyes and raised my arms in front of my face, kind of expecting the worst. What I got wasn't the worst. It wasn't even anything any of us ever really expected at all.

"Eat you guys? I'm not going to eat you at all. I don't like eating things alive!"

The werewolf spoke to us in a very friendly and civilized voice. It was miles away from the bellowing cries that he gave out. He actually sounded like some kind of gentleman. None of us could believe what we were hearing.

"What...?"

"Did you just say that you wouldn't eat us?"

It was Mario who gathered the courage to ask the werewolf about his motives. The werewolf continued to answer in a friendly tone that was miles away from his howls of terror.

"Why would I want to eat you guys at all?"

"Uhm, you did howl and growl earlier. What did you expect us to think?"

It was me asking this question. I couldn't understand any of it, so I just had to ask the werewolf up front what this was about.

"That stuff earlier? You guys were scared of that stuff? Come on! That's just how werewolves say 'hi.' I was surprised that you guys ran off when I was just introducing myself, so I chased after you all. I finally managed to corner you."

None of us couldn't believe what the werewolf was saying. This was something else.

"For real?" I asked.

"Why would I want to eat you guys?"

"For starters, you're a werewolf and that's what everybody thinks about werewolves. Everyone knows that werewolves eat anything alive," Kaz said.

"Oh, is that so? So, you're going to believe everything that everyone says about me and my kind? That is really incredibly mean of you to do so. So, if everyone said that bees were evil creatures that only wanted to sting people to death, you would believe them?"

"No way! That's different! Nobody thinks that way of us! We're all known for being cute and cuddly hardworking creatures that make honey all day!"

I nudged Kaz in the back.

"Uhm, actually he's right. Some guys actually do think bees are mean."

"For real? No way, boss!"

"Yes, you have a stinger attached to your butt, don't you?"

"Noob's right, and I kind of get what the werewolf is saying. Maybe he isn't as dangerous as we thought," Mario said.

"That's better. You guys can't believe everything they say about us. By the way, I'm not just "the werewolf " here. I've got a name too you know. I'm Melvin."

Melvin stretched out his paw to us. For a moment, I thought that he would rake or claw us with it, but it became apparently clear that he just wanted to shake hands, or paws, with us.

"Uhm, nice to meet you, Melvin. I'm Noob, and this is Mario, and my bee, Kaz."

"Nice to meet all of you guys. I'm glad you were all passing down here. After all, I don't really get too many visitors in here."

"That's not really surprising, but yeah, I get it," Mario said.

"Well, what brings all of you here?" Melvin asked.

"We're looking for a bumblebee. He's my bumblebee actually. A pretty fat one with a nice smile, and pretty friendly too. His name's Nate. Maybe Nate passed through here?"

Melvin reacted with excitement at my inquiry.

"Yeah! Yeah, I know him, He was delicious."

We all stood in terror. Maybe he didn't eat people but bees. What kind of game are we playing?

"I'm joking! I spoke with him earlier."

"Really? What did he say?"

"He said that he was looking for the way to the Pine Forest. He said that he was looking for the legendary Super Jelly generator."

Now I was excited too. We were on the right track, and there was still a good chance that we could find Nate.

"That's wonderful! What did you tell him?" I asked.

"I told him to go past the pumpkin field. The pumpkin field is just outside this cave, but you could get lost in this cave because there are many side routes and tunnels here. I know the way out since I live here. I showed Nate the way out. I could do that for you guys, too."

"You would do that? For real?"

Now I was really excited. We all were. This werewolf, or Melvin, had actually spoken with Nate. This was a really big development. Perhaps he was the key to finding and saving Nate. I had now a great team and I didn't have to hold Mario's sweaty hand anymore.

Entry #7

The Giant Mantis.

Melvin was kind enough to honor his word and show us the way out of the cave. Melvin was actually a very friendly sort, just as he had described himself. He was in no way the terrible or terrifying werewolf that the stories made him out to be. Because of this, I did feel kind of guilty for immediately judging him as some kind of scary, fearsome creature. I could see now that Melvin was actually a very kind and friendly guy. Remind me never to judge someone in the future until I really get to know them better.

"Boy, this cave sure is confusing! There are a lot of tunnels and it's so dark. It all looks the same to me," Kaz said.

"That's just what I said earlier. The cave has so many twists and turns inside that it's easy to get lost in it. I showed

Nate the shortcut out of here, just as I'm showing you guys."

After some time, we finally came to the end of the cave.

"Well, here we are. This is the end of the cave, and this is where the pumpkin field starts."

We reached the end of the cave, and just outside was a field full of pumpkins. It was just as Melvin had described it. We were really getting close to Nate now.

"Just get past this pumpkin field and you'll get to the Pine forest. I better accompany you guys all the way."

Mario shook his head.

"No, you don't have to, Melvin. You've already done enough for us by showing us the way out of your cave. We don't want to take up any more of your time. You've probably got something better to do."

Melvin shrugged his shoulders.

"Yeah, like what? It's not as if a werewolf like me has a busy schedule or anything. I really don't have anything better to do. Besides, I think you guys are still going to need my help."

"Why is that so?" I asked.

"Well, because we're approaching the pumpkin field, and it's guarded by a mantis."

"Oh no! I had almost forgotten about that mob! There's always got to be some kind of dangerous creature blocking our way, hasn't there?" Kaz said.

"Well, if you insist, Melvin. We really could use all the help we could get," Mario said.

We all walked through the pumpkin field. There were pumpkins as far as the eye could see. I was amazed at all the fields that the server had to offer. For the longest time, I was just stuck in my field with my hive, and with Mario and his. I kind of thought that the world was just limited to us. Boy, was I ever wrong.

"All these pumpkins look so yummy! It would sure be great to get pollen here!" Kaz said.

"I wouldn't really recommend that, Kaz. After all, this is the pumpkin field, and there is a big, bad mantis that lives around these parts," Melvin said.

"Well, I'm sure you'll be able to protect us if ever it shows itself."

Mario started picking up pumpkins and carrying them.

"What are you doing?" I said.

"In case we get hungry later, who knows how long until we reach Nate."

"You don't need five pumpkins Mario!"

"No, four of them are for me!"

Kaz didn't have long to wait for that. Before Melvin could say anything in response, we came across the giant mantis. It was lying behind a considerably large pile of pumpkins that were stacked on top of each other. Just as we passed the pumpkin stack, the mantis knocked all of them down, exposing himself to us. He was, well, a giant mantis. He was a little bigger than the giant ant, and that said a lot about his size!

"Whoa! That's the biggest mantis I've ever seen!" Mario said.

"You guys get moving! I'll distract it! Don't stop for anything! Believe me, it's not as friendly as I am," Melvin said.

"No way! We're not leaving you behind!" I said.

"Don't be silly, Noob! That giant mantis really will eat you guys up if you give it the chance, and there's no reasoning with it!"

I shook my head. I was firm about this. After all, I had

already lost Nate because of my bad attitude. I wasn't going to get Melvin in trouble for it too.

"That giant mantis isn't going to be easy to stop! How are we going to stop it?" Kaz asked.

"Exactly my point! That's why you guys should have run while you had the chance!"

Mario shook his head. Now I was seeing the old Mario again. There was no fear in his eyes, even with the giant mantis standing right in front of us.

"Noob's right! We're not leaving anyone behind here, not after what happened to Nate! Besides, I think stopping the mantis is a lot simpler than it seems!"

"Is that so? How?"

Melvin was getting a little frantic now. The giant mantis swiped at him with one of its giant legs. He leapt away just in time to avoid being swatted away like a fly. Keep in mind he was still carrying the pumpkins. He started juggling them like a clown.

"The answer is all around us, literally! Grab some pumpkins and throw them at the mantis!"

"I get what you're trying to do, Mario! It's brilliant!" I said.

Melvin did say that the mantis was crazy about pumpkins, and pumpkins were just about everywhere in the field around us. I grabbed some pumpkins and tossed them towards the mantis. They immediately drew the attention of the creature who started to munch on them.

"It's working! Keep tossing the pumpkins!" Mario said.

"Amazing! You guys sure are smarter than you look!" Melvin said.

Before long, even Melvin got into the act and started tossing pumpkins towards the mantis. It was so distracted that it couldn't even think of fighting anymore and, tossing a final load of pumpkins towards him, we strolled out of the field.

"Amazing that it completely forgot about us once it focused on the pumpkins!" Kaz said.

"A giant animal like that mantis is easily distracted," Mario said.

"Exactly! Now you guys can go straight to the Pine Forest. As I'm here with you guys too, I might as well join with you and go on all the way."

I could really see now that Melvin was anything but a scary werewolf. If anything, he was a friendly dude. I was really happy to have him come along with now as we neared the end of our journey.

Entry #8

A Great Surprise.

Well, we made it to the Pine Forest. This was the last stop in our journey to find Nate.

"Well, we're here. Now, we just have to find Nate and we can get back home," I said.

"If we find the Super Jelly generator, it could be a really big thing for all of us," Mario said.

I shook my head.

"If we find it, it's yours, Mario. I really don't care about that legendary item anymore. All I care about is the safety of Nate."

"You've really come a long way since we started out in this journey, boss. Nate will be glad to see that you're not who you used to be," Kaz said.

It was a grim reminder from Kaz, even if he didn't mean it. We wouldn't even be in this situation if I had been nicer to Kaz, Nate, and all my other bees in the first place. I just hoped that we were not too late.

The Pine Forest was full of trees; it seemed impossible to find a bumblebee like Nate in a large forest like this.

"How are we going to find Nate now? This forest is so big!" Mario said.

"Leave that to me! As a bee, I know Nate's particular scent and I can zero in on him through that, even in a place like this," Kaz said.

"Well then, it's up to you now, Kaz. Can you catch Nate's scent?"

Kaz flew up into the air and sniffed around for what seemed like an eternity. Finally, he answered me.

"I've got it! Follow me!"

Kaz flew as fast as he could towards the scent. We all followed close behind him.

"I heard that there are werewolves here too! What are we going to do if any of them come out of the trees?" I asked.

"Leave them to me. You're with a very sociable wolf here. They won't harm you as long as I'm with you guys," Melvin said.

"Are we getting closer, Kaz?" Mario asked.

Kaz kept sniffing the air around him. His wings fluttered furiously and sounded more like a plane's propellers than wings. I had never seen him fly this fast and with this much purpose.

"We are! Come on!"

We dashed through a lot of bushes and plants. I almost stumbled along the way trying to keep up with Kaz, but we all kept going.

"Here! I found it!"

Kaz had brought us to a candy store. He must have sniffed my mint and followed the scent. I can't believe that there was even a candy store here. Kaz immediately flew in and ransacked the place of its candy, eating as much as he could in seconds. He came back out, his belly the size of a balloon.

"Oh I also picked up Nate's scent too, he is over there."

Kaz pointed towards a small tree and behind it was Nate. I was so relieved that he was all right.

Nate turned and saw us, and I could see the fear in his eyes. I really regretted seeing it there. It was my fault that he was so scared. I had treated him so badly and I was sorry about that. I knew that I had to change.

"Nate! You're all right!" I said.

"Boss! Kaz! Mario! And Melvin, too! What are you guys doing here?"

"Never mind that! I'm just glad you're all right!"

I ran up to Nate and hugged him. Kaz came with me, and it was a group hug now.

"Boss, are you all right?"

"I'm fine, Nate! Listen, I know I've been really mean to you and the other bees, but I'm not going to do it anymore. I've realized the error of my ways. I'm not going to treat you like trash anymore. From now on, things are going to change around the hive!"

"For real, boss?"

I could see the look of shock and confusion on Nate's face. I guess he couldn't really believe that I was serious.

After all the times I was so mean to him, I guess I couldn't really blame him for that.

"Yes. Don't worry, Nate. I mean it."

"Thanks, boss. I'm really sorry I ran off, but I was looking for the Super Jelly generator. I didn't find it. I'm not even sure it's a real item."

I shook my head and smiled at Nate.

"I told you, Nate. That doesn't matter now. You guys just keep up the good work at the hive. I'm happy that you're all my bees."

"Thanks, boss. Really. Thanks."

"Look, guys! Maybe we can still go home with something after all!"

Kaz pointed to a small egg on the ground. No one had noticed it at first because it blended in with all the other rocks around it. We moved the rocks and saw it clearly. I couldn't believe what Kaz had found!

"Look, boss! It's a Tabby egg!"

"That's a rare event egg, Noob! That hatches into a Tabby bee! An event bee! Usually, they can only be purchased... But somehow, you've found one! That means..."

I smiled at Mario.

"That I'll finally have an event bee. Yeah."

"I'm so happy for you, Noob!"

So, I managed to get an event bee after all. That was all great and wonderful but, for me, it was just a bonus. The important thing was that Nate was safe, we all went home happy, and we even made a new friend in Melvin. It was a really great adventure that ended well for everyone!

UNOFFICIAL

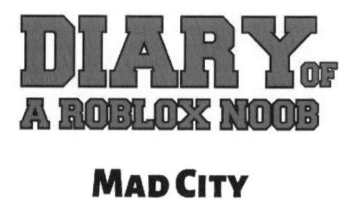

MAD CITY

BOOK 3
ROBLOXIA KID

Entry #1

One Small Step for Noob, One Giant Leap Into... Mad City?

Hey y'all! It's everyone's favorite Roblox hero here: Noob. I've got a new series of adventures to share that I just had to jot down in my trusty Noob Diary. And believe me, they have all the twists and turns and excitement that you'd want from a classic Noob adventure! Plus, you might even learn a thing or two along the way... I'm sure I did! Yup, I was just as surprised as you are now. I told you: these adventures have got it all!

I know that the description makes it sound really fun, but in all honesty, I wasn't thrilled at all when these adventures came my way. You've got to understand where I'm coming from here. The thrilling adventures you read about are my own death-defying experiences!

In other words, while you find them thrilling, I'm the one risking my neck out there so you can enjoy all the thrills and spills of a Noob adventure... so, you better appreciate it! Another important thing to mention is that exciting, unexpected adventures are not quite as exciting when you're retired!

Well, introductions aside, let's get to the meat and bones of it all then, shall we? It's time for me to tell you about my adventure in Mad City.

Yeah, you read that right. My most recent adventures took place in Mad City, the most dangerous city in all of Roblox! And I'm sure you're wondering how on Earth I might have found myself having an adventure in a place as *mad* as Mad City. Well, too bad! I haven't gotten to that part yet...

Looking back, this was probably the most exciting venture I've had so far! But it didn't start with me climbing up walls or shooting down cops in high-speed car chases. This story began with simply chilling on the couch and chowing down on some pizza. Oh, don't worry, though— all the car chasing and shooting bits still happened later!

I've realized that the greatest journeys begin with a single step. Sometimes that step can be so small it's barely noticeable. But a step is the beginning of a road to an epic journey and sometimes an even better destination!

It's just like Neil Armstrong said during the moon landing of 1969:

"That's one small step for man. One giant leap for mankind."

See what I mean about small steps leading to much bigger things? You never know. Even the smallest step could send you to space!

So there I was, taking the "first small step" of my adventure, chilling in my house and enjoying the pizza. It was really something else too! Salmon with root beer pizza! Yeah, I know what you're thinking, it sounds really weird. I prefer the term "exotic." I heard about the toppings from a food video I saw online. It sounded really strange, and I like strange things, so I decided to try it out. Hey, don't judge... the other suggestion was apple and ketchup. I think I made the right decision. I'm sure some would say they were both very bad decisions.

Anyway, I'm getting a little off track. This took place a little while after I'd returned from my vacation in Bee Swarm Simulator. Well, if you can call it that. I'm sure you remember. I've had my share of adventures in that server as well. It turned out to be anything but relaxing, so I was taking my time chilling at home and trying to get my life here in Mad City in order.

In any case, this new adventure begins with me just sitting on my couch. And little did I know, I was a sitting duck.

"Move! Move!"

"Target is inside!"

"Fire in the hole!"

My ears were suddenly assaulted by a barrage of military-style commands. The sound of SWAT soldiers' voices was accompanied by the sound of my front door suddenly being kicked open. I dropped my pizza in shock. It was heartbreaking. Even if it was salmon.

"Hey, what's going on?"

The SWAT soldiers didn't bother to answer me. My small home was suddenly flooded with SWAT soldiers! Definitely not cool!

Oh, and one of them had shouted, "fire in the hole," right? Well, that's what they always say as they toss some kind of grenade in their enemy's face.

"What is this? I didn't do anythi…"

I hadn't even finished my sentence when a thick cloud of smoke suddenly sprouted in the middle of my living room. It filled the room, preventing me from seeing or breathing! All I could do was cough—hard.

"What's… the… meaning of… this? I…"

I spat out words between the coughs. There was no way I could focus. The smoke was everywhere.

"You're coming with us, Noob!"

I heard the SWAT soldier's voice in front of me. His voice sounded muffled and hollow like the rest of the soldiers. They were all wearing gas masks which made them sound as if they were speaking from the inside of a tree trunk. But more importantly, the gas masks meant that they weren't coughing their brains out like I was!

"Target is within area! Repeat, target is within area!"

"Target is incapacitated! I'm going in!"

Inca-what? These crazy SWAT guys were invading my house! I couldn't believe what was happening. What had I done to deserve any of this?

"Stop! What are you…?"

Before I knew what was happening, one of the SWAT

guys rushed up to me, tackling me hard. In my current state, there was no way that I could avoid it.

I went down on the floor. The SWAT guy had me pinned!

"Neutralizing the target now!"

"Hey, whoa!"

The SWAT guy moved fast. He spun me around so that my face was on the ground and grabbed both my arms and held them together. I heard the sound of a pair of handcuffs snapping shut, and I knew that I was truly helpless now.

"Target is neutralized! We've got him!"

One of the other SWAT guys came up to me. I felt him stand over me as I lay face-down on the ground.

The smoke was starting to clear now and he took off his gas mask. I looked up and saw him smiling maliciously down at me.

"This is just 'cause I can."

As he spoke, he brought down the handle of his rifle onto my head. It was a hard strike that would give me a nasty bump and headaches for hours. I was knocked out cold.

Entry #2

Welcome to Mad City.

When I woke up, I wasn't at my house anymore—I think I had seen that one coming when the dude knocked me out! I was somewhere else. Likely somewhere I wouldn't be by choice.

I could feel that I was in a moving van. A team of SWAT guys were sat beside me and my wrists and ankles were all cuffed up.

"Who are you guys? Why did you invade my home? I've done nothing to deserve this. I'm no criminal! I even served in the police force for some time!"

One of the SWAT guys looked over at me. I immediately recognized his features. It was the guy that had whacked me with his rifle. He had a really nasty grin on his face that told me he wouldn't hesitate to do it again.

"It doesn't matter. KingPat wants you tossed into the slammer."

"KingPat? Who's KingPat?" I really didn't know who KingPat was!

"You say you were on the force, and you don't know KingPat? What were you doing all that time? Eating doughnuts?"

The SWAT officer was hitting a little too close to home here. I'd served on the force, and I'd served well. And it seemed like yesterday, but it had been almost a year now since I had served as a cop in Mad City. Considering the high crime rate, not to mention that bizarre time I was kidnapped by Granny, well, I just couldn't take it anymore. The stress was too overwhelming, so I did the only thing any sensible person would do: I resigned from the job. It had been a whole year since I had left the force and I had been living quietly until this happened, not looking for any trouble. Now, trouble was coming to me.

Another SWAT guy was talking to me now. He was still wearing his gas mask and helmet, so I didn't recognize him. He sounded a little nicer than the last one at least. It actually sounded as if he felt sorry for me, as if he wouldn't have broken into my house if he had had a choice. That just made me feel even worse.

"Who's KingPat?"

"Go ahead and fill our ex-cop in on the details, George. Might shut him up! It doesn't really matter what we tell him now. When KingPat has you in his sights, you're as good as dead from the start!"

The dude without the mask seemed to be having a blast. I didn't even know the guy, but he was rejoicing at my misery. I had so many questions in my mind. What was this guy's problem with me? Why did the SWAT guys barge in and capture me like this? And the biggest question of all: who was this KingPat dude and why did he have me arrested?

"The captain's right, man. You're in really big trouble. KingPat's the guy that runs the whole city. He controls the cops, the businesses and everything in between. He owns Mad City."

"And now he owns you, too," the nastier SWAT member added.

All these questions were swimming around in my head, like fish crowding a small bowl. I hope you liked that fishbowl simile, by the way, I'm really trying to make my adventures sound more exciting. Plus, all the descriptive writing makes me sound kind of heroic— Sorry, getting off track again. Anyway, the fact that I had never heard of KingPat was disturbing. I wondered how he had managed to get a hold on the police force and the whole of Mad City, in only a year. The way the SWAT cops spoke about him, they sounded really afraid of this guy. Whoever he was, he was clearly powerful, and most importantly, I had caught his attention somehow. I didn't like the idea that this powerful man was after me, an ex-Mad City cop. What did I ever do to him? I didn't even know him!

"I don't get it! I'm no criminal! I'm an ex-cop in this town! I even feed stray cats and dogs! Why would this KingPat guy want me arrested?"

The captain shrugged his shoulders.

"Hey, do I look like I care? I don't know, and quite frankly, I don't really want to know. All I know is this: I sure don't envy you."

"The captain's right. KingPat's not someone you want to be enemies with. Man, I'm sorry, but I'm just doing my job. We all are. You have to understand."

Understand? I didn't understand any of this. This was exactly the kind of thing I was trying to avoid now. I had experienced more than my fair share of danger and craziness as a Mad City cop. Just a year in that job drained me completely. Now, I was being dragged back into it once again.

I stared out the small window. The big city looked a little darker, a little meaner, and a lot more dangerous to me now. I never realized how different things could appear when you were the one being arrested. I looked outside and saw the usual Mad City stuff. In this city, crime was an ordinary occurrence, and there was a lot of it. There seemed to be some kind of street fight taking place on every corner we passed. There were even some dudes shooting at each other. This didn't look like a city. This looked more like a warzone.

"I never noticed just how crazy this town was."

"When you're a cop you try to block all of the crazy stuff out. You view it as just a part of your job, I guess." It was the sympathetic one, George, who spoke.

Before I even joined the force, I had already heard rumors about Mad City. Everyone had. The crime rate was sky high, and unpredictable didn't even come close to describing how crazy life was in Mad City. It really earned its name. If this KingPat ran the city then he must be pretty tough and fearsome.

"We're taking you to Mad City prison. The worst prison in the worst city. Welcome to your nightmare!" the captain said.

I could hear clearly the delight in the captain's voice. I had never met him, but he seemed to be enjoying himself. This guy was trouble.

"Who are you, and what's your problem?" I asked.

My question really angered the SWAT captain. He whipped out his bat, and struck me across the head. The small riot bat hit a lot harder than I had expected it to.

"Ouch!"

"Think you're somebody, little man? Think you're still worth anything? Well, let me tell you now, you're not! First, you quit the force. Why was that, by the way? You a coward? And now, KingPat wants you jailed. So that puts you right at the bottom of the food chain in all of Mad City! So, don't go get started on me, you got it? And the name's Captain Tracy. But that's sir to you!"

Captain Tracy. I knew I would never forget this jerk's name. He sure wouldn't let me.

Entry #3

What's My Name?

"What's your name?"

The prison guard was asking a simple enough question, but he barked it at me like an insult. Is being in a bad mood part of the qualifications you need to work for the criminal justice system? Anyway...

"My name's Noob and..."

"Wrong answer! You're nobody now! Once you enter Mad City prison, you're less than nobody! You're now just prisoner number 1568!"

Prisoner 1568. It sounded intimidating, like I wasn't even Noob anymore. These dudes were making sure that I knew my place.

"Here! Wear these at all times!"

The guard threw a bunch of clothes over to me. I tried to catch them but missed, and they fell all over the ground in front of me.

"Bad catch!"

It was Captain Tracy. He approached me from behind and struck me on the back of the head with his bat. It was the kind of bat that prison guards use, and it hurt really bad. I fell to the ground as he continued to hit me over and over again.

"That's enough!"

The voice came from behind me. It sounded like the voice of a mountain, if a mountain could speak. It was deep and seemed to make the entire ground shake a little.

"Sorry, Sir." It was the first time I'd heard the captain sound weak. "I tend to get carried away sometimes. I just love my job."

Captain Tracy was apologizing to the large man and was on his knees. On his knees! The sight of a tough and rotten dude like Captain Tracy on his knees, almost begging for forgiveness, well, that kind of thing stays with you. Even with my head still aching, I nearly burst out laughing on the spot! But I covered my mouth in case I had to take another beating. My head really hurt!

As I watched him begging for mercy from the figure that towered over him, something told me that this had to be KingPat.

"Please, sir, I'm sorry! I'll make it up to you, I promise!"

KingPat dismissed Captain Tracy's apology with a wave of his hand.

"I expect you to follow my orders to the letter. Do you understand, Captain?"

KingPat spoke in a slow and deliberate manner. He didn't raise his voice but there was something commanding and intimidating about the way in which he spoke. Whatever it was, he sure spooked Captain Tracy, and it was a scary thing to watch.

KingPat smiled at Captain Tracy in the same way that a dog handler smiles at a faithful canine that has just sniffed out some treats.

"You'll have to pardon Captain Tracy here. He's a bit on the violent side. Like he said, he kind of gets carried away a lot, and it's all I can do to keep him in check."

I looked up and got a closer look at the huge dude

standing over me. He was round, like an egg. Exactly like an egg, in fact. You could say that he looked like a huge walking egg with arms and legs stuck on each side! Hey, I know I'm making him sound funny-looking, but seeing him in person did not make me laugh one bit. He was completely bald and wearing an expensive suit. The big guy looked calm, but his eyes looked as if they could bore holes right through you.

"You're KingPat."

"Guilty as charged. I am the man who brought you here to the Mad City prison."

It *was* KingPat! *This* was the man who had made my life so miserable recently! He was here in the prison with me, along with Captain Tracy.

"You're KingPat? You're the one who landed me in this place! What do you want with me? What did I ever do to you?"

KingPat shook his head and smiled at me.

"There there, Noob. A good man does not reveal all his secrets all at once. Rest assured, all will be revealed to you in good time; you'll learn everything, and more… if you survive your time in the Mad City prison that is. Bwahahaha!"

KingPat's laugh chilled me to the bone. He really was a scary big boss type of guy. I had no idea what I had done to make him want to throw me in jail, but here I was.

"Good luck, Noob. Oh, sorry, I forgot, I mean prisoner number 1568. Take the prisoner away, Warden. He's all yours."

"With pleasure, boss! Get up, prisoner! Time to take you to Maximum Security!"

To my surprise, it was Captain Tracy who spoke. I couldn't believe this! How could Captain Tracy be the warden of this place when he was also the SWAT captain?

"You're the warden, too?" I asked.

Captain Tracy nodded and smiled at me.

"Yeah, sure! What are you going to do about it? It's like I said earlier. I just love my job! Both of them!"

"Captain Tracy is quite the overachiever. He's just like that student in school who gets the highest grades in all subjects," KingPat said.

I smirked at them both.

"Yeah, the teacher's pet."

My remark turned Tracy's face red with anger. He looked

like a tomato that was about to explode. Before this could make me laugh—he really did look like a tomato—he struck me once more on the head. Hard. Again. Before he could go again, KingPat stopped him.

"That's enough for now. I like you, 1568. You've got a lot of spunk in you, just as I hoped you would. Maybe you will survive this after all."

"Get up, prisoner! Put on your uniform! It's time to go to Maximum Security!"

And so the warden/SWAT captain/guy I was already fantasising about knocking out with his own bat, picked me up and led me to the bathroom. I closed the door and changed quickly while they waited outside. The windows in the bathroom were all boarded up so there was no chance of escape.

"Don't even try to break out of that window!" Warden Tracy commanded from outside.

Once I was done, Warden Tracy led me to the maximum-security wing. I'd seen enough movies to know this couldn't be a good thing.

"The maximum-security wing? Isn't that the place where they keep all the super-dangerous criminals? The ones that can really do a lot of harm?"

"Yeah, that's the place! I'm surprised you even know what it is!"

"Yeah I guess I watch a lot of cop shows… There must be some misunderstanding here! I'm not supposed to be in a place like that. I'm not a danger to anyone!"

"I agree. I don't think you're a danger to anyone," Tracy chuckled with a cruel smirk.

The warden continued to lead me through a series of long and seemingly endless corridors packed full of cells. The cells themselves were full of prisoners who banged on their bars and shouted insults as we passed by. I was really scared here. We hadn't even reached the maximum-security ward yet, and already the criminals looked pretty tough and dangerous. If the normal prisoners were this bad, I wondered what kind of crazy criminals were housed where we were heading.

"Just give me a chance to break out of here Warden and I'll really cut you up!"

"Lemme outta here!"

"You're going down, Warden!"

"Who's the newbie? I'll break him to pieces!"

"Shut up, all of you! KingPat's watching!"

At the mention of KingPat's name, everyone suddenly went quiet. Jeez, what had KingPat done to make everybody so scared of him?

After a really long walk, we finally reached the ward. As we entered, I expected everyone to go crazy as they had before. In fact, it was quite the opposite. The place was so quiet you could hear a pin drop on the floor. None of the inmates said a word as Warden Tracy led me inside.

"This is it? This is the ward? It's not what I expected!" I said.

Warden Tracy smiled at me.

"Yeah, I know what you're thinking. You were probably expecting a riot, or to see loads of crazy loons locked inside their cells. Well, it's a bit different around here, but you'll soon realize why it's the maximum-security ward."

Warden Tracy shoved me inside a cell and slammed the cell door shut.

"See you soon, Prisoner 1568. I'm sure we'll be seeing a lot of each other. In fact, I guarantee it."

I didn't doubt that. I slumped down in the corner of the pitch-black cell and tried to grow accustomed to my new surroundings.

"Noob? Noob, is that you?"

The voice came from the shadows on the opposite side of the room and made me jump backwards, hitting my head on the exact same spot Tracy had been pummelling over the last couple of hours. I didn't even notice that the voice sounded familiar.

"Hey, take it easy. I'm not going to hurt you. Don't you remember me?"

My eyes slowly began to get used to the dark until I could just about make out the outline of a tall, male figure.

"Don't you remember me? It's me, Decks!"

Decks. It had been awhile since I had heard his name, let alone seen him in person. I took a good, hard look at him, and saw that he was telling the truth. This was definitely Decks, the same man that had survived Granny's house of horrors with me. I couldn't believe it!

"Decks! It's really you! What are you doing here in this place?"

Decks walked over and stood in front of me. He didn't look like your average prisoner. It wasn't like he was built like a tank or anything and he didn't seem particularly intimidating; in fact, he was pretty friendly-looking. I noticed he kept shuffling his fingers around, and I looked down to see a deck of cards held tightly in his hands. It was the Deck of Fate, the same mysterious deck of cards that he had acquired from Granny's bottomless pit.

"I should be asking you that same question, Noob. After all, you're the cop."

I shook my head.

"*Former* cop. I retired shortly after that incident with Granny. I was never really the same after."

Decks shrugged his shoulders as he fumbled with his cards. "I can't say that I blame you, Noob. Something like that can change a man. Change him for the better or the worse."

The way Decks spoke, I began to wonder which way the experience had changed him.

"Noob, why are you here? You're a straight-up kind of guy. You don't belong here."

I shrugged my shoulders.

"I know, prison orange isn't my color at all." I can't actually remember what I said, but it was something cool like that. "Honestly, I don't know why I'm stuck here. A bunch of SWAT guys arrested me on no charges at all, if you can believe that. The only thing they keep saying is that KingPat wants me here."

"KingPat? That big menace that controls Mad City? If he wants you here, you're in real trouble, man!"

Wow, I guessed I could always rely on Decks to say something reassuring...

"And you really have no idea what he wants with you?" Decks asked.

"I wish I knew. It sure would make my life a whole lot simpler. How about you? Why are you in here?"

Decks shook his head.

"If it's all the same to you, Noob, I would rather not say. Let's just say I deserve to be here, and I'm willing to do my time."

I didn't push Decks for more answers. I could see he meant what he said. Clearly he had been quite busy since the incident with Granny. Was Decks a criminal? Well, he'd said it himself; something like that can change a person, for better or worse.

"Still love playing with those cards of yours, eh?"

He stopped shuffling the deck and answered my question

with another question.

"Do you trust me, Noob?"

Whatever had happened to Decks, I had no choice but to trust him.

"Yes."

"Good. I'm going to break out of here. Care to join me?"

Decks asked the question so casually that it sounded more like he was inviting me for a cup of tea than to do something tough like break out of the place. But what choice did I have? I wasn't going to stick around to find out KingPan's plans for me!

"I'm in."

Entry #4

Yard Fight!

"Everybody get up!"

A loud voice boomed through the corridors, accompanied by a loud bell which woke me from my uncomfortable sleep. I had tried hard to get a good night's sleep. I'd spent ages thinking about my old place and all the great comforts I'd had there so I could lull myself to sleep. Looking back, it was pointless to picture a comfy place back home when in reality I was asleep on the hard prison floor. I didn't get much sleep.

"Everybody get up, already! It's time for your yard break!"

"Come on, sleepyhead! Rise and shine!"

It was Decks. He was standing right beside me, looking strangely refreshed and eager to start the day. Me? I was already in a bad mood upon hearing the sound of that awful bell and Warden Tracy's voice on the loudspeaker.

"Ugh! Is this how they wake everyone up in this place?"

Decks nodded, still looking annoyingly upbeat and perky.

"Yep! You sure look grumpy."

"Why wouldn't I look grumpy? This is no way to wake anyone up!" I replied.

"I guess I can't blame you. I was like that too at first. You kind of get used to it though. By the way, you better get up off that bed of yours."

"What if I don't want to get up? What if I'm really sleepy and just want to lie down here for a bit longer?"

I'll be honest with you. I'm not really much of a morning person at the best of times, and waking up like that was, well, beyond awful for me.

"I don't think you want to do that," Decks said.

"Why not?"

I was still lying in bed, my ears ringing from Warden Tracy's voice and the morning bell, when it happened. Suddenly, Warden Tracy himself was standing right beside Decks inside our cell. I don't even know how he managed to get inside so fast; he'd been pacing the corridors shouting down the megaphone just a few minutes earlier.

"Get up off your lazy butt, prisoner!"

"Warden Tracy! Go easy on him, Sir! It's his first day in jail, and..."

Decks was trying to plead my case, but the warden was having none of it.

"This'll get you up and moving!"

The warden pointed a long, thin rod at me. This wasn't his usual bat but something far worse. The rod tapped me only lightly, and I suddenly felt a sharp electric current run through me. There were sparks everywhere. I yelped in pain and jumped up out of bed.

"Yikes!"

"There you go! That got you out of bed! If you want some more then feel free to keep lazing around in the morning! There's more where that came from."

He didn't need to say it again. I was out of bed now, my butt smoking from the electric charge. Not a good start to the day at all.

"Owww...."

Decks shook his head. I noticed that he was still shuffling his deck of cards in his hands. He looked a little concerned about me.

"I tried to warn you about that."

"Get to the yard now, before I shock you both!" He waved the rod in our faces, and we both scampered out of the cell like mice, heading for the yard with the other prisoners.

"That prod the warden's got is amazing! All it is is a magnet and electrical wires. Those are the two main things you need to generate an electric current. Touch the magnet with the wires and hey presto, you've got electricity!"

"Yeah, and presto, you've got a burnt butt. No offense, Decks, but I'm not really in the mood for a science lecture right now."

The warden watched us both like a hawk as we marched out to the yard. Something told me that he would have liked to have increased the power on his prod and fried me right there on the spot, but he didn't. Warden Tracy was smiling; he clearly took a lot of pleasure in seeing me squirm.

"You know, I think there's a word for what the warden's doing to you. A specific word that means "being happy when other guys suffer" or something to that effect. I think it's in German though…"

I shook my head.

"I said I'm not in the mood for any lessons right now, Decks."

I was already feeling sore after the warden's electric shock. I had no idea things were about to get a whole of a lot worse. Just as we stepped outside, everyone started laughing and pointing in my direction.

"What on Earth is so funny? Why are they all laughing at me?"

Decks laughed.

"What's going on? Why is everyone laughing at me?" I asked, going slightly red. It was so embarrassing!

"Look behind you. Or maybe you can smell it already."

I sniffed behind me. Decks was right. I could smell something. It was the smoky smell of something that had been burned.

"My butt! The prod. It…"

Decks laughed and shielded his eyes.

"Yep. It burned your uniform right off, somewhere where the sun don't shine, if you get my drift."

I suddenly realized that my underwear was exposed to the whole yard. I desperately tried to cover myself up with my hands, but I knew it was too late. Warden Tracy had really done it now.

Decks shook his head and shuffled the cards in his hands.

"I'm warning you, boys. Stop laughing at my friend, or you're all going to be real sorry."

Decks was challenging them for me? I had decided on two things. One, I was fairly certain Decks had my back. I guessed he sort of bonded with me because of everything we had been through with Granny. Two, Decks wasn't completely sane. I mean, let's face it, you would have to be more than a little unstable to challenge a whole yard of prisoners all by your lonesome. Yep, Decks was definitely not the sanest person in this place, but I wasn't going to tell him that. It was everything he had been through with Granny. That had to be it. After all, he survived falling into a bottomless pit, and he basically took down one of gaming's scariest monsters. I mean, if you go through all that, you're bound to get some screws loose, right?

And to my astonishment, most of the prisoners actually

backed down from Decks's threat. I couldn't believe it. I thought that they would be all over us after he challenged them, but most of them actually stopped laughing! I guess they sensed that Decks was a real threat too. It was hard to say who or, more accurately *what*, Decks was!

Decks might have got some of them to back off, but a lot of them weren't happy with what he'd said, including a large bruiser type who started to approach us.

"Are you talking to us, Decks?"

The inmate was built like a tank and looked really menacing. He had arms that almost popped out of his prison shirt, and a body that looked like it was carved out of rock.

"Yeah, you know I am, Rock."

Well, I'm not surprised his name was Rock...

Rock walked right up to Decks, followed by several other prisoners. They were all in front of us now, and we were definitely waaay outnumbered.

Rock was up close in Decks' face, but he didn't seem bothered. Other guys would have been terrified at a giant prisoner standing right in front of them, but not Decks. Nope, he was just standing there playing with his cards as if he didn't have a care in the world. I'm not going to lie, I was starting to think that Decks was kind of cool. Mainly nuts, but cool as well...

"I'm just going to tell you this once, Decks. "Take it back," Rock said.

Decks smiled at Rock.

"And I'm warning you, Rock. Back off now. You're standing way too close to me."

Rock stared intently at Decks. Decks looked right back at him, still smiling. He was clearly not afraid of Rock in the slightest.

"No way," Rock replied.

Decks giggled like a boy that was about to open a Christmas present.

"Oh, you're really going to regret that decision."

Decks moved so fast, it was like watching lightning. He was so fast in fact that I didn't even see him move. Before Rock knew what was happening, it was already over.

"What...?!"

Rocks looked down in time to see his pants suddenly fell off. He was exposed to the rest of the yard in just his underwear, and he looked just as bad as I did now, or even worse.

The inmates behind him howled with laughter at the sight of a fearsome dude like Rock covering his underwear. Even I couldn't help but laugh at the sight. Who wouldn't laugh?

"Yikes! What did you do? What did you do?" Rock cried.

Decks grinned at Rock. He was clutching a single card in his hand. He flashed it at Rock. It was the Jack of Spades.

"Jack of Spades. Mmmm. Those spades cut really deep, right? Nasty what a papercut can do."

Rock growled at Decks like an angry pit bull raring to bite someone. He was scowling and snarling now. And I was terrified.

"What are you all laughing at? This ain't funny!"

The other inmates behind Rock stopped laughing immediately as they realised the Rock had shifted his attention onto them for a moment.

"I beg to differ, Rock. It does look pretty funny from where I'm standing. That was for laughing at my friend Noob here. You all best back off now."

"Hey, uh, Decks!"

I nudged Decks' arm and he turned to me, grinning from ear to ear. You could see that he was loving it all! Decks didn't seem to worry that Rock was furious. He actually looked like he didn't have a care in the world.

"Yeah? What's the problem, Noob?"

"What's the problem? What's the problem? Uh, you've really ticked off Rock!" I whispered angrily. "You know, the huge guy who's about to rearrange our faces. Look, I appreciate you standing up for me. I really do! But he's a big dude, and he's got a lot of prisoners backing him up!"

"Your friend's a lot smarter than you are, Decks! But you're both done for now! Get them, boys!"

As soon as Rock gave the order, the prisoners charged towards us, ready to tear us apart. It was not looking good at all.

"Yard fight! Yard fight!"

The prisoners came at us, charging like those pit bulls I mentioned earlier. Even Rock charged at us. He was still holding onto his pants to keep them up, but he was still charging and even madder for it.

"Tear them apart!"

"We're done for!" I cried.

I'm not ashamed to admit that I was scared witless. Who wouldn't be? Well, Decks, that's who.

Decks didn't run from those guys. Instead, he ran right towards them. It was like watching someone run through a storm. Or maybe it was more like he *was* the storm. Yeah, I have to admit it was a little awesome to see him do that. And he wasn't done. Far from it.

Decks moved rapidly through the mob. They all tried to grab him, but he was just too fast. They were like an angry gang of farmers chasing a loose chicken running in all directions. They couldn't even lay a hand on him. They were so focused on him that they completely forgot about me.

"What's wrong with you guys? He's just a single prisoner!" Rock shouted.

Rock was still there too, but he couldn't do much to help. I mean, he was trying to keep his pants up for crying out loud! If the other prisoners didn't stand a chance then there was no way that he did. Not like that!

And speaking of the other prisoners? Well, they soon found themselves with the same dilemma. When Decks was done, Rock wasn't the only one with missing clothing.

"Hey, my pants are all ripped!"

"They can see my underwear!"

"Why did I wear my rubber ducky underwear today?!"

Decks had somehow managed to cut the fabric of every attacking prisoner's pants. The other prisoners watching all erupted into laughter. I couldn't help but laugh myself. Decks had turned a potentially dangerous situation into a hilarious one. And his speed was just amazing. What couldn't this guy do?

"How did you do that?" I asked.

Decks winked at me.

"What can I say? It's magic."

"All right everybody! Break it up!"

It was Warden Tracy. He was angry and full of himself as usual, but there was nothing to break up. The fact was that Decks had soundly defeated Rock and his gang of thugs. They all raised their hands up in surrender as the warden and his men arrived.

"Everybody, hands in the air! That includes you two!"

Warden Tracy and his men set their sights on me and Decks. I raised my hands immediately. As usual, Decks wasn't scared one bit. He was still smiling at Warden Tracy and his men.

"You look really pleased with yourself," I said.

"Why shouldn't I be? I put that bully Rock and his gang in their places."

"Yeah, that's great and all, but Warden Tracy and his guards are here. We'll have to answer for this."

Decks giggled. He was the only one in the yard now without his hands in the air. A fact that had not gone unnoticed by the warden.

"What's so funny? Put your hands up, prisoner!" Warden Tracy yelled.

I had to agree with him on this one. I couldn't understand why Decks was laughing. At the time, it was hard not to assume this guy was a complete lunatic.

"Have you lost it, man?"

Decks smiled at me. His hands were still by his sides, and I was beginning to get really scared now.

"Ah, Noob. You really don't understand, do you?"

"What? What don't I understand? You're speaking nonsense, Decks! Just put your hands up already!"

"Listen to your friend, prisoner! This is your last chance! I'm not going to warn you again. Raise your hands now, or you're going to be sorry!"

Decks shook his head.

"My, my, is that so, Warden? You seem so agitated."

I cringed as Decks continued to wind up Tracy.

"So now I guess I've got no choice. I might as well raise my hands and do as you say."

The warden nodded, his gun pointed at Decks.

"Noob, hold your breath," Decks ordered.

"What? What are you talking about?" I asked.

Decks didn't answer me. That didn't mean I ignored his command. I had no clue what he was about to do, but I figured even with all the loose screws in his head, he was probably trying to protect me. So I held my breath. He raised his hands in the air and dropped all his cards on the ground.

All except one card.

Decks tossed the remaining card into the air. Before the warden or anyone knew what was happening, the card dissolved, and a large gas cloud covered the entire yard.

It was just like the smoke grenade that the SWAT had used in my home, only ten times thicker.

I couldn't see a thing. Judging by all the shouting and the commotion around me, it seemed everyone else was having the same problem. It was crazy!

"Somebody get them! Get them!"

I could hear Warden Tracy shouting in the middle of the chaos. I tried my best to hold my breath, but it wasn't really doing me much good.

Suddenly, someone grabbed my arm and pulled me towards them. I was too confused and out of it to even resist.

We were running, jumping and jolting in every direction. I had no idea what was happening. I felt like a leaf being blown around in the wind. There was nothing I could do, and I was just hoping for the best.

Suddenly, I became aware that the smoke cloud had cleared. Actually, it hadn't. Whoever this person was, they had simply pulled me away from the gas.

"Boy, you're a lot heavier than I thought."

I looked up, saw Decks's face and stood hunched over, trying to regain my breath.

"This is a lot of exercise for a retired cop, Decks."

"Ha!" Decks laughed. "Is that any way to talk to the person who's going to save your electrocuted butt?"

"Don't speak too soon. What do we do now?"

Now, Noob, we escape."

Entry #5

Escape from Mad City Prison.

You would think that tagging along with Decks would be the obvious decision. And I know this is coming from a guy who eats salmon and root beer pizza, but I put a lot of thought into most of the decisions I make. So I had to think for a second about the path I was going to choose. On the one hand, who would want to stick around in a place like this, right? I mean, he said he was breaking out, and it was clear that Decks was capable of doing just about anything he put his mind to! So I should have jumped at the opportunity, right?

But there still remained the fact that this man was completely insane. It was clear that something wasn't right about him, and he was super-duper powerful too! I mean, we're talking about a dude who took out prisoners and guards with just a deck of cards. A deck of cards for crying out loud! A guy like that was obviously dangerous.

I was trying to make my decision when I heard Warden Tracy and his men approaching from behind us. They had already gotten past the smoke cloud and they were headed our way! So, what was it going to be? Leave with a crazy, deadly guy and a pack of cards? Or stay here in the Mad City Prison and rot? Looking at it that way, the decision suddenly became a whole lot easier.

"All right, lead the way!" I shouted with false confidence.

We slipped through a door in the corner of the yard, and I followed him down a few corridors until we came to a locked door.

"Luckily, these idiots who work here give us gun-cleaning duty," Decks started to explain. "It's supervised, of course. But what they didn't think about was the fact that all it would take would be one curious prisoner to sneak a peak at the door code." He punched in four numbers and the code screen said:

"INCORRECT."

"Oh." Decks sounded defeated.

"What's the matter? Is this the gun room?" I started to panic.

"They've changed the code! Blast! Okay, err... " He began to look around the corridor.

"What's happening, Decks? Why do you want to get into the gun room? Decks?"

Decks picked up a fire extinguisher.

"DECKS!" He wasn't listening, so I tried to take back some control. "If you don't talk to me, then I can't trust you!"

He stopped and turned to me.

"We're both going to die if we stay here, Noob. We have two options. We let that happen, or we take a risk. You and me, shooting our way out as partners, loaded with the guns from inside that room. I've been here for a long time, and trust me when I say this is the only chance we have. I didn't want to do it alone, and now I've got you! What do you say, Noob? Come out of retirement for one last showdown?

At this point I couldn't argue with him. I had hoped for a more fool-proof plan than this. But it was better than rotting in a cell.

"Okay, Decks," I said reluctantly.

"Smart move."

Still holding the fire extinguisher, he smiled and then turned around, smashing it onto the door lock and breaking it clean off. Once busted, the lock hit the floor as Decks kicked his way in.

The room was full of guns! These were high-powered guns, too. Decks was dealing with more than just his cards now.

"Come on, Noob! Grab what you can!"

I wasn't completely sure how we were going to do that, but I didn't question Decks any further. It was time to just wing it and hope for the best.

There were several guns in the cabinet to choose from. They sure looked scary, and I didn't know which to pick. I finally settled for a high-powered automatic rifle. Decks seemed to approve.

"An AK-47. Provides a balanced grip, great reload speed, and low recoil. A popular choice for a lot of guerrilla fighters too. Medium-range with a great rate of fire. All in all, a pretty well-rounded gun. You made a good choice, Noob! Pick a sidearm in case of close-range encounters."

I settled for a heavy pistol with a large barrel and a larger chamber. It looked as if it could carry really heavy ammo, and it even had a scope to help in aiming and handling.

"Whoa! A magnum! A really high-powered pistol with short range and powerful recoil. All in all, a really tough gun to handle, but boy, does it pack a wallop! Anybody that gets hit with that baby ain't going to be getting up anytime soon!"

I had tried to pick the best guns that I could for the situation at hand. After all, we were attempting a prison breakout, and I had to be armed correctly! I wasn't surprised that Decks was so familiar with the guns and what they could do. You had to assume a dude like him was knowledgeable on such matters.

Decks was impressed with my gun choices but he picked the biggest, baddest one of all for himself: an automatic machine gun. It was big and heavy, and the ammo looked big enough to fell an elephant or any large animal. It also looked more than capable of mowing down anyone in our way.

"Whoa! That's a really powerful gun there!" I exclaimed.

"You bet it is! This baby can mow down those cops like a lawnmower through grass!"

"Nobody move!"

It was Warden Tracy. He and his men filled the room behind us.

"So, you two managed to get to the armory. Good for you, but we've got you both outnumbered. Just put your guns down, and we'll play nice. Or at least we'll try to," Warden Tracy said.

Warden Tracy and his guards stood there in front of me and Decks in the armory. Yeah, I know what you're thinking. This whole idea was starting to seem even more foolish than I'd originally thought.

That was until Decks opened fire with that huge machine gun of his. I remembered what he'd said about the gun cutting down enemies like a lawnmower ripping through grass. Turned out that was a pretty accurate description.

The huge machine gun cut through them easily. The sound of automatic fire rang through the air, and I just stood back while Decks let loose on the guards. He had used up a large amount of the gun's ammo in around five minutes, but five minutes was all it took.

Decks was done, and the large barrel of the machine gun was smoking from all the bullets that it had fired. A silence filled the air, but it was broken by the roar of the prisoners in the yard.

"Come on, Noob! There's going to be a huge riot in this place now. I wouldn't want to be around here when it erupts. It's going to be the prisoners versus the guards, last man standing!"

I followed Decks as he made his way out of the prison. He was right. I could already hear the sounds of fighting getting louder and louder behind me.

It didn't take us long to get to the front of the prison now that the guards of that sector were out of the way. There were a few posted there but a lot fewer than I expected. I guessed most of them were already too busy trying to handle the riots in the prison.

"Freeze, you two! You're not going anywhere!"

The guards pointed their guns at us, and Decks pointed his huge machine gun at them. I pointed my AK at them as well. The guards were all that stood between us and the main doors. It was a standoff, like in an old-fashioned Western movie.

"Really boys? Do you really want to try and play with us? You've got pea shooters and we've got this big baby here. We've just got past a lot more guards than you. They were better armed too, but I still mowed 'em all down. What makes you think you stand a better chance of stopping us than they did?"

Decks made a valid point, though he seemed to be enjoying himself too much, which was a bit unsettling. I could see the guards hesitate as he spoke. They looked at each other, and then at us. Decks smiled as he continued to point the large machine gun at them. He was more than eager to use it again.

"What's it going to be, boys? I've still got more than enough rounds to play with you."

The guards dropped their pistols to the ground and raised their hands.

"Forget it! I'm not getting paid enough to stand up to that thing!"

"You win, Decks. You two can walk out of here."

"Smart choice, guys. Come on, Decks," I said.

I moved towards the front door, but Decks was refusing to budge. He still had his gun pointed at the men. His trigger finger was getting itchy.

"Decks? Decks, come on. We've won. We're free!"

Decks didn't respond. The men were frozen in fear. They had all dropped their guns and there was no way that they would be able to reach them in time if Decks decided to open fire on them. I didn't like this at all.

"Decks, I said come on already! It's over! What are you standing around for?"

Decks blinked and stared at me. It was almost as if I had woken him up from a strange dream.

"What? Oh okay, Noob! I'm coming!"

Decks followed me out the front door, much to the relief of the guards. The moment had passed, but I kept thinking, had Decks really been about to gun down those unarmed men? What would I have done? I realized that I was still dealing with a loose cannon of a partner.

"Okay, here we are! Hop in!"

We came out in the parking lot, and Decks led me over to an expensive-looking violet sportscar.

"Whoa! Is this your car? How did you set this up?"

Decks smiled at me.

"It's not mine. We're stealing it!"

We hopped in, and Decks had no problem hot wiring it to start. The engine roared to life and he drove us out of the prison gates. Was it over? Was it all done? That was what

I kept thinking, but you know how it is; I'm usually wrong about these things.

This was no exception.

Entry #6

I Want to Go Home!

We drove around the crazy town that was Mad City. Decks was behind the wheel, and he was anything but a cautious driver. Several pedestrians were crossing the street as we roared out of the prison. Decks didn't bother to slow down for them; instead, he accelerated faster and drove right towards them. I was screaming at him to slow down but he wouldn't. The car kept moving at the poor pedestrians like a bull that saw red, and they only missed being flattened by inches as all scattered and dove out of the way.

"Whoopee! That was fun!" Decks screamed loudly.

"Are you crazy? You could have run those people over! And for what good? They weren't trying to stop us!"

"You don't understand, Noob! This is Mad City!"

"I don't care where we are! We've got to follow some rules!"

Decks grinned at me as he drove the car even faster.

"That's just it, Noob: in Mad City, there are no rules."

It was hard to dwell on the realization as we sped through the city, but my fears about Decks were quickly coming true. He continued to drive the car at breakneck speed, barely avoiding other vehicles on the road. I was holding on to the edge of my seat now.

"Whoa, slow down Decks! What's the rush anyway? We got away already!"

Decks looked at me as if I was crazy.

"What kind of a question is that? There's always a rush! If there's no rush, it's pretty much boring!"

Decks' words proved that he wasn't completely sane. I mean, what kind of guy would drive around the city at that speed just because he felt like it? A crazy guy, that's who! I started to see why Decks had been placed in the Max-Security wing now. To say that he was dangerous was an understatement. I decided to just come out and say what I was thinking.

"Look, Decks. I appreciate you standing up for me and breaking me out of prison. I really do. But this is getting to be a little too much for me now. This is your thing, and, erm, I get it. If you want to go around running people over, well, I won't say I agree with it, but I'm not going to stop you. I just want to go home, and that's what I'm going to do. Pull over here; I'll get a cab back to my place, and that'll be the end of it."

Decks did just that. He pulled the car to a sudden stop that almost had me flying through the front windscreen. The car's brakes kicked in and the tires screeched and screamed in protest as the car came to a halt.

Decks looked at me from the driver's seat. It seemed like I had touched a nerve. His face was getting red, and he seemed angry. This wasn't good. By now, I knew that Decks was not the kind of dude that you wanted to make angry. And he was right beside me. Not good at all. He scowled at me like an angry dog. And then, just as I thought Decks was about to let it all out on me, his expression changed in an instant. This creeped me out, big time!

"So you're telling me you just want to get out and go home. Is that it, Noob?"

I was really scared of him now, but I didn't know what else to do! I had been dragged into all of this by KingPat, a powerful and mysterious man I didn't know much about. Of course, I just wanted to go home!

"Yeah, Decks. I just want to go home."

"Look, Noob. I understand where you're coming from. I really do. I mean, I would be pretty upset too if I got dragged out of my house by SWAT agents, but let me tell you now, going home is not a good idea."

"Decks, you said you understand where I'm coming from. I need to get back home. Back to normality. I've got TV shows to binge-watch and weird pizza toppings to try. I'm tired, Decks. I retired for a reason."

"KingPat wants you, Noob. I don't know why, but he dragged you out of your house and threw you into prison. You don't know KingPat. He's a ruthless kind of guy. He'll come after you. You can't just go home. It's all different now."

Decks was telling the truth of course. KingPat was not the kind of guy who would let this slide. I wasn't thinking straight though, and I refused to listen. I was scared and tired, and all I wanted to do was go home.

"Look, Decks, it's been a long day. I just want to get back

home, and that's what I'm going to do."

I opened the door of the car. Surprisingly, Decks didn't try to stop me. I got out and walked away from the car. We were on a busy road, and a taxi came into view almost immediately.

I gave the cabbie the directions to my place and sat back in the passenger seat. I took a deep breath and forced myself to relax. Perhaps this nightmare was finally over!

Of course, that wasn't how it would play out. Decks had said it himself earlier; this was Mad City, and nothing ever played out that easily here.

We had been driving for a while before I realized what was happening. The driver wasn't taking the route back to my place. Instead, he was driving around the city.

"Hey, this isn't the way home," I said.

The cabbie ignored me.

"Hey, I'm talking to you!"

There was still no answer. I realized that the cabbie had no intention of taking me home.

I was starting to panic now. I tried to unlock the doors but they wouldn't budge. They seemed to be controlled by some kind of inner mechanism in the car itself.

"Hey! Let me out!"

Of course, the cabbie didn't listen to me. He continued to drive, ignoring my protests. I started to bang on the glass screen that separated us. My fists pounded at the glass, but it did not shatter. It was hard, maybe bulletproof!

"Don't even bother pounding on the glass, Noob. There's no point."

"You know my name! How do you know my name? Who are you, and why are you doing this?" I asked.

"It was pretty simple getting the lowdown on you, Noob. I mean, KingPat's after you. He's made sure that everyone in Mad City knows who you are. He's even posted a huge reward for anyone who catches you and brings you to him. You're wanted, buddy! Dead or alive. And I'm no killer, so I'm gonna have to take you to him."

Dead or alive? That was the second time that day I'd felt like I was in a Western! I had a price on my head!

"KingPat! I'm such a fool! I should have listened to Decks! He was right!"

"Decks is your friend? KingPat's posted a pretty high reward for his capture too. Everyone in Mad City is after the two of you. I want you to know Noob, that I don't want you to do this. I just need the reward for my family. We're barely scraping by. The reward will really go a long way in making sure we don't starve."

Great! What was worse than being on the run from KingPat? Getting caught and feeling sorry for your captor! I couldn't get angry at him for seizing me. His family needed the money. He was just desperate.

"Look, I'm armed! I've got my magnum with me. If you don't let me go, I'll blow a hole through this window. I can easily jump out from here!"

"Yeah, good luck! The windows and the panel behind me are made of reinforced glass. They're bulletproof! Your bullets won't even make a dent, no matter how powerful they are."

"Why does an innocent cabbie who says he's not a killer have bulletproof windows, huh?"

"You know, I remember seeing you around Mad City. You were a cop. You probably didn't live in the *real* parts of Mad City, though, did you? Never truly experienced what life's like here when you're not protected by the law! Every cab in this city has bulletproof windows, pal. Cost more than I could afford, but they've saved my butt more times than I can count. Definitely more times than the cops ever did."

I felt for the guy, but I had to watch out for my own neck. I also wasn't sure that I believed the cabbie. He could easily have been bluffing and I was determined to go home. I took out my magnum and fired a single shot at the car window. I immediately regretted it.

The cabbie wasn't lying about the glass. The shot only left a small mark. It echoed and vibrated through the entire backseat area of the cab, making my ears ring. It sounded like a thousand bells going off in my head, and for a moment I thought I'd gone deaf.

"Aaagh!"

"I told you not to try it. Don't blame me."

I clutched my ears with my hands.

"I just want to go home already!"

"I'm sorry, Noob. I can't let you do that. I just can't."

The cabbie was dead serious. This was it. I was in a taxi ride to my own death. I was just about ready to give up when I felt a powerful force hit the back of the cab, making me jump out of my seat.

"What the...?"

I turned around and saw a familiar sight... Decks' violet sports car. I could see him waving at me from the car as he continued to ram the cab from behind!

"Is that guy crazy? He's trying to run us off the road!"

"Oh, he's crazy, all right!" It was the first time I'd found myself happy about this fact!

Decks rammed the taxi twice more, and the cab swayed and shook dangerously with the impact. Somehow, the cabbie managed to keep control, even as Decks continued his relentless attacks.

"What is he doing? Does he want to kill us?"

I shrugged my shoulders.

"I gave up trying to figure that guy out a long time ago! And I'm sorry about your family, but you asked for this!"

The cabbie was clearly terrified of Decks, and I did feel sorry for him, but he had meddled in a dangerous world by choice!

Even while I'm writing this now, I still haven't been able to think of a single way I would have made it out without Decks. I'm not ashamed to say I even tried to make a few versions up because it would have been a super awesome story if I'd busted out of there all by myself! You know, purely for story-telling purposes... But I couldn't come up with imaginary ones, either. It was an impossible situation. Anyway, now at least I had a fighting chance... assuming Decks didn't kill me, of course!

I could smell smoke coming from somewhere inside the taxi. That had to be a bad sign.

"I don't think your cab can take much more of this. You'd better just pull over and let me go. It'll be a lot easier for you," I said.

The cabbie shook his head and continued to grip the steering wheel.

"No! No way am I letting you go! You're my family's meal ticket! I've got to get you to KingPat!"

"Look, Mister! You don't know this guy like I do! He's not going to stop until your cab stops running. And I'm worried he might not stop there. So it's best that..."

Before I could say anything more, it finally happened. Decks picked up speed and rammed the side of the taxi hard. It swerved out of control before tipping over.

Stuck inside that small cab, the whole world suddenly

turned upside down. My head slammed against the roof of the cab as it rolled over in the road, but I managed to stay conscious even as I was being tossed around.

When the cab finally came to a halt, it was lying on its roof. The cabbie was squirming in the front seat.

"Oww! Your friend's crazy!"

"Tell me about it."

With miraculously only a couple of bruises, I forced myself out of the now upside-down cab. The window may have been made of reinforced glass, but it made no difference now that the collision had unhinged the car door, and I was able to kick it open.

I looked up to see Decks standing over the cab. He looked pleased with himself, as usual. And he still had that big, intimidating machine gun with him.

"Hello, Noob! How's it going? I don't want to say I told you so, but I definitely told you so! I said that trying to head home was a bad idea but did you listen? Nooo."

"All right, all right. I admit it. You were right, Decks. I was wrong. Thanks for the save."

"Don't mention it. After you ran off, I knew I had to follow you. I figured trouble was bound to find you, and I was right! Now, it's time to make this guy pay."

Decks pointed the machine gun through the open cab door at the cabbie, who hunched over in terror and covered his face with his hands. I couldn't let this happen!

I stood directly in front of Decks and that big gun of his.

"Whoa, whoa! What are you trying to do?" I asked.

"Shoot him! That's what!"

"There's no need for that, Decks! He's just a cab driver trying to look after his family in this awful town!"

"Not if you ask me. He was trying to kidnap you and take you to KingPat! For that, he deserves to be sprayed with bullets!"

I shook my head.

"No way, Decks! No way! If you want me to come with you, you'll have to do things my way! And I know you want me to come with you. You wouldn't have bothered to follow me if you didn't!"

Decks hesitated before finally putting his huge machine gun down. I saw the cabbie heave a sigh of relief. Still uncomfortable, but at least he was alive! Why did my only friend in this scenario have to be that psycho?!

"All right. You win, Noob. For now. We can't play this nice though when KingPat sends his goons after us. I'm just saying."

I nodded at Decks.

"But you don't need to shoot at everything that moves either. Let's keep moving."

Decks shrugged his shoulders.

We were heading towards Decks' sports car when two black vans screeched to a halt on the road. Men got out and started shooting.

"More of KingPat's men! Get behind the car!"

The car was close enough for both of us to take cover. I could see now that having a bounty on your head made life pretty difficult, to say the least. It was strange being on the other side of the law after all my time as a cop! Not that I had any clue what I had done to wind up on this side of it.

The men continued to fire at us as we ducked behind the sports car. The car had already taken a lot of damage from the cab. Its windows were shattered, and the body quickly became full of dents and bullet holes.

"They've got us pinned down!" I said.

"No, they don't!"

The fire ceased, and Decks stood up, pointing his machine gun at the men.

"You boys spoiled a perfectly good paint job!"

He started to fire, spraying several rounds at anything in front of him. The sound of the gunfire was deafening.

After several seconds, it was over. Decks lowered the gun and there was complete silence.

"Is it safe to come out now?" I asked.

Decks turned to me and smiled with that creepy smile of his.

"Yup, they're done."

No one fired at us anymore, so I knew that Decks was right.

"Let's get out of here!" I shouted, ears still ringing.

We jumped into the sports car. Despite taking a beating from the gunfire, it started up straight away. The doors had several dents and bullet holes and the windows were shattered, but it still moved as fast as ever.

"Okay, so where do we go now? You said it yourself. The

whole city's after us."

Decks kept his hands on the steering wheel and his foot on the accelerator.

"Don't sweat it, Noob. You're with Decks, the craziest, maddest guy in Mad City! But you're in good hands. We're going to go to my super-secret hideout to plan our next move. And also chill a little bit. It's been a heavy day."

Decks sounded as if this was all just a game to him. I was uneasy but had no choice but to go along with his plans. We had escaped prison, only to end up on the run in Mad City. And I couldn't go back home until this was all somehow settled. That nutjob's hideout sounded like my only option.

I'd had no idea when I sat down to eat pizza the day before that over the next twenty-four hours I'd be involved in a prison riot, a prison escape, a shootout, and a car chase.

I told you that this story would have all the excitement you'd expect from a Noob adventure! And it was far from over. I just couldn't wait to get back to that pizza! Maybe I could still reheat it...

RO GHOUL

BOOK 4
ROBLOXIA KID

Entry #1

Not an Entry!

Hi there, Noob fans, or Noobers (I thought of that name myself. Sounds cool, eh?) It's Noob here again with the pulse-pounding, slam-bangin' sequel to my last adventure. This is going to be big, even bigger than my last adventure, and let me warn you, it's not for the faint of heart!

The last time you Noobers checked in, I was on the run from the really nasty crime lord, KingPat, with my new, slightly unstable friend, Decks. We had just escaped from the Mad City prison and were lying low from KingPat in Mad City. Now, this is where the next adventure begins!

It all began with something that was not in my diary! Yeah, you read that right. The start of the adventure wasn't from my diary, so I wasn't in it. Hard to explain, eh? Well, to make it simple, it began with a news clipping from Mad City's paper, the Mad Times. I cut it out and stuck it in my diary because of some strange news that popped up. It was this strange piece of news that started my next adventure: The Strange Case of Roblox Ro Ghoul!

The newspaper article was written about Freddie Foxy. Freddie was a small-time crook in Mad City. In a place like this, well, Freddy was nothing special; there were lots of small crooks, just like Freddie, running around doing small-time crook stuff. So boy, were the cops of Mad City surprised when Freddie turned himself in!

Yeah, that's right. Freddie turned himself over to the cops. He went to the station and personally surrendered, but that wasn't the only strange thing that happened. The cops said that poor Freddie was shaking like a leaf at the station and rambling about some really scary stuff.

"A monster! There's a monster on the loose!"

"A monster? What are you saying, Freddie? Before anything else, cuff him!"

Police Chief Herman couldn't believe any of this. First, a criminal had walked into a precinct full of cops. That in itself was a first for a city so notorious for its crime. Secondly, the criminal was terrified and ranting about a monster.

"Cuff me? Please! Take me to prison! Lock me up already! It'll be safe there!"

"A crook like you, asking to be handcuffed? Now I've really seen everything!"

The police chief was hardworking enough, but Mad City was just too crazy for him. Now, there was a small-time crook in front of him, just begging to be arrested.

Still, two of the officers were happy to oblige and immediately cuffed Freddie, who looked relieved by their actions.

"Okay. You're handcuffed now, Freddy. Why you would want to be arrested is beyond me, but I'm not complaining. It's crazy enough outside as it is, and I'm not letting you get away. So now maybe you can tell me more about this "monster" you're talking about?"

"It was terrible! So terrible! The creature came out of nowhere and killed Foxy Foxy!"

Police Chief Herman was stunned at what he was hearing. Foxy Foxy was Freddy Foxy's twin brother. The two of them were known small-time muggers who often robbed and shot at people. That was nothing out of the ordinary in Mad City, but now he was hearing that Foxy Foxy had just been killed by a monster...

"Your brother was killed by a monster?"

"That's what I said! The monster was a human at first, then it suddenly sprouted sharp tentacles on its back! It killed my brother!"

"It was human?"

"Yeah! It looked Japanese when it was a human. Just like a tourist or something! Foxy and I were just chilling in a back alley when the human, or monster or whatever, passed us! We didn't even give it a second thought. But then it sprouted those crazy sharp tentacles on its back and I knew we were in trouble!"

"Tentacles on its back? Seriously?"

Chief Herman still couldn't believe what he was hearing from Freddy. It sounded crazy, but he could see that the poor kid was genuinely terrified. Whatever had happened, he didn't seem to be lying.

"I ain't joking around, Chief! We thought he was just some Japanese tourist that had got lost or something. He, or it or whatever, approached us, and asked if we knew where Decks and Noob were!"

"Decks and Noob? The two escaped convicts from prison? How would you know where they are?"

"Well, exactly! And that's what I told the Japanese dude. After we said that, well, that's when the crazy stuff happened. Suddenly, the Japanese dude wasn't a Japanese dude anymore! He sprouted two long tentacles on his back... tentacles! With sharp claw tips at the end!"

Some of the other cops at the precinct couldn't help but laugh as they heard Freddy recall his story. You couldn't blame them. After all, it did sound more like the plot of a fantasy or horror movie than a real experience.

"I'm not making any of this up! Why would

I want to go to jail for crying out loud? The man started ranting that he was no ordinary dude and that he was really a "ghoul." He also said that there would be more people like him coming to Mad City to look for Decks and Noob!"

"And your brother?"

"I told you chief: he killed him! He grabbed him with one of his tentacles and crushed him good! Said he didn't have any use for someone with no information! It was awful! I only just managed to escape! You guys can go to the alley and see for yourselves!"

Freddy was a crook, but it sure didn't look like he was lying. He was genuinely terrified, and that was something you couldn't fake. The police chief had seen his fair share of craziness in Mad City but this was off the roof.

"I'm going to head there right now personally with some of the boys. Come with us and show us where it happened."

"All right, but you've got to protect me!"

Remember what I told you about how crazy it all sounded already? Well, it was about to get a whole lot crazier!

Entry #2

The New Decks.

"Did you read this, Decks? And check out the video! It's gone viral already!"

I was really eager to show Decks the article. I was all pumped up and didn't really know what to make of it. Decks? He just didn't really care. Ever since we had gotten away from KingPat, he didn't really seem to care about anything anymore.

Decks was where he always was in our secret hideout: sitting on the couch in front of the TV, binge-watching all of his favorite shows. He had with him his frequent companions: a huge bag of chips and a tower of soda. Yeah, Decks wasn't exactly raring to go outside anymore. He hardly went out for fear of getting caught by the cops. I mean, we were escaped prisoners, after all. It wasn't just the cops we had to watch out for either; just about every big and small crook in Mad City was after us too. There was more than enough reason to lie low.

"Dude, did you see all of this? Come on, you've got to check it out!"

Decks yawned at me and took another chip from the bag of.

"I'm sleepy, man. I don't read the news or watch all those crazy vids online."

"This is different, man! Some small crook says there are monsters calling themselves ghouls in Mad City! They can disguise themselves as people and..."

"And you believe a story coming from that rag of a paper? Heck, who even reads newspapers these days?"

Decks stretched out further on the couch. This was a guy who used to do insane stuff in prison with just a small pack of cards. The cards? They were just sitting on the table now gathering dust. The man? Well, he was doing even worse. Decks was a shell of his old self. He was way out of shape now and was as round as a balloon. Overweight from eating too many chips, the couch sagged under his weight and he could barely move thanks to all the extra pounds he'd put on. All Decks ever did was eat and sit on the couch all day. It was pretty sad seeing him like this, but I guess this was what hiding out for so long had done to him. He'd turned from a deadly and unpredictable assassin-type to, well, a couch potato.

"Come on, Decks! You have to check it out! Ghouls in Mad City? This is big news!"

Decks rolled his eyes and slapped his forehead in frustration.

"That's big news? Ghouls in a city like this is big news? A city where shootouts, robberies, and all sorts of crazy stuff happens every single day! You're right, that's really big news, Noob!"

"Come on, man! I know what you're thinking. I know you've gotten tired of moving because we're hiding in here, but you've got to move sometime! The original plan was to chill here while we made some kind of plan to take down KingPat! This news..."

"Is related to that? How?"

I stopped short for a moment. Decks was right. I couldn't really see how this was related to KingPat in the slightest, but I also refused to just stand here and watch Decks rot away on the couch.

"Oh, just take a look already!"

"Man, you can be rough, you know that?"

I guess Decks was surprised that even a guy like me could lose his temper now and then. Finally, he took my phone and watched the video.

"Whoa, this is crazy stuff all right."

The video showed the cops coming into the alley. They found poor Foxy Foxy's body right where Freddie had described it would be.

"Look at that, Decks. The poor guy looks like a tiger has had a fight with him!"

"I've seen worse. It certainly doesn't mean that there's any ghoul running around the town."

"Wait up. It gets better. Keep watching."

The video continued to play, revealing Freddy pointing anxiously at someone in the distance

"It's him! That's the guy I was telling you about! The dude who said he was from Tokyo!"

The police chief and his men approached the Japanese-looking man. It was clear that some of them were struggling to keep a straight face.

"Yes, officers? How can I help you?"

"Sorry to bother you, Sir, but our suspect here says th you killed that man over there. He also says you turned into some kind of monster while doing it. We'll have to take you to the station just to answer a few questions and..."

That was when the Japanese dude smiled. You could see that there was something different about him just by looking at those eyes of his. They were glowing red and his grin was almost evil. This was no ordinary dude from Tokyo.

"I'm sorry. I can't answer any questions."

That was when it happened. The dude sprouted two tentacles with sharp claw tips from his back. It was exactly as poor Freddie Foxy had described. The cops saw it all for themselves, and there was no doubt now that he was telling the truth.

"What did I tell you? It's a ghoul! A real..."

The policemen were all in shock. For a moment they just froze there, like several deer about to be run over by a ten-wheeler truck. Doom was right there in their face, but there was nothing they could do. They were too terrified by what they were seeing to react.

The ghoul grabbed poor Freddie with one of its tentacles and began crushing his body. It was a sad sight, and the cops were all still frozen in fear.

"Do something! That, that.. ghoul is killing him!"

It was Police Chief Herman who finally managed to snap out of it. He whipped his gun out and began firing at the creature. After several tense moments, his men finally responded and began to fire as well.

You would think that the sight of several armed cops would intimidate the ghoul. It would definitely intimidate any normal man, but this creature was something else entirely.

The ghoul tossed aside poor Freddie who went flying across the alley like a ragdoll. I wasn't sure how badly hurt he was but one thing was for sure: he was definitely not all right.

After the ghoul had tossed aside Freddie, he waded into the gunfire like some dude walking into the rain. The bullets seemed to hurt him, but only a little. They didn't really seem to be doing any real, significant damage. It was almost as if he were being stung by mosquitoes which was definitely not what Police Chief Herman and his men wanted.

"Our bullets are barely having an effect on that thing! It's still standing!"

"Thing? Thing? I'm not just any thing. I'm a ghoul! Get it right!"

The ghoul swung his two tentacles around in a violent fashion, swatting away most of the men like rag dolls like Freddie earlier. One thing was for sure: this ghoul could hit really hard.

Police Chief Herman was one of the poor cops that were tossed aside. He was violently thrown to the pavement, but somehow he managed to stand up. His men, however, were still on the ground. The ghoul had wiped them all out with a few swipes. It was like nothing I had ever seen. Even Decks was starting to take notice now.

"What.. what are you? What do you want?"

Police Chief Herman raised his gun at the ghoul, but it was clear that this was a hopeless situation. His hand was trembling so badly that it was unlikely he could aim straight. Even if he did hit the ghoul, it was clear that bullets wouldn't stop it. And he was already beaten up pretty badly.

"Are you that dense? Didn't you listen to what that dumb petty crook told you? I kept him alive for one reason and one reason only: to tell you about me and my purpose! If you didn't hear it before, I'll tell you again now. I'm here for Decks and Noob. I know that they're hiding here somewhere in your sad little city. Give them to me and maybe, just maybe, we'll spare the city!"

"We? We? You're not the only ghoul here?"

I could see the fear in the police chief's eyes now, and that was really scary to see. Decks and I knew Police Chief Herman's rep in the city. He was known as a tough cop who tried his best to somehow bring law and order to the city. Yeah, I know what you're thinking: that's an impossible job! The police chief knew that too, but he never showed any fear when battling with the criminals of Mad City. He was known as a fearless cop. But now, standing in front of the scary ghoul? Well, he wasn't so fearless anymore.

"You heard me! There are others coming to your city now, as we speak! You think I'm bad? Wait until you see my brothers and sisters! They're all coming here to your Mad City to find Noob and Decks. So, if I were you, to spare all sorts of heartache, I would surrender them to us immediately!"

"I don't even know where they are! This is a big city,

and they're hiding somewhere! Why do you want them, anyway?"

The ghoul smiled at the police chief and swatted away his gun. Whatever little defense he had had was now gone. He was completely at the mercy of the foul ghoul.

"Why we want them is not important! What's more important is saving your city from us! I'll spare you, Police Chief Herman. I know you're an honorable dude, and you'll do what needs to be done to save your city. I'm only going to spare you on the basis that you will share this message with everyone. We want Decks and Noob, and if we don't get them, we'll tear your city apart!"

The video ended, and Decks and I were left speechless. We stared at each other for a long time before speaking again.

"Man, I told you that was some heavy stuff! We've got monsters out there looking for us."

"If it wasn't already bad enough with KingPat after us, now these freaks are after us too? This is bad, Noob. Really bad. Bad, bad, bad, bad."

"Way too many bads for me, Decks. What do we do now?"

"What do we do? It's simple. Get me another bag of chips.

I finished this one while watching that stuff."

I looked at the empty bag that Decks was holding. He was right; he had finished it all. I couldn't believe what I was seeing. How could any dude finish a bag of chips so fast? And to think that this was once some feared criminal. Now, he was just an overweight couch potato. A couch potato that couldn't care less about anything that was happening in the outside world.

"Are you serious, Decks? You want us to just stay here while you gain even more weight? Look at yourself already!"

Decks shrugged his shoulders.

"What do you want us to do, Noob? You said it yourself. Look at me. I'm overweight. I can barely get up from the couch. I could have taken on those cops and anyone else in my best days, but you saw those ghouls… I'm not sure I ever could have taken them on. My best days are already far behind me. We can't stop that thing; this is way over our heads. The best thing to do in a situation like this is bury our heads in the sand like ostriches and hide here where it's safe."

"Are you serious?"

I couldn't believe any of this. First the police chief, and

now Decks. These were two men who were known to be fearless. Depending on which side of the law you stood, both men inspired fear in their enemies. And now, they were both afraid of this ghoul – a ghoul who had said that it was just getting started.

"Whoa! Look! My notifications just went crazy!"

My phone started pinging over and over again. It was my news notifications. I opened the app and watched some of the videos streaming onto my phone.

"Look at this, Decks! Can you believe this?"

The news was all about Mad City. There were reports of more ghouls arriving and attacking people on the streets. The ghouls were going crazy and causing chaos everywhere. There were so many reports, my phone was getting flooded with them.

"It's already started. These ghouls are tearing the city apart."

Entry #3

Just a Deck of Cards.

The ghouls got to work on the city faster than anyone could have imagined. From inside our apartment, we could hear screams from outside and the sound of cars and buildings being blown up. Chaos was raging.

"It sounds like a war out there! I think the ghouls are a lot closer to us than we thought!"

I was really starting to freak out now. I mean, those crazy ghouls had arrived in the city a lot faster than anyone thought they would.

"We've got to do something, Decks!"

I was really worried now, but Decks just continued to sit on that couch of his. He didn't look afraid or concerned at all. If anything, Decks actually seemed annoyed.

"Oh, stop bothering me about all of this ghoul stuff, Noob."

I couldn't believe what I was hearing. It was one thing to see Decks slowly get out of shape, but it was another thing entirely to see him suddenly not care about anything.

"Are you serious, Decks? What are you saying? Aren't you aware that ghouls are tearing up the city? They're tearing up the city because they're looking for us!"

"So what? The city's always been crazy! Let them tear it apart already!"

"Look, I've never been a crook in my life. Ever. Even when we got jailed, I was never really into a life of crime or anything. I never really knew why KingPat had it in for me, so I'm not used to this kind of stuff. If you don't care about the city getting trashed, fine. But these ghouls look like really dangerous dudes. We can't just sit here and keep hiding. If you ask me, they're going to find us sooner or later and..."

"They're not going to find us, Noob. Our best bet is to just stay here and hide. None of them could possibly discover where we are."

Decks' words seemed to make some sense. I mean, even if those ghouls were dangerous, there was no guarantee that they would find us. After all, it was a big city. How could they possibly know where we were?

It was right about that time that we heard a knock on the door.

"Pizza delivery!"

"Finally. It's about time!"

Decks was relieved but also a little annoyed that the pizza delivery was late. Considering what was happening all over the city, it was amazing that the pizza he'd ordered arrived at all.

"You ordered pizza? You ordered pizza now, in the middle of all of this madness? I can't believe you, Decks!"

"What's wrong? I ordered the pizza before all of this craziness broke out. I'm just glad it's finally here!"

"You do know that the city is in the middle of some kind of ghoul invasion, don't you?"

"Yeah, yeah. What I do know is that I'm really hungry, and I can't wait to dig into that pizza!"

This was really not the old Decks I knew. Hiding out had

given Decks a very unhealthy appetite. This was really all getting out of hand.

"I can't believe you're more concerned about getting your pizza than working out how we can away from these ghouls tearing up the city!"

"What did I tell you earlier, Noob? There's nothing to worry about! They'll never find us here. You worry way too much. Now cool it already. I don't want you spoiling my pizza!"

Decks tried to get up but failed. He was so big now that he had difficulty just getting up from his couch.

"Uh, maybe you could get that pizza for me? I'm having a little difficulty getting up here. Please?"

"You really need to lose weight. You know that? I'm serious!"

I didn't want to get the pizza, but there was no way that Decks was getting up from the couch. It was terrible seeing him like this, but there was really nothing I could do.

I opened the door and the delivery boy was standing right in front of me.

"Hi there! You ordered some pizza?"

I almost snapped at the poor pizza delivery guy but I kept myself in check. After all, he had nothing to do with Decks' behavior.

"No, my friend did."

"A party size pepperoni. Well, that'll be 300 robux."

"Yeah, okay. I'll just go and get the money from Decks."

"Decks? I knew this was the place!"

Okay, wait… something didn't sound right. I immediately knew something was wrong when I heard the pizza boy speak.

"What did you say?"

"You heard me. I knew this was the right place to find you and Decks."

Before I knew what was happening, the pizza boy suddenly sprouted two huge tentacles with sharp tips. They looked just like the ones from the videos. Yeah, somehow one of the ghouls had managed to find us.

"This can't be happening…"

"Oh, you bet it is! Looks like I've finally found you and your friend Decks! I heard rumors about a fat man ordering a lot of pizza at this place. I heard he was good at cards too so I just had to check it out! Well, well, turns out my hunch was spot on!"

"Decks, we've got a big problem here!"

The ghoul didn't give me a chance to say anything further. He reached out for me with one of his huge tentacles. I don't know how but I managed to duck before it hit me, and the tentacle smashed up one of the tables instead. I didn't want to think about what would have happened if it had caught me.

"Stand still! You're only making this much worse for yourself when I finally catch you."

"Sorry, but my mama always told me not to trust some dude with long tentacles sprouting from his back!"

The tentacles were like some kind of crazy, living obstacle course. They kept swinging around, and it was hard to dodge and keep one step ahead of them. Our place was getting trashed. First it was the table, then some chairs, then our mirror. They all got smashed pretty good by those long tentacles. The mirror was the worst part. I'd heard you'd get seven years of bad luck or something for smashing a mirror. Oh well. In my life, I've probably had much more than just seven years' worth of bad luck anyway.

"Decks? I need you man, and I need you now!"

"Stay away from my friend!"

Decks had finally decided to show.

The ghoul saw Decks and noticed just how round he had grown. He paused, but finally couldn't help himself. He started guffawing loudly.

"Hahaha! This is Decks? I'd heard that you'd both been hiding out for some time so I expected him to be kind of out of shape. But this? This is something else! He's so overweight!"

"That's what I've been trying to tell him."

Great. The ghoul and I actually agreed on something. This situation was getting crazier and crazier by the minute.

"I thought I would be up against a great assassin. Turns out this is going to be a piece of cake!"

"You think I'm a pushover now? You think you can just walk all over us and trash our hideout? Well, I'll show you I've still got it! You're..."

Before Decks could even finish, one of the terrible tentacles reached out and swung at him. It hit him hard, right flush in his face. There was no way Decks could dodge them at his current size. If he were lighter and in better shape, he could have easily ducked out of the way; sadly, that wasn't the case anymore. Decks went flying, smashing into one of the cabinets with tremendous force.

"Decks! Are you all right?"

"Ugh. Not really…"

"You're lucky that KingPat wants you both alive. If he didn't, I could easily kill you both here right now. Instead, I'll just hand you over to him in really bad shape."

KingPat! So, it was him all along. He was the one who had sent these awful ghouls after us. I wasn't really surprised. A man like that would stop at nothing to get what he wanted.

"I can't say that I'm surprised. I knew KingPat had to be behind this, somehow!"

"What do you want me to do, Noob? Pat you on the head and give you some treats? Yeah, you figured it out. Smart. Real smart. I can do all that after I've handed you both over to KingPat!"

With those long and powerful tentacles swinging around, there was no doubt that he could definitely do that and more. Decks and I were in a really tough bind here. How could we stop a rampaging ghoul like this? Decks was far from his old self, and I was no fighter.

"Noob! Use my cards!"

I heard Decks' voice loud and clear. I already knew where his cards were and I raced towards them. The ghoul, however, wasn't finished with trashing our place. Somehow, I kept one step ahead of those awful tentacles of his as he smashed up just about everything remaining in our little place to try and get to me.

"What are you going to do, Noob? Whatever it is you're trying, you better just give it up already!"

I ignored the ghoul's taunts and kept moving. Finally, I saw the cards. Decks hadn't used them for a long time now, and they were gathering dust on a small table.

"Get the cards and use 'em, Noob! They pack a mean punch, enough to knock that ghoul out!"

I reached for the pack of cards just as the ghoul whipped at me with its tentacle again. He barely missed me. His tentacle struck the floor, leaving a large dent in the concrete.

"Got 'em!"

I had the cards, but I had no idea what to do with them

now. These cards were Decks' tools of choice, not mine. To Decks, they were potential weapons of mass destruction. To me? They were just a pack of cards.

"What do I do with them now, Decks?"

I shot a glance at Decks. He was wiped out on the floor, and looked both pained and annoyed at me.

"It's a pack of cards, dude! Just toss one of them at that thing already!"

It sounded really silly to me. I mean, how could a pack of cards hold up against a raging ghoul? How could a single card do anything against a tentacled monster like this? I had so many doubts and questions in my mind, but I decided to just throw caution to the wind.

I picked one of the cards and tossed it at the ghoul.

That was when it happened. When the card made contact with the ghoul, smoke and mist suddenly appeared. The card was a smoke and gas bomb of some sort. Don't even ask me how Decks had managed to get hold of such a powerful set of trick cards!

The gas and smoke quickly got thicker and I was struggling to see in front of me. It was also getting tough to breathe, and I started coughing really badly. I couldn't see the ghoul, but I couldn't hear him coughing. Apparently, the card had just made things worse for me!

"Great! I can't see! I can't see anything Decks! Where's the ghoul?"

"A trick card? Pathetic! You're the one getting gassed out here, not me!"

The ghoul was mocking me now. Things seemed to be going from bad to worse. Suddenly, I felt something grab me in the thick cloud of smoke. The ghoul had hold of me with one of its claws. Its grip was so tight, I felt like I was being squeezed like an empty aluminum can.

"Arrgh! That hurts!"

"Like it? My claws can crush the breath out of you! I've got you now!"

It was pretty hard to argue against that point. It felt as if a giant snake was choking me out.

"Noob! Toss another card at him!"

I really didn't know if tossing another card at the ghoul was a good idea. After all, it seemed as if the cards had crazy, unpredictable effects. Then again, what choice did I have? He had me by the claws, and I really didn't have many options left.

I tossed a second card at the ghoul. It wasn't hard to aim; even with all the swirling smoke around me, he was right up close to my face.

The card struck the ghoul flush in the face, just as he had struck Decks earlier. This time, there was no smoke or gas. Instead, I heard a sound like a loud "pop" or "bang." It was almost like a gunshot or a firecracker had popped right in front of the ghoul's face.

This time, he wasn't just annoyed by it. I heard the ghoul cry out in pain as the card exploded in his face, and he released me from his tentacles.

"Aaaahh! That card! It hurts!"

I dropped to the floor. The gas and smoke were clearing now, and I could see the ghoul stumbling around the mess that was once our little hideout. He was clearly still feeling the effects of the card.

I looked at Decks. He was still on the ground, but he was smiling with satisfaction now.

"Nasty stuff, ain't it? I call it my exploding card. And for good reason..."

The ghoul continued to stumble around, clutching at his face. He was clearly stunned and in pain. I couldn't just stand around; I had to press the advantage. Even Decks knew this.

"Throw another card at that freak, Noob! Now, while he's stunned!"

He didn't need to tell me twice. I threw another card from the deck. The card struck the ghoul again with a loud boom.

It was much louder than the last explosion. A whole lot louder, and stronger. The explosion engulfed the ghoul and blew him to bits, throwing me to the ground in the process. I was sure that there could be nothing left of the ghoul after a powerful explosion like that.

I rolled my way over to Decks who was still on the floor. The smoke was clearing now but there was no sign of the ghoul; he seemed to have vanished in the powerful explosion.

Unfortunately, our hideout was disappearing too. The explosion had started a fire that was now engulfing the whole place. It had been trashed by the ghoul, and now it was going to be burned to the ground.

"Decks! We've got to get out of here! This place is done for, and we will be too if we don't move fast."

Decks was still lying on the ground. He was still weak and in rough shape, but he saw the urgency of my words.

"You're right. Come on. Help me up, please!"

Let me tell you now, lifting up Decks was no easy task. He had gained so much weight that it was like trying to lift a solid oak tree that had been chopped down. Fortunately, he still had enough strength to help himself up; if he'd have been completely out of it, I doubt that I would have been able to move him.

"That's it. Come on. Let's get moving already..."

I could smell smoke all around me. The fire was spreading at a rapid pace, and we were still in there!

"Phew! If we make it out of this alive, remind me to lay off the junk food!"

"That's what I've been trying to tell you all this time!"

We both scrambled to our feet and started making our way out of there. Decks was still weak, but you'd be surprised how much energy a man can find when he's running for his life. It was as if he had gotten a shot of pure adrenaline as he started making a dash for the door. I was right behind him.

We dived out of the front door like there was no tomorrow.

The whole place was burning behind us. Just as we dived out, the hideout finally burned down. Everything fell apart in one awful blaze of glory.

"Looks like we're out in the street again. At least we've still got my deck of cards. That gives us a little edge."

I shook my head. Decks lost all the color in his face.

"What are you saying? What do you mean?"

"The deck of cards got lost in there."

"Are you serious? You've got to be kidding me!"

"Well, not all of them."

I whipped out one card from my pocket. It was the Ace of Spades.

"They were all destroyed in the explosion. All of them except this one, that is. I managed to keep it with me."

Decks sighed in relief. He took a deep breath and looked a lot calmer now.

"Well, at least you managed to save one card. It's better than nothing. Still, it's best to keep hold of it and really just use it in case of an emergency."

I looked around. The whole city was burning, and there

was chaos in the streets. People were running for their lives, and the ghouls were just causing trouble for the fun of it.

"Don't you think this pretty much counts as an emergency?"

Decks frowned.

"You know what I mean, Noob. Let's just try to lie low in all this madness."

Entry #4:

Decks and I were facing the terrible prospect of being on the run again. We had no hideout, he was out of shape, and we had no trick cards to help us. We were basically on our own. You would think that the odds were against us, but we actually had one thing in our favor. With the ghouls running down the whole city, it was easy to lie low in the chaos.

"We're really done for now, Noob! If any of those ghouls find us, we're dead! We've only got one card, and I'm no good so out of shape like this! What are we going to do?"

Decks was right. It really wasn't looking too good for us.

"I don't know, Decks. I don't know. I'm trying to think of something."

I was struggling to think of anything. It wasn't easy to think rationally with an entire city burning in front of us.

Everywhere I looked, people were running. There were overturned cars in the streets, and I could see a lot of cops and ghouls battling. The cops were on the losing end of course, and they could barely keep the ghouls at bay. In all the confusion, they barely noticed us. Decks was so out of shape that he looked like a different person, and I looked like an average Joe. It was pretty easy for us to just blend in, which made what happened next even more surprising.

It all happened so fast. A huge spotlight was suddenly flashed towards where we were. Both Decks and I were stunned by the light.

"What's happened…? What's going on?"

"What's going on, is that you're both coming with us!"

When we opened our eyes, the light was gone, but there were several policemen standing in front of us. They were all decked out in riot gear and heavy weapons, and they had their guns pointed right at us.

"Man, is that Decks? I remember seeing him before! I was glad he didn't kill me! He looks, well…"

"He's out of shape, Morris. Yeah! Keep that gun pointed at him. If the trackers say that it's Decks and Noob then it's them all right! Those trackers don't lie."

Decks and I knew that there were too many cops to outrun. With their guns right in our faces like that, we really didn't have any options left. Well, we did have one option; we still had that last card.

Decks and I looked at each other. He nodded at me, and we both silently reached an agreement. This wasn't the right time to use the card. I could have whipped it out and used it right then and there, but I decided to keep it for now. There would be a better time to use it, and Decks agreed. We both just raised our hands.

Even the riot cops noticed how different Decks looked. That was something, but the real story was, how did they suddenly find us?

"Trackers? What's going on here? How did you guys find us?"

"Stop asking questions and come with us already! We're already doing you a favor!"

"Doing us a favor, eh? You're just going to throw us at the mercy of those ghouls!"

"We don't have time for this!"

One of the cops handcuffed us both, and we were both quickly hauled into a waiting armored car. Once inside, the car drove swiftly through the streets of Mad City.

I looked out the window. The ghouls were everywhere now. They were determined to have their way with the city, and the cops couldn't do much to stop them.

One of the cops barked orders at the driver.

"They're tearing up the city! Drive faster before one of them actually notices us!"

"I'm already flooring it!"

The driver was right. I could see that he was going as fast as he could. He weaved through the mess that was the road, avoiding abandoned cars, burning cars, and cars that had collided with each other.

"Watch out!"

Suddenly, a giant tentacle lashed out at us from out of nowhere. The driver spun the steering wheel around as hard as he could. Somehow, he managed to dodge the tentacle. Despite his best efforts, however, it was still stretching towards us.

"That thing seems to be several miles long. It just keeps stretching and stretching!"

"This should stop it dead in its tracks!"

One of the cops took out a heavy machine gun. Its bullets looked large enough to take down an elephant, and it could fire several of these, one after another.

"Hold on, everyone! It's time to knock this thing down a peg or two! This is going to be nasty!"

The cop kicked open the back doors of the van. The tentacle was right behind us now; it seemed to have a life of its own as it kept stretching and chasing after the van.

"Eat this, freak!"

The cop unloaded on the tentacle with his heavy machine gun. There was a loud roaring sound as the machine gun erupted with gunfire. The bullets struck the tentacle repeatedly, and it drew back. It looked as if it were in real pain from the gunshots.

The van pulled away.

"Yeah! Did you guys see that? That dumb tentacle ate all the bullets! I bet you he'll never be crazy enough to..."

The poor cop never had the chance to finish his words. Before we knew what was happening, another giant tentacle reached out from nowhere and coiled around him. He dropped his heavy machine gun on the floor, a look of sheer terror on his face.

"Noo! Help me, somebody!"

The other cops were about to draw their guns and fire at the thing, but it was too fast. It pulled back, yanking the cop away.

"Did you see that? These things are crazy! They just won't stop!"

Boy, was Decks ever right. One tentacle had just yanked the cop out of sight when another struck. It coiled its claw into a fist and slammed into the side of the van. The blow was so strong that the van went flying on its side and skidded and landed on the side of the road.

Decks and I crawled out of the van.

"Those things just don't stop, do they? They'll stop at nothing to catch us!" Decks panted.

"Calm down. We're almost at the station."

It was one of the cops. He too had survived the impact of the crash. Unfortunately, he was the only cop remaining.

"Come on. I'll take you both to the station. It's not far from here."

"What are you going to do? Turn us over to those things? Well, I can't say I wouldn't do the same thing if I were in your shoes. You should know though that KingPat is behind all this. He's the one who sicced those things to get us. As cops, you guys should just go after him. He's the dirtiest and most powerful man around. I can't see what he would want with two losers like us."

It was a valid point. Decks and I already knew that the ghouls wanted us for KingPat.

"You don't understand. We already know all of that. We're not going to give you up to KingPat."

"What? What are you saying?"

Before the cop could answer, another long tentacle came out of nowhere and snatched him up.

"Help!"

Before we could do anything, the cop was tossed away like a broken toy. Another ghoul walked up to us.

"You guys are done for now. I'm taking you out. Permanently."

Decks and I didn't like the sound of the ghoul's words.

"Whoa, whoa, whoa! Ease up there. Permanently? I thought you guys were out to get us and give us over to KingPat?"

The ghoul laughed as I spoke. His voice was like broken glass.

"Boy, don't you two watch the news? The deal with KingPat is off! Us ghouls have decided to just trash the city for kicks! We're going to kill you all and take the city for ourselves!"

Okay, that really didn't sound good.

Entry #5

An Old Friend Returns.

The ghoul was right in front of us, and the situation was looking really bad.

"I'm going to tear you both apart while my fellow ghouls are taking apart your city!"

He reached out and grabbed both of us in his tentacles. Decks and I squirmed frantically to free ourselves, but it was useless; his grip was like iron.

The ghoul was really overconfident now. He was sure that he could kill us both.

"You're both done for! I just wish Decks was as strong and dangerous as he was before! I'll take no pleasure in killing this fat pig!"

"Really? Too bad, because I'll take a lot of pleasure doing this!"

I managed to wriggle one of my arms free from the ghoul's grasp. It was the arm that held the ace of spades. In one powerful downward motion, I slashed at his tentacle with the card. It was like a knife slicing through butter.

The ghoul was shocked to see that part of his tentacle had been cut off. I fell to the ground, as the ghoul cried out in pain.

"There you go! That'll show him!"

Decks was overjoyed that I had chopped off that ghoul's tentacle; the ghoul, unsurprisingly, was not so pleased.

"You'll pay for that! I'll rip you apart!"

The ghoul charged at me, and I knew that he could do just that. I had a bad feeling that I wouldn't be able to pull off the trick with the card a second time.

Luckily, I wouldn't have to.

Just as the ghoul charged at me, he was struck down by a powerful blast. The blast wasn't gunfire. It was a very powerful laser that roasted the ghoul where he stood. The ghoul was done for; he disappeared, dropping Decks to the ground.

"Decks! Are you all right?"

"I'm fine, Noob! Who took down that ghoul though, and with what? That looked to be a powerful laser beam. I haven't heard of any weapon that can fire a laser that powerful."

"You haven't heard of my new prototype G-Blaster? It's a gun that's specifically designed to take down ghouls! If you haven't heard of my gun, then it's a safe bet that you haven't heard of me either! Shame on you!"

I recognized immediately that voice. I only knew of one man who was that full of himself, but who could also back it up. I couldn't believe he was back!

"Major Creative! It's you! What are you doing here?"

Major Creative was decked out in full armor. His "G-Blaster" as he called it looked like a heavy cannon and I was amazed that he could lift it. It was still smoking from the powerful laser that had been fired.

"Me? I'm here to save both your sorry butts. After all, someone's got to do it, eh? Believe me, before the day is over, this big cannon of mine is going to taste plenty more ghoul!"

I knew Major Creative well enough to know that this was

no empty boast; he would take down more than his fair share of ghouls before all this was over. I was relieved to see him.

Entry #6

Not the Same Man He Was.

"You know this dude, Noob?" Decks asked.

"Pretty well. We had our fair share of adventures before. The Major's a pretty in-your-face kind of genius, but believe me, Decks, he's the best kind of guy to have in an awful situation like this."

The Major smiled behind his transparent helmet. It was round like a fishbowl and it complimented his heavy armor.

"Glad to see you still remember me, Noob. Follow me. You guys were in the station already!"

Major pointed at the police station. I hardly recognized it at first; it looked like it had taken a real beating.

"Those poor cops already got you here. I've established a small base of operations in the basement. We'll be safe there!"

The major led us both down to the station's basement. We followed with no complaints. Being underground was definitely a lot safer than staying up in the city right now.

In the basement were several cops, including Police Chief Herman.

"You managed to get them down here, Major. That's great! But the other cops..."

The Major didn't answer. His silence said it all.

"Those ghouls are going to pay! A lot of good cops have gone down because of them already!"

The police chief was so angry about losing his men that he didn't notice Decks at first. Decks was so out of shape that he looked like a completely different person. When the police chief finally noticed, he could not believe what he was seeing.

"Whoa! Is that you, Decks? I can't believe you've gained so much weight! This is crazy!"

I frowned.

"Hey, I've been telling him to lay off the junk food, the soft drinks and the pizza. Did he listen? No way!"

"Look. You guys can make fun of my physical fitness later! I want some answers, and I want them now! Tell me Police Chief Herman, why did the ghouls suddenly decide to tear up the city? We know they were hired by KingPat so why the sudden change of heart?"

"And why is Major Creative here? Not that I'm ungrateful for his saving us back there, of course," I added.

The police chief shook his head.

"I think Major Creative is better suited to answer all those questions."

"The ghouls changed their mind because it is simply in their nature to do so. Ghouls aren't really intelligent creatures. They live for battle and would rather fight and devour people than negotiate or follow orders. Their breed is a special mixture of man and monster. They aren't easy to control, but KingPat was too full of himself to notice this when he summoned them."

"Summoned them?"

Major Creative nodded.

"Yes. He summoned them by stealing one of my own

inventions: a powerful magnet that can attract lifeforms from other dimensions. He summoned the ghouls from another dimension where they existed. That's why I had to come here to stop them: KingPat is using my equipment. He stole the powerful magnet and a lot of other inventions of mine. That just makes me mad, and now, it's personal. I've got to stop him."

Decks shrugged his shoulders.

"I can understand where you're coming from, Major. I mean, even I would be really angry if someone stole my stuff. What I don't get is this: why did you even invent something like that magnet in the first place?"

"He's Major Creative. The man's a mad genius, and that's putting it mildly," I replied.

"That still doesn't answer my question, Noob. Why would someone create something as powerful as that? As far as I can see, a magnet that can suck dudes from another universe isn't particularly useful. From what we've seen here, it's actually harmful even."

Major Creative bowed his head and looked ashamed.

"You may have gained a lot of pounds, but you've gained even more wisdom, Decks. You're right. I probably had no business creating such a device. It has no real practical use and it's only brought everyone trouble. I'm sorry. It's just that I'm an inventor, and I can't help but invent stuff. It's just what I do, and this time it really got your city into trouble. I'm really sorry."

"I think everybody here will agree with me when I say the time for saying sorry is over, Major. We just have to face this head-on and defeat the ghouls. We have to take back our city."

I was glad to hear Police Chief Herman speak. He was starting to sound like his old self already, and he was right; it was time to take back the city.

"We're going to take back the city all right. And I've got just the toys we'll need to do the job."

I knew that Major Creative meant it. It was time to tackle those ghouls head on.

"All right! Let's do this! Those ghouls are going down, and we're taking back our city!"

A triumphant roar sounded from everyone in the basement. It was time to take it to the ghouls.

"Okay, so how are we going to take it to those crazy freaks?"

"With a guy like me, you can take it to anybody! I've got a

tool for every situation."

That wasn't hard to believe. I knew the Major well from our past adventures together; the man was a genius and he could do just about anything he set his mind to. Plus, he had already taken down one ghoul that had attacked us with relative ease.

"Here, everyone, take these guns. They were designed by my great genius to take on ghouls specifically."

The Major passed around several guns that resembled his giant cannon. They looked smaller and more compact, almost as if the giant cannon he held onto was their big brother.

"So, this stuff is supposed to do the trick and take down those freaks?" Chief Herman asked.

"It took down that ghoul chasing after Noob and Decks, so it should do the trick against the others."

"You've got a bigger one."

The chief was pretty observant.

"Yeah. This is the more powerful version. I admit I had to make some compromises on the original design to allow for mass production in such a short time. It won't pack as much of a punch as my cannon, but it should be enough to take most of them out."

"I hope it'll be enough. I guess we'll just have to trust you on this, Major."

"Hey, I have a question for you! How did you guys even manage to find us?" Decks interrupted.

"It was me, Decks. I was the one who designed your cards."

"You what?"

Decks couldn't believe what he was hearing. He had never seen Major Creative before, and now he was saying he was the one who designed his cards? Yeah, even I admit it was something of a stretch all right.

"How could you have designed them? I bought them from..."

"From one of my old customers, yes. He told me that he'd sold you the cards, and you've definitely made the most of them since then! The trick cards were an original design. It was a relatively simple chore to trace the cards back to you."

"Okay, so you are every bit the smart dude that Noob says you are. Cool. I don't mean to sound ungrateful or anything, but I notice you weren't going to give us up to

KingPat, and you weren't going to haul our butts back to jail. So, what gives? I mean, I wasn't born yesterday. Why would you guys suddenly take all the time and effort to find us in the middle of this war with the ghouls?"

"I'll answer that," Chief Herman volunteered.

"We wanted to find you two because of you, Decks. You are one of the best and most dangerous criminal assassins that have ever lived. I don't mean to inflate your ego or anything, but you were a real legend back in the day. Everybody feared you, and I mean really feared you. You were the baddest man in Mad City or anywhere. When the Major revealed the ghouls' natural love for violence, and how they wouldn't surrender you to KingPat anymore, we knew we would have a war on our hands against the worst possible enemies. To help us out, we wanted to get the best and most dangerous man on our side."

Decks shook his head. I noticed he suddenly looked really small and ashamed of himself.

"That man was me. Yeah, it WAS me. I'm not who I once was."

Police Chief Herman shrugged his shoulders.

"Hey, you said it, not me. Let's face it, you're not exactly as dangerous as you used to be..."

The police chief spoke slowly. He didn't want to embarrass Decks, but it was the truth.

"You're right, of course. I hid for so long that I lost my edge. I'm not the same man I used to be. I would be useless against these ghouls now. I don't even have my deck of cards anymore!"

Major Creative placed a heavy hand on Decks' shoulder.

"Don't worry. You're not going to be useless. Not if I can help it."

"What do you mean?"

"I've made these tools especially for you, Decks."

The Major whipped out another set of playing cards. Decks' jaw almost dropped as he placed them into his hands.

"Whoa! A new set of cards! That's so awesome!"

"Hey, awesome is the Major's middle name! I've seen the dude make miracles! I'm not even kidding," I said.

The Major shook his head.

"Look. As much as I would love to keep this praise about me and what I can do going on, it's not healthy, and we've got ghouls to take down! It's best we start doing that instead!"

"Now that's what I'm talking about! It's time to take our city back from those freaks!" Police Chief Herman shouted enthusiastically.

Everyone in the basement roared their approval. It was time for the final battle against the ghouls to begin. This time, we were determined to take them all out.

Entry #7

The Final Battle.

We stormed out of the basement, the special blaster rifles that the Major had created in our hands. Don't even ask me how he manages to come up with such crazy toys. That's just the Major for you. That's why he's long since earned his name. Inventing all sorts of crazy stuff is what he does best.

When we reached the street, we started firing at any ghoul we encountered. The new cannons quickly proved themselves. Any ghouls we met were taken down immediately and with ease.

"These guns are an absolute blast! We're taking them down!"

More ghouls were coming our way. I pointed my small

cannon at them and the laser knocked them flat. This was not like before when the ghouls took the gunfire the cops threw at them and just laughed it off; this time, the Major had created a truly fearsome weapon.

"It's working! They don't stand a chance against these new weapons!"

The new cannons were not the only weapons causing all sorts of problems for the ghouls.

"Yahoo! This is great!"

Decks was in his element, tossing his new playing cards at every single ghoul that he came across. The cards exploded on impact, releasing powerful gas and producing many more strange and powerful effects. The ghouls were no match for Decks, who was starting to look a bit like his old self again, even with the extra weight. That was pretty amazing to see.

"I can see you really outdid yourself this time, Major!" I said.

"Noob, I always outdo myself! I'm always making something bigger, better and more efficient than the one before! That's just who I am!"

We tore through Mad City with the crazy weapons that

the Major had created, taking down every single ghoul that we encountered. We really didn't get any kind of real struggle from them. The weapons were that good that the ghouls were now reduced to pests that we were exterminating.

However, as with all these things, it wasn't going to last.

"These new toys you've made are amazing, Major! We could revolutionize the police force with these and finally stomp out all crime in the city!"

"Are they really that good? They haven't really been put to the test. They haven't taken on me!"

Before we knew what was happening, Police Chief Herman was snatched up by a pair of tentacles. And he wasn't the only one. Most of the other policemen were snatched up too. The sheer number of arms coming at us now was just incredible.

"What is this? There are so many arms!" I shouted.

"You bet there are!"

They came from a single ghoul. Like all the others, he looked just like any ordinary dude. The only difference between him and the other ghouls was the insane number of tentacles he had on his back.

"This is crazy! How many arms does this guy have?" I asked.

"More than enough to take out the entire police force apparently!" the ghoul replied.

He was right. It was just me, Major Creative and Decks who were left standing and being forced to deal with those crazy arms of his; they were all over the place, swinging and coming at us like some crazy circus obstacle course.

"Noob! Decks! This is what it's all been building up to! We've slaughtered all the ghouls around the city but this is their most powerful one! We have to take it down! If we don't, everything will have been for nothing and..."

Major Creative was going to say more but one of the ghoul's tentacles swatted him away. He went flying and his armor apparently short-circuited. He couldn't move! It was now just me and Decks.

"He talked too much, don't you think? Now, this is better! Me, the most powerful ghoul, versus the two of you! Two nobodies!"

I have to admit, I was scared out of my mind. I had no idea how Decks and I were going to take this monster of a ghoul out. He had single-handedly taken down the whole police force and Major Creative! What could an overweight former assassin and a Noob like me do?

A lot apparently.

"Noob! Shoot him!"

Shooting at the ghoul seemed like the most obvious, and yet the silliest, thing to do. It seemed too powerful and completely, well, unbeatable! Still, it had to be worth a try!

I pointed my cannon at the creature and started firing. Even if it wasn't so powerful, I probably wouldn't have been able to hit it. My hands were shaking in fear and it was almost impossible to hold my gun straight.

"Is this some kind of a joke? I'm the baddest ghoul around, and you're trying to shoot me? I guess I should show some respect for your initiative and bravery and blah, blah, blah, but nah! I'll just kill you instead!"

The powerful ghoul swatted away my cannon, sending it flying to the ground. He grabbed me with one of those many terrible tentacles of his. I felt the life being squeezed out of me as he gripped me harder and harder.

"Ouch! Let me go!"

I was starting to turn pale. I couldn't breathe!

"Now, why would I do a silly thing like that? The great Noob, one of the greatest Roblox players ever, is going to be taken out by me, the greatest ghoul ever! You are so done for and..."

"Hey you!"

The ghoul turned around. Decks was standing right behind him.

"You're the one who talks too much!"

Decks ran up to the ghoul and jammed several cards in his shirt. I don't know how he managed to run so quickly. I guess he still had some of his old skills buried under all those excess pounds. They were just waiting to be unleashed. And now was that time.

"What have you done?"

"I've just jammed all my cards into your shirt! You fell for the most basic trick ever! Noob was just a distraction. A distraction that distracted you long enough for me to act. Now, you're the one that's done for!"

"No!"

It was too late for the ghoul. Decks had done exactly as he'd said; the ghoul had no choice but to take the full brunt and power of all the cards combined.

285

To say that there was a big boom would be an understatement. A series of large explosions followed. Huge gas clouds filled the air, and an assortment of nets, sharp spikes and other traps were generated. The last ghoul standing had no chance at all.

As he disappeared into the explosions, the ghoul released his grip on me. I landed on the ground with a loud and painful thud, but at least I was still all right.

I couldn't see anything in front of me. I covered my eyes and started coughing like crazy. There was smoke and all sorts of crazy stuff everywhere, but the ghoul was done for and taken care of. As the air slowly cleared, I started to look for Decks.

"Decks! Decks, where are you?"

"I'm here!"

Decks motioned to me. I found him close to a fire where the ghoul had once been standing. He was on the ground and clearly exhausted. He was breathing hard and panting.

"You did it! You saved us all! How did you do that?"

Decks shook his head.

"Don't ask me, Noob! I don't know how I did it myself!"

"Well, whatever! You did it, and you saved us all! You've still got it!"

Decks smiled at me and I knew that it would only be a matter of time before the old Decks would return, badder and even more dangerous than before.

"Come on! We've got to check if the others are all right!"

We ran towards Major Creative.

"I'm here! Help me out of my suit of armor! It's damaged and I can't get out!"

It took some effort, but Decks and I eventually managed to peel the Major out of his battlesuit. He wasn't joking about the damage. As far as anyone was concerned, his high-tech battlesuit was now simply a hunk of scrap metal.

"That ghoul really did a number on your suit, Major!"

"It doesn't matter, Noob. I'll make a bigger and better one! Come on. We have to tend to the policemen!"

We did just that. Police Chief Herman was badly injured, but he would be okay in time. Most of his men were also in a bad way, and the city was in ruins. All of this just because of KingPat's mad obsession with me! It just wasn't right!

"What are we going to do now? The city's in ruins!"

Major Creative did not hesitate to answer me.

"That's simple, Noob. We help to rebuild the city. And once we're done with that, we take down KingPat, once and for all!"

UNOFFICIAL

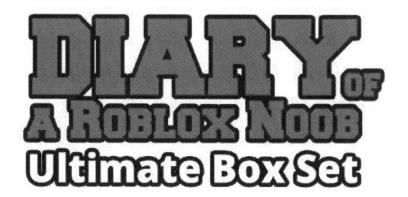

DIARY OF A ROBLOX NOOB
Ultimate Box Set

+3 BONUS STORIES

ROBLOXIA KID

UNOFFICIAL

JAILBREAK

ROBLOXIA KID

Chapter One

Doing Hard Time.

I woke up in the middle of the precinct. There were handcuffs on my wrists, and I was seated on a bench. There was a grumpy police officer in front of me. He sat behind a desk, and looked real busy. There were other policemen and they all looked just as busy and grumpy as that guy.

The entire precinct was a beehive of activity. The grumpy cops were escorting and taking a lot of other prisoners all around. The prisoners protested loudly and the other officers ignored them as they brought them to wherever they take prisoners. As you could imagine, the prisoners were not very happy with how they were being treated. To tell the truth, I wasn't very happy with where I was, either.

"What is this? Where am I, and why am I in these handcuffs?" I demanded.

Yeah, I was beginning to sound just like the prisoners already. I was really going to fit into this place, really nice.

"That doesn't matter, Noob! You're here now, and you're going to do hard time!"

"What did you call me?" I asked.

"Noob! That's your name, and it suits you really fine, considering you're headed straight for the pen!"

The police officer that was handling me was the picture of friendliness and courtesy. It was clear that I was not going to get any answers from this guy. Still, I could not help but ask some important questions. I needed to get some idea of where I was, and what was going on.

"Hard time? Come on man, what was my crime?"

The police officer shrugged his shoulders and waved me away with his hand.

"What are you talking about? This is Roblox Jailbreak! In this server, you don't need no crime to be sent here to do hard time! Lucky for you, eh?"

That was a nice joke at my expense.

"I'm not serving any time for nothing!" I protested.

The police officer shook his head.

"If it's any consolation, most of these guys haven't done anything wrong either, but they're serving time all the same! Some of them, though, actually have committed some kind of crime. I'm just not sure about your case."

"I don't even know how I got here! I just woke up with these chains on my wrists!" I said.

"Does it even matter? Look kid, the important thing now is you're here, and you're doing time! So get up already, Noob!"

Yeah, it was a command and not a request. I had no other option but to get up from the bench. The policeman grabbed me by the arm and pulled me up.

"Come on, already! I've got a long day, and I want to go home to the wife and kids already. Let's go."

There was a slight hint of pity in the police officer's voice as I got up. It was there for a moment, but only for that moment. It passed quickly enough, and he frowned. I could see that this guy simply wanted to do his job, and that was that.

I really had no choice and simply followed the police

officer. My hands were cuffed, and he led me away from the noisy precinct.

Chapter Two

A New Cellmate.

I knew that he was not going to lead me anywhere better, and I was right. I passed through a metal detector that scanned my entire body. They made sure I wasn't carrying any custom parts that could start trouble in the prison.

"Okay. Dude's clear," the guard behind the metal detector said.

"His name's Noob," the police officer said.

"Heh. Noob. Suits him just fine."

"Never got to ask you your name, boss," I said.

The police officer smiled at me.

"Boss will do just fine. Here."

Boss handed me a new set of clothes. At that moment, he was like some kind of magician. I never saw where he pulled those clothes from. It was almost like pulling several rabbits out of a hat, or something like that.

"Change into these. They look better on you."

It was a prison uniform. The color was a very plain and boring light brown. Well, I was really doing hard time now.

I had no choice but to change to the prison browns. Yep, I know what you're thinking. It was really tough to change clothes with my wrists handcuffed like that, but somehow I managed. When I was done, I was looking really good.

Boss nodded and smiled at me.

"Yeah. You look good in prison browns, Noob," he said.

I frowned at him.

"Shut up, Boss."

It all happened so fast. I felt something hard and solid strike my tummy. It was a well-placed kick from Boss' boot, and let me tell you now, I really felt it. I thought that I would throw up, right then and there. Somehow, I managed to hold my breakfast in.

"You don't talk to me like that, ever. You got that, Noob?"

I shot a really angry look back at Boss. I guess I wasn't really thinking straight then. It was a bad move, for obvious reasons. After all, I wasn't the one with the power here.

Boss quickly made me pay for the dagger looks, as he struck me down with his baton. It looked like a plastic toy, but it really hit hard. I was knocked down, and the dude behind the metal detector just smiled and laughed it off.

"I said, did you get that, Noob?" he repeated.

"I got it loud and clear, Boss," I said.

"Good. Now let's get you back up on your feet. Come on, the boys are all dying to meet you, Noob."

I got up and started walking. Boss started walking beside me. Suddenly, he slipped hard on the floor. There was a loud thud as Boss fell right on his butt. Boss was a heavy sort, with a big belly to match. When he fell, the entire ground shook, and I thought that there was a minor earthquake. Well, seeing Boss fall flat on the ground was too much, and I couldn't help but giggle just a little.

Boss immediately got up. With his heavy frame and

imposing presence, it seemed as if it was his pride that was hurt more than anything. A guy that big and powerful could fight a tank head-on and still be standing. He dusted himself off and growled.

"What's so funny? Ain't never seen anyone slip before? Keep walking, already!"

I stopped laughing and continued walking, just as Boss said. I looked behind, and it became clear what happened. There was an errant banana peel that was right where Boss took a step. It was the culprit behind his very epic fail. I turned and saw the guard behind the metal detector. He smiled and winked at me. Boss never saw any of it.

I smiled back at the guard. I didn't know the guy at all, but it was clear that he didn't seem to like Boss very much. Well, I was happy to see Boss tripped up, in any kind of way. It was nice to know that not everybody liked Boss. Perhaps this would come in handy for me later on.

Boss and I marched on until we came to a large row of cells. There were several prisoners all around the cells, and there were as many as 5 floors all full of cells and prisoners.

"All right. We've got yard time in the afternoon where you can meet up and socialize with the other prisoners.

You can do that if you're the friendly type. Personally, I wouldn't recommend it."

Yeah, it didn't take a genius to see that Boss was right. I immediately saw why he would not recommend me socializing with the other inmates. They were all in their cells, but they were all hooting and shouting all over the place. To say that they were noisy and rowdy was, well, being mild. They were all acting like a bunch of caged monkeys.

"Are they always this noisy?" I asked.

Boss turned and smiled at me.

"Only when there's a new inmate in town. Like now."

"Oh-kay."

A few more steps, and Boss led me to the second floor. I was led right smack into the cell in the middle of the cell block. There was a single inmate in the cell. There were also two beds stacked on top of each other in the cell. There was also a sink that was built into the wall. That was about it. Yeah, the cell was very well furnished. I guess I couldn't complain. It wasn't like I was checking into a 5-star hotel with all the luxury in the world.

"Pablo! You've got a new cellmate!" Boss barked.

The other guy lifted his head up and smiled at me.

"Pablo Santana, esse. Nice to meet you."

Yeah, with that accent, and with the way he talked, he definitely sounded like a Pablo. Pablo was surprisingly very friendly and smiled at me immediately. He offered me his hand, and he smiled. I could see that Pablo would be pretty easy to get along with. Well, that was definitely nice to see in a place like this.

I shook hands with Pablo and my mood brightened, just a little bit.

"Nice to meet you, Pablo. I'm..."

"Noob. His name's Noob," Boss said.

I was a little relieved to hear Boss mention my name. For some strange reason, I couldn't remember my real name, so I guess Noob it was, for now.

"Hi, Noob. Let's try to make our stay here as pleasant as it can possibly be," Pablo said.

It was actually quite refreshing to see someone like Pablo in a place as depressing as this. He had a kind of positive energy that was actually quite easy to catch. He kinda didn't fit in a prison like this, and I wondered what a nice guy like Pablo could have done to be in a place like this.

"Don't get too friendly with Pablo. You'll have to do a lot of hard time here with him."

"A man's got a right to smile and enjoy himself, doesn't he?" I said.

Boss glared at me as he approached. Suddenly I felt like a rabbit being chased down by a large grizzly. Boss stood in front of me, and I could see just how large he really was. His big tummy only made him look even bigger and more intimidating.

"I've only met you now, Noob, but I already don't like you. Too bad for you. You better be nice here in the prison, because I'll be watching your every move," he said.

"Take it easy, Boss. I don't want any trouble. I just want to do my time."

Boss nodded and turned away. He closed the cell door in front of me. It was just me and Pablo inside.

"Good. You better just keep it that way. For your sake."

Boss walked away, and this time there were no banana peels in front of him. Eventually, even the other prisoners got quiet. I guess it was time to settle down in my cell with Pablo.

"Hey esse, what did you do to get on the Boss' bad side?"

Pablo asked.

I shrugged my shoulder.

"Beats me. Boss was on my case the minute I stepped in here."

"That's too bad, esse. In case you hadn't noticed, he's the warden. Boss runs things around here, with an iron fist. If he doesn't like you, that's instant bad news for you."

I shook my head.

"It doesn't matter. After all, he won't be seeing me around here for long."

Pablo smiled and giggled at me.

"What do you mean, esse? Are you planning on getting out of here? Let me tell you now, esse, lots of other guys have tried it before, and they all failed. You better just forget about any fancy ideas of escape. You'll just get burned and make things worse."

I smiled and winked at Pablo.

"Is that so, now? Well, I say, they call this server 'Jailbreak', right? I think it's time that we make it earn that name."

Chapter Three

Something Loose.

"Heh. I like your style, esse. You've got spunk, guts. All the stuff that makes for a tough guy. Too bad all of that doesn't amount to much down here. All it's going to do is make Boss angry, and you'll see soon enough that he doesn't like getting angry."

Pablo spoke to me with caution, and I could see that he was very serious. It didn't matter to me, though. I was not going to spend time in jail for nothing. For me, the whole point of doing hard time was making amends for some kind of crime or bad stuff you did. Well, Boss simply couldn't pin anything on me, so there was no reason for me to stay locked up like this. I was determined to get out, one way or another. I just had to find out how to do it.

I immediately looked around the bare cell that I shared with Pablo. I observed all of our surroundings and took them all in very seriously. There wasn't much to look at. The walls were made of thick bricks and Roblox concrete, tough stuff to be sure. The only thing that passed for furnishing in the room was the sink. I immediately thought that perhaps there was a way to crack through it.

I went around it, and felt around the sink with my hands.

"Looking for weak spots in that sink, esse? I really wouldn't bother. It's wedged shut. The guards also do their rounds around here every hour, and they're always inspecting the cells, looking around for trouble. If you think we can dig through that sink, or somehow yank it out, well, I just don't think it's possible."

I smiled at Pablo.

"Anything's possible, Pablo. We just have to make a plan and follow through with it."

Pablo shrugged his shoulders.

"You're a different sort, all right, Noob. I just don't see how you can do it."

"We. It's we, Pablo. I can't break out of this place alone, papi. What do you say you help me, and we can both break out?"

Pablo's cheerful demeanor suddenly turned very serious. I could see the change in his mood, and it was almost instant.

"And get on the Boss' bad side? No way, esse! I don't want no trouble! I just want to do my time!"

"Doing your time, eh? Speaking of that, what are you here for anyway, and how long is your time in the prison supposed to be?"

"I got caught stealing some diamonds at the local jewelry store, esse."

Pablo's answer raised my eyebrows.

"Stealing diamonds, eh? Whatever for? You going to sell them somewhere?"

Pablo shook his head.

"No. That's not exactly what I wanted to do, esse. I wanted to steal them diamonds, but I didn't want to sell them."

"Really now? What were you going to do with them? Give them to someone special?"

When I mentioned someone special, Pablo's eyes lit up

again. His cheerful mood came back almost instantly, and he was like a car that had just gotten a refill at the local station.

"Something like that, esse. It was for Maria and me."

"Maria? So you've got a special someone outside of the jail?"

Pablo nodded.

"Yup. Me and Maria, we wanted to get out of the server. Those diamonds were our ticket out of here."

Okay. Now it was really getting interesting. I could imagine Pablo giving those diamonds to someone special. Pablo looked like a really romantic sort, even if I didn't really care about such things. I just wanted to get out. What really got my attention was what he said. How could you possibly get out of the server with just diamonds?

"I think you lost me there with the 'getting out of the server part,' papi. How were you and Maria going to get out of the server with diamonds?"

Pablo began to speak a lot faster now. It was Pablo's habit to speak like a jackrabbit when he got excited. He was so excited that he piled the words all over each other. It was more than a little difficult to understand what he was saying.

"You haven't heard, esse? This server's gotten an upgrade, esse! An upgrade! That's big news! An upgrade! Do you what that means? I was the first one who discovered the upgrade, and now it's all over the news! It was that upgrade that was our ticket out of here!"

"Whoa, whoa. Slow down there, Pablo. I heard you the first time you mentioned the upgrade. You're liable to choke on your own words. Why don't you take it easy and explain this upgrade to me?"

Pablo did just that, and slowed down. He took some deep breaths, and finally began to make some sense.

"All right, esse. I get it. This is how it goes. There's a 'trains' upgrade to the server. Simply put, they'll be adding a whole slew of cool vehicles to the server. They're a lot of cool stuff that inmates like you and me, or anybody for that matter, never really got to use in the first version. They've got cars, a helicopter, a cool motorcycle, a snowmobile, and other stuff. It's the works, esse! But the best part is this."

"Go on. I'm listening."

"They've got trains too, ese!"

"Oh-kay. Trains are pretty cool all by themselves, but I still don't see what that has to do with the diamonds that you stole."

Pablo put his hands together in an excited fist pump kind of thing. I clearly got him excited, and I already found Pablo to be quite a lovable character. At least hard time here wouldn't be so bad with Pablo around, right?

"Come on, esse! Put two and two together! The whole trains upgrade thing is just the start. It's just the tip of the iceberg, so to speak. The trains, the new vehicles, they're all cool, but they're not telling you something. They're not telling everybody something. It's something only yours truly, Pablo Santana, found out! All this, and I can speak Spanish too eh, esse? Estoy bien, genial!"

All this, and modesty, too. Yup, that was good old Pablo for you. A real character.

"So please, enlighten me, Pablo. What aren't they telling me?"

"The train has a supercar at the end, esse! It has a real badass engine and can run by itself! The supercar is experimental, and it's powered by diamonds, esse! Maria is good with all this mech stuff, esse. She and I found out, and we realized we could escape the server! That's why

I stole the diamonds in the first place. We were going to use it to power the supercar to break out of the server."

"Whoa, whoa, whoa! You're right, Pablo. This is big stuff. You're telling me this supercar can travel so fast it can break out of the server barrier? That's kind of like breaking through the barriers between servers. Science fiction stuff!"

"Time travel, faster than light, all that stuff. It's there in that supercar, esse. It can break out of the server. It's a big secret, and that's why they simply disguised the supercar as a simple piece of the train. The train runs around the prison, on its tracks. The entire facility was built around the prison, esse. It would have been perfect."

Now it was me who was chuckling.

"Sounds to me like you took this escaping thing a lot more seriously than you first led on, Pablo," I said.

"You got that right, esse. Me and Maria, we wanted to get out of this server and start a new life together. That was until I got really sloppy, and the police caught me red-handed with the diamonds."

Pablo turned sad again. His shoulders hunched, and it seemed like a giant weight was placed on his shoulders. He really started to feel bad again.

"It would have been perfect but I got caught. Now I'm in prison, and Boss and the other guards won't take their eyes off of me. It's hopeless, esse, and it's all my fault."

I placed a hand on Pablo's shoulder and smiled at him.

"There's always hope, Pablo. Cheer up. We will escape this place, and you'll get your new life with Maria. We'll both escape together."

I leaned on the sink, and as luck would have it, I immediately felt it budge. It moved, but ever so slightly. It was so slight that you could barely notice it, but it was there. There was a weak point in the sink. My heart immediately jumped for joy inside of me.

"Did you feel that, Pablo?" I said.

Pablo shrugged his shoulders.

"Feel what, esse? You must be getting delirious or something."

"Look!"

I motioned my hand towards the sink. I grabbed it firmly with both hands, and so did Pablo. It shook, just a little bit.

"Did you feel that, Pablo? The sink is loose!" I said with

excitement.

We both managed to make it budge, but it still wasn't enough to make any kind of a difference. The sink was still firmly attached to the wall, and it was impossible for me and Pablo to rip it off of its foundation. We simply weren't that strong.

"That's cool, esse. It really is, but I can't see where this is going. That sink is still wedged tightly to the wall. We're not dudes with superpowers. There's no way we're going to be able to yank it off."

"No, of course not. That still doesn't change the fact that it's loose, just a little bit. All we need to do is find something to pry it loose."

Pablo smiled at me.

"Something, or someone."

Chapter Four

Yard Time.

It was my first time at the yard, and I intended to make the most of it. All the prisoners were outside at the prison yard, and for a few moments we could soak in the sunshine and fresh air. It was quite refreshing to be out of our cells, but I wasn't here to take things easy or get lazy. No, I intended to make the most of yard time while I had it.

I looked outside the wire fence around us. The train tracks were right beside the prison, and the train rumbled right beside us. The sound of the train was loud and booming. It sounded like some kind of angry dragon that was stretching its wings outside. Well, I was determined to ride that angry dragon out of the prison and to my freedom. I deserved as much, and so did Pablo.

The other inmates all did their thing around me and Pablo. Some of them lifted weights to keep in shape. Others played basketball at a nearby rusty goal and basket. A few others took in the sights like me. I wondered if they were planning some daring jailbreak like myself. Well, it didn't matter. The only thing that mattered for me now was getting out of there.

"All right, esse. You asked me yesterday for a way to yank that sink clean off. I've got that something for you, esse. Something, or more accurately, someone."

"Who is that someone, Pablo?"

Pablo pointed to one of the inmates lifting a large barbell above him. He was lying on a makeshift bench and doing some bench presses with it. The man was built like a tank, and he lifted the heavy weights with ease.

"That's Paquito over there, esse. Paquito Bonito's spent a lot of time here in jail, esse. He was arrested by some cops when he was driving his van. The poor guy claims he's innocent, and I have to agree with him, esse. He says that he was just busy picking up his wife when they nabbed him. Poor Paquito was so big that five officers had to yank him out of his van."

"I can see what you mean about Paquito, Pablo. The guy

is a powerhouse. What did they nab him for?"

"They arrested him for hit-and-run, esse. Story goes that Paquito was so caught up in picking up his wife on time that he ran over an elderly lady on the road. The poor old lady spent a lot of time at the hospital."

"Whoa. That's tough."

Pablo shook his head.

"You know what's tougher? Getting Paquito to even agree to all of this. The one person he's more terrified of than his wife is the Boss, esse! I don't know how you're going to convince him to help us. And even if you manage to do that, how are we possibly going to get him into our cell to do the deed?"

"I'll figure that out later, Pablo. First things first. Let's talk to the big man."

We approached Paquito. He got bigger and bigger as we got nearer. I could see that the man wasn't built like a tank. He was built like 5 tanks. It was pretty obvious that Paquito wouldn't have a problem yanking that sink out of the wall. The only question now was would he be willing to do it?

"Absolutely not, Pablo!"

Well, we got our answer right there. The words came right out of Paquito's mouth the moment we approached him.

"Come on, Paquito! If you yank that sink out of the wall, it will be easier for us to crawl through there, out of this prison!" I said.

"You look like a nice enough dude for a new inmate, Noob. I'm sure you mean well and all, but I can't see how this is going to work," Paquito said. "If that thing is loose like you said, I won't have any trouble yanking it off. Why, I probably wouldn't have any trouble yanking it off even if it was screwed on tight. All that being said, how do you know that we can crawl out of the prison from there?"

It was a valid question from the gentle giant, and I immediately had an answer for it.

"Our cell is located directly beside the tracks. Me and Pablo can hear the trains roaring beside us. If you yank that sink from the wall, it will punch a hole through it. From that hole, we can make it to the train, and freedom."

Paquito shook his head and retreated from us. It was kinda funny watching a huge man like that retreating like a little mouse in fear. It was both funny and scary. It got scary when he explained why he was so frightened.

"So you guys want me to get inside your cell and yank that

sink off? No way. Nope. No! It's just out of the question."

"Take it easy, big guy. Why are you so scared of doing it, anyway?" I asked.

"The Boss. If he finds out about it, he's going to have my head! If he even knew what we were planning, we would really get it for sure!"

There it was again, or more accurately, there he was again. It was the Boss. Pablo was afraid of him, but Paquito was simply shaking in his boots at the mere mention of the Boss' name. I began to wonder what kind of a man Boss was to have such a hold on all these men? These were hardened criminals, men who should have not been afraid of anything. They were not afraid of anything, except the Boss. What kind of a man could command such fear and respect? I didn't know the answer to that question. All I knew was that this Boss was really something of a terror in the jail.

"Look, Paquito. Come on now! This maximum security prison isn't what it really is, you know. It's got a real weak point, and me and Pablo here are literally sitting on it! We just need your strength to knock that sink out of the wall and we're free! Don't you want to be free? Come on!"

I saw a look of hope come over Paquito's eyes. There

was real hope and a fire that wasn't there before. I really saw something and it was just a matter of fanning those flames so it could get Paquito to move. Unfortunately that moment lasted much too short. The flames were there and gone again. The moment simply came and went, just like that.

"I do. I really do. I'm just too afraid of the Boss to try and escape like that."

"Come on now, big guy! If you don't overcome that fear, you'll stay in prison here. We all will! You've got to…"

"All right! Yard time's over! Everybody back to their cells!"

The loud and booming voice of the Boss came over a loudspeaker. He was announcing the end of yard time. The other guards were already moving to get us all back into our cells.

"All right, Pablo. Paquito. Noob. You guys heard the Boss. Your friendly chit-chat time is up. Let's break it up and get going."

The guard moved us all back to our cells, and there was really nothing we could do. We just went back like quiet sheep. You couldn't really blame us, and you couldn't really blame Paquito, I guess. I was asking him to take something of a leap of faith. That wasn't easy for anyone.

The guard led me and Pablo back to our cell. He silently slid our door closed. The bars were between us and the cell block again.

"Well, it was a nice try, Noob. I'll give you that. You tried to talk the big man into going with our plan, but he just backed out. Nothing you can do about that, and there's no shame in it. You did your best."

I shook my head. Yeah, I was frustrated over the results of our talk with Paquito. I wasn't completely out of hope, though.

"It's never over until it really is over, Pablo. Something tells me that Paquito will come around sooner or later. When that happens, we'll have our chance to get out of here."

As it turned out, that chance came a lot sooner than I expected.

Chapter Five

The Choice.

"What do you mean I have to build a new wall in 3 days?"

We all overheard Paquito arguing with the Boss. His voice was loud enough so that everyone in the yard heard what they were all talking about. Paquito did not even bother to hide the frustration in his voice. This was just my 8th time at the yard. I had spent around a week in prison.

"Come on, Paquito. You know you're the strongest one here in the prison. No one can match your strength. That's why I need you for the job. You're the only one who can do the job right," the Boss said.

"I know what you need me for, Boss, but what you're asking me to do is just plain unfair. You're asking me to do the job of ten men in half the time! Even my strength has its limits!"

Paquito was protesting really hard, but the Boss would not be swayed. There was a reason why he was the jail's warden and known as the Boss.

"You know, Paquito, I've been asking you nicely all this time. However, you're a pretty stubborn fellow, and my patience has its limits."

"What do you mean, Boss?"

The Boss looked Paquito in the eye. There was no hint of fear in his entire body. Most men would be terrified of such a giant man like Paquito, but not the Boss. He simply stared him down, and did not budge from where he was standing.

"I tried to be nice and polite to you, Paquito. I just didn't want to hurt your feelings or anything, but that doesn't mean that I'll go soft on you. If asking you nicely won't do the trick, I'll simply have to force you to do it."

"What? I don't understand..."

"Understand this! If you don't do the work and complete that new wall in three days, I'll make sure you spend the rest of your sentence in solitary confinement!"

Paquito trembled at the sound of solitary confinement. It

was every prisoner's worst nightmare. No one wanted to go into solitary confinement, and for good reason.

"All right already! I'll do it!"

The warden smiled when he heard Paquito agree to build the large wall. He smiled and looked very pleased with himself. I also smiled at Pablo.

"There you go. I knew you were a reasonable dude, Paquito. You can start working immediately."

"All right, Boss."

The Boss left Paquito feeling very miserable, while he felt like a winner in every sense. Well, the Boss was definitely a bully in the yard. Paquito was anything but enthusiastic when he answered the Boss. It was clear that he was anything but happy to work on that wall. That was a good thing for us, and the chance that we had been waiting for.

"You heard that, Pablo?" I asked.

"How could I not? They didn't even bother to keep their conversation to themselves, esse."

"Well, remember how you were asking me how we could possibly convince Paquito to help us? I think we've just found our way."

I sounded really pleased and very hopeful, but Pablo did not share my good vibes. He still had his doubts about everything.

"I still don't see how we can use any of that to our advantage, esse. Paquito still doesn't look like he wants to be helpful."

"You leave the convincing to me. Just tell me now. How much time do we have before yard time ends?"

"I think we still have some time."

That was the answer that I was waiting to hear.

"Great. Come with me, but let me do the talking."

Pablo shrugged his shoulders.

"All right, esse. It's your call. You're the man with the plan."

I approached Paquito with full confidence. The Boss was long gone, and he was also very confident that he had a good worker with Paquito.

"Hey, Paquito. I overheard you and the Boss talking about that wall you're going to make."

"Hey, Noob. Pablo. I guess everybody in the yard heard us talking. I can't believe what he's asking me to do, but

I've got no choice. If I don't do it, I'll be stuck in solitary! You know what that's like? It's terrible!"

"I gotta admit, big guy, I don't. That's because I've just been here at the prison for less than a month. I don't know what it's like, and frankly, I don't want to know."

"It's terrible, man! You're just sitting there all alone and..."

"Get it together, Paquito! I didn't come here to compare notes about solitary. I came here to remind you about my offer again."

"The breakout thing? Again? Come on, Noob! I already told you that I'm not interested."

"Listen here, Paquito. The Boss is a bully, plain and simple. I know how bullies are, and take it from me, he's not going to change. You finish this wall for him, and you avoid solitary, that's great. It really is. However, it's not going to end there. The Boss has seen that you're a strong guy, and he's going to keep taking advantage of that strength, over and over again. That's simply how bullies are. This wall won't be the end of it. There will be a lot of other stuff in the future, and you won't be able to say no. You can keep taking all that from the Boss, or you can choose to end it by breaking out with us."

For a moment, no one said anything. The three of us just

looked at each other, and I could see that the big guy was really thinking about what I said.

"It's your choice, esse," Pablo said.

Finally, Paquito spoke up.

"That's a great offer, guys, but I still can't do it. I'm sorry."

Chapter Six

The Plan.

I didn't hear the end of it from Pablo after that. It got so bad that he just kept ranting about my epic fail, night after night. Worse than that, I even heard it during the day.

"Well, that was a nice speech and all, esse! It really moved the big guy, and gave us the results we wanted, eh? What did I tell you, ese? I told you that big ox was an idiot! I told you we're trapped here in this prison. We might as well accept it. It will be a lot easier for all of us, that way."

Pablo spoke his mind, and there was really nothing that I could say. He was right. I seemed to have expected too much out of Paquito. Pablo ranted like that, over and over again, night after night. Yeah, I really lost a lot of sleep because of Pablo's disappointment.

"Ok, ok! I get it, papi! I really do! You've been ranting about this for 3 days and nights, Pablo. Give it a rest already."

I was literally covering my face with my arms now. It had been the third day since the Boss spoke with Paquito. The wall was almost done now, and we were outside at the yard. Pablo would not let me hear the end of it.

"Yeah, you heard me right, esse! Sure sucks, doesn't it, esse? I told you to stop filling our heads with hope and all that stuff! We're just going to stay here and rot! It's awful, esse!"

Pablo was starting to sound as if he was more angry at himself than he was at me.

"Are you done, Pablo? It's been three days already, and you've done nothing but rant over and over again about Paquito and the yard!"

"I'm sorry, esse. I really am. I guess I just thought the big ox was better than that. I thought that he would actually, well, help us, you know?"

Yeah, so he was angrier at himself than he was at me. More accurately, I guess he was angrier at Paquito for not helping us.

"Look, I feel you, bro. I really do. I gave him a great offer and he refused. There's really nothing we can do about it. We just have to move on and..."

A huge and imposing figure approached us. We immediately recognized him as Paquito.

"Hi guys," the big man said.

The big man looked very down. Well, I guess that was usually the case with Paquito, so there was no surprise there. The big surprise, however, was Pablo suddenly blowing up at him. I thought he had gotten tired of ranting for 3 straight days and nights. Apparently not.

"Hi yourself, esse! How's that wall of yours coming, esse? We gave you a chance to help us escape! A genuine chance to escape, and you blew us off! I hope you're happy with yourself!"

"That's just it, Pablo. I just wanted to say that..."

"Say what? That we suck and you rock because you made that wall? I really hope you're happy with yourself, Paquito! I mean, for a guy as big and strong as you are, you really lack brains! You should have helped us!"

"Pablo..."

I tried to calm him down, but there was no getting to

Pablo. Yeah, that was Pablo for you. The guy was lovable and all, but he had a temper too, and he didn't like being pushed around or rejected like that.

"No! This guy's got a lot of nerve coming back to us, Noob! After what he did…"

"Pablo, let's let the man speak, shall we?"

Somehow, I got him to shut up for a few moments, and Paquito finally did speak. He spoke plainly, and straight to the point.

"Guys, I'm in."

When I heard Paquito, I was surprised, and I felt awesome! Finally, the big man came to his senses! Super cool!

"Whoa. Did I get my hearing straight? Did I just hear what I heard? Did you just say that…"

Pablo's jaw dropped, and he was at a loss for words. I guess I couldn't blame him.

"Yeah. You heard me right. I'm in. I'll help you guys break out."

"I gotta ask, man. Why the change of heart all of a sudden?" I asked.

Paquito answered with a frown on his face. Something

obviously went wrong here.

"I'm about to finish the wall and all, but the Boss is still getting on my case. He says once I'm done here, I'm supposed to construct a new wing for the prison in 3 days more. A new wing! Can you believe that? He's turning me into his one man construction crew! And at no extra cost! That ain't fair at all!"

"What did we tell you, esse? Boss will just take advantage of you."

"That doesn't matter anymore, Pablo. What matters now is that he's on our side. Time to break out of here."

"Great! Great! We're getting outta here!"

Pablo was so happy that Paquito finally accepted and he could hardly contain his excitement. The big man knew exactly what I was thinking, and he silently agreed. He placed one of his giant hands on Pablo's mouth. Pablo was always a very emotional and passionate person. Many times he was just too much.

"Go ahead and shout little louder, esse! I guess you want everyone else to know what you're planning! With a little luck, you'll reveal the entire thing to the Boss and we'll be done before we even start!" I said.

"Noob's right! We were just lucky that no one heard you shouting like that because there's a pickup game of b-ball that everyone's betting on!" Paquito said.

The big guy was a lot smarter than he looked.

Pablo silently nodded. When we could see that he would keep his mouth shut, Paquito finally let go.

"Sorry guys. Don't know what came over me. I can get a little carried away, eh?"

"Well, keep it together, esse! I can't do anything if everyone finds out about this plan before it even happens!"

"Uh, Noob? Speaking of keeping it together, I was just wondering right now."

It was Paquito. He had something on his mind.

"Yeah?"

"Just how are we going to break out? Like I said earlier, I can't just waltz in your cell and yank that sink loose."

I smiled at them both.

"I've already got that covered. You see, I've got a plan."

Chapter Seven

The Big Swing.

A plan is the most important thing to have anytime, and anywhere. If there's anything that I've learned, it's that you've always got to have a plan. A plan is the most important thing to have, if you have any kind of problem. See, the plan's like a map. Your solution to the problem is the destination you want to go. The problem itself is the whole wide, unfamiliar land. It's full of obstacles and strange stuff. A plan gives you direction and a clear means to get to your destination. Without the plan? You might as well be a lost babe in the woods.

Like I said earlier to Paquito in the yard, I had a plan, and it was time to execute it.

The Boss' loud voice came through the speakers.

"All right, losers! Time for roll call!"

Roll call was when all of the prisoners left their cells and stayed inside the cell block. A head count was made to make sure all the prisoners were still around the prison. Kind of like attendance in school. Well, attendance was the perfect time to make a break for it.

The guards all slid us out of our cells and we all stood at the center of the prison area. There we were, several of us all standing there as a few guards, and the Boss himself, counted us off.

Pablo stood beside me nervously. He could barely stand still and stay calm through it all.

"The guards are counting off, esse. You think he'll do it, esse?"

"Calm down, Pablo. Have a little faith in Paquito. I'm sure he'll come through," I said.

The Boss called out everyone's name, and you had to answer with a loud and resounding 'Present!' That was how roll call went, and so far, Paquito had not made his move yet.

"A2K!"

"Present!"

"Big Stimpza!"

"Present!"

"Da Shiek Ha!"

"Present!"

As you can see, roll call could take more than a while to get done. There were so many of us, and we would all be called out one-by-one. Well, Paquito would simply not wait that long.

Before any other names were rattled off, the big guy made his move, just as we planned. I saw it all go down.

Paquito socked the nearest prisoner beside him. The impact of his fist knocked the poor guy out. Once he was out, Paquito did something only someone with his strength could do. He picked up the poor guy by his ankles and began to swing him around like a baseball bat. I think they call that move a 'big swing' in pro wrestling, but I'm getting ahead of myself here.

As you can imagine, Paquito's wrestling move knocked down several prisoners, and immediately caused mayhem. Chaos and craziness erupted everywhere, and all the prisoners were immediately riled up. Several of them started to try and beat up Paquito.

He was more than capable of fending them off. With one swing of his fist, he knocked down three of them. A few other prisoners came to his defense and utter chaos erupted.

"What is that moron Paquito trying to do? Order! Let's get some order around here!" the Boss said.

The guards all jumped into the chaos, but they were only a few men. They were soon overwhelmed by the sheer number of the prisoners. Everyone was knocking, punching, or kicking someone else, and order was simply impossible, at least for the moment.

I socked one prisoner in front of me.

"Come on, Pablo! That's our cue! It's time to head back to our cell!" I said.

"What about Paquito? We won't be able to yank out the sink ourselves!"

"You called?"

It was Paquito, and he was standing in front of us, smiling. He had bulldozed through several guards and prisoners, and was now standing in front of us.

"Come on! This madness won't last forever!"

We made a break for the now empty cell blocks. We reached our cell, and like the others, it was open. The cell doors had all slid open for roll call, and we easily got in. I pointed at the sink.

"There's the sink, Paquito! You think you can..."

"Done."

Paquito didn't even let me finish my sentence. Before I could finish, he simply yanked the sink from the wall. He yanked it as easily as someone would slide a drawer open from a desk. It came off with a large chunk of the wall. His strength was amazing.

When he was done, there was a large hole the size of Paquito. It was a hole that would fit all of us, considering me and Pablo were much smaller than Paquito.

"Well. He's efficient, isn't he?" Pablo said.

Paquito grinned at us. He was very proud of the damage he had caused.

"Like taking candy from a baby!" he said.

"All right, you two. No time to pat everyone on the back. We can do that when we're outside," I said.

The gust of wind outside and the sounds of the city

blasted us from through the hole. The train tracks were literally right beside our cell! Everything was working, just as I had planned.

It was then that we realized just how close we were to escaping the prison. For a moment, we were all struck by what was happening. We couldn't help but savor the moment. We were so close to freedom now!

"Do you hear that? Do you feel that? It's everything outside! We're free!" Pablo said.

We all felt really good, but I wasn't kidding when I said that there wasn't much time to pat everyone on the back.

"Hey! What are you three up to?"

We looked down from our cell and saw Boss. He had seen what we had done, and was already moving up the steps towards us. The commotion was already dying down, and several guards were already taking the place of the ones who had been struck down in all the chaos. I had to hand it to him. The Boss really had this prison under his strict control.

"It's the Boss! He's on to us! We've got to get moving!" I said.

"No kidding!"

The roar of the train from the outside sounded, and we all heard it. The cell shook all around us as the train approached.

"It's coming! I hope Maria will do her part of the plan!" I said.

Pablo smiled at me.

"Have a little faith in my mami, esse! She will come through on this!"

Pablo smiled from ear-to-ear. With a smile like that, how could I not doubt him? Right as he smiled, the rumbling and shaking got louder and louder.

"You hear that? It's the train! It's coming right on schedule! I told you my Mami would come through for us! She always does!"

I was very happy to see that Pablo had so much faith in Maria. With the train rumbling closer towards us, it was hard not to have faith in her.

"It's coming!" Pablo said.

"That's great and all, but it's got to slow down for us to jump inside!" I said.

"Have a little faith, esse!"

The rumbling and the shaking began to get weaker. I felt the floor under us go stable again. It could only mean one thing; the train was slowing down!

"The train's slowing down! How is that even possible?" Paquito said.

"Noob and I planned this all out! When you agreed to break open the wall through the sink, we already told Maria to board the train and slow it down!"

"She did that?" Paquito said.

Pablo shrugged his shoulders.

"Hey, that's my mami for you, esse!"

The train rumbled on, and it finally began to approach our cell. Within a few moments, the train came into sight. It was huge and painted bright orange. The giant train was an amazing sight to see, especially for prisoners like us.

"It's right there in front of us!" Paquito said.

The train was now moving at a snail's pace. It would be a lot easier for us to jump onto the train from where we were because of its decreased speed. Only a few things needed to be fixed now.

"Come on, come on!" I said.

"Hold it right there, you crazy cons!"

"Oh no! Not now!"

It was the Boss. He had managed to enter the cell along with several guards behind him. Yeah, his timing could not have been worse.

"No! Not now! Not when we're so close!" I said.

"Not a problem!"

Paquito moved towards them and punched the Boss flush in the face. The Boss went flying back, knocking his men over. They were down on the ground but they would not stay down for long.

The car that we had been waiting for was now almost in front of us. It was the supercar that Pablo had told us about. It was right in front of the cell and its door was open. There was a nice lady waving from the car.

"Mami!"

"Pablo! You and your friends must jump in now!" she said.

"Go! Go!"

Pablo went first. He took a huge leap of faith and managed to land in the car. I looked back and saw Paquito was still busy fighting off the guards.

"Paquito! Come on!" I said.

"Go already! I'll hold them off!"

I didn't like it, but I had no choice. I jumped and landed on the supercar's floor. It was definitely a rough landing, but I was inside.

The train was already gaining speed. I got up and saw Paquito take the final leap. Just as I stood up, he leaped right at me. He landed on top of me. The impact was incredible. It was like getting hit by the train. My breath was knocked out of me.

"Noob!"

"Noob, man, I'm sorry! Are you all right?"

I looked up and saw Paquito sitting on top of me.

"I will be once you get off me!"

"Oops, sorry!"

He got off me, and my breath rushed back just in time. I thought I would get choked, but I managed.

"Guys, this is Maria. Maria, this is Paquito and Noob, my friends from the prison."

Maria smiled at me and Paquito. I was happy to meet her,

and even happier that she and Pablo were back together. Well, it was all's well that ends well, right? Not really.

"Guys, we've got trouble! Look!"

Paquito pointed out the supercar's window. There was a large helicopter flying above us. I could make out Boss sitting inside beside the pilot.

"Stop this train now! There are escaped felons inside!" he said over the helicopter's loudspeaker.

Yeah, there was more trouble.

Chapter Eight

The Big Explosion.

"All right, Pablo. We've gotten this far because of your knowledge about this secret supercar. Now we'll really see if it's all that it was hyped up to be!" I said.

Pablo nodded.

"Don't worry Noob! I studied all about this car and what it can do. Look!"

Pablo pressed a button on the car's wall. The car shook violently, and we were all knocked to the ground. There was a powerful heave, and it felt like the supercar was breaking away from the train. With one powerful heave, it did just that.

I looked out the window and my eyes almost popped out. There were clouds and the blue sky all around us.

"Whoa! It's flying!" I said.

"How is this even possible?" Paquito said.

"I told you guys! This supercar's an experimental prototype that can do all sorts of cool things! Once it gains momentum, it can blast us out of the very server!"

It probably would have done just that, but it was not meant to be. We felt powerful gunfire hammer the supercar's walls. We all knew what it was. It was the police helicopter, and it was opening fire on the supercar.

"They're shooting at us!" I said.

The supercar took heavy damage from all that gunfire. There was no way that it was going to stay in the air with such an assault. The supercar shook violently, and we felt the air rushing all around us.

"We're going to crash! Everyone hold tight!"

Paquito held onto one of the car's railings, Pablo embraced Maria, and I just tried to stay standing. This would be a violent landing, one way or another.

The supercar crashed to the ground with terrible intensity. We felt the ground hit the car, and we were all thrown and knocked about the supercar. It was simply not possible to stay standing as it hit the ground.

The supercar skidded and rocked the ground, crashing out of control. We were bounced around inside, and I thought that the supercar would never stop. Somehow, it did.

We were all on the floor as the supercar finally stopped skidding. The windows were all smashed, and there were several dents in the walls around us. There was also smoke coming from somewhere. The supercar was a total wreck.

"Everybody all right?" I asked.

I looked around. Paquito, Maria, and Pablo were all still in one piece. They were pretty banged up, that was for sure, but at least everyone was okay.

"That was the roughest landing ever! Even I can't take a pounding like that again," Paquito said.

"The supercar's trashed! We have to get out!" Pablo said.

We all left the car, and stepped out into thick woods. There was a trail of fallen trees and burnt ground where the supercar crashed. It was still smoking behind us.

"Go! Go!"

After we had run a considerable distance, there was a powerful explosion. The supercar blew up in a ball of fire.

Thankfully, none of us were inside.

"Whoa! That was one heck of an explosion! The boss is sure to see that!" Paquito said.

I smiled at the three of them.

"That is all to our advantage," I said.

Pablo looked at me with wide eyes that did not understand anything that I had just said.

"Did I just hear you right, esse? How can any of this be for our good? The supercar's completely destroyed and we can't escape to another server!" he said.

Good point. I was still smiling.

"I know all that. But it's still okay. That's because the explosion has guaranteed our freedom. The Boss should believe now that we all kicked the bucket with that blast, and for good reason. No one could have survived a blast like that, right?"

We all looked up and saw the police helicopter. It was already flying away from the scene of the explosion. I smiled at everyone.

"We may not have escaped this server, but we definitely broke out of the prison, and we're free!" I said.

"We, we did it. Didn't we?"

Pablo and the others couldn't believe it, but I was right. Our freedom was right there in front of us.

"Give me some skin, guys!"

High-fives were exchanged all around. Everyone was happy and in good spirits. We had escaped the prison and the Boss thought that we were all done for. Everything ended up pretty good, don't you think?

It was a long walk out of the woods to the next town, but none of us really minded any of that. After all, we were free. A whole new life and maybe a new set of adventures awaited us all. Anything was possible now that we were out of jail.

UNOFFICIAL

TREASURE HUNT

ROBLOXIA KID

Chapter One

The Key to the Treasure.

Noob took a moment to look around him. He stood over the shore, and there was miles and miles of white sand as far as his eyes could see. Further from him were thick patches of woods that were filled with trees and greens of all kinds. Where the white sands ended, the blue sea stretched out as far as he could see. It was an amazing sight, and Noob took it all in.

"This place is amazing! This server looks really great! The scenery, the stuff all around, it's kinda a bit much to take in!"

"Treasure Hunt Simulator can have that effect to any newbies who first enter it. Most of them are just overwhelmed by the sheer scope and beauty of everything around them."

Noob turned around. The voice was just as unfamiliar as his new surroundings. A man approached him. He looked friendly enough with his smile, but Noob didn't really know what to make of the parrot that was perched on his shoulder. The bird cackled and then spoke.

"Awkk! Most of them are just overwhelmed by the sheer scope and beauty of everything around them."

The man patted the parrot on the head.

"Shut your trap, Borris. Show some manners to our new friend here."

"Awkk! Show some manners to our new friend here."

The man shook his head.

"Sorry about Borris. He does have that annoying habit of repeating a lot of things I say. I don't know how I've put up with him this long."

"Awkk! I don't know how I've put up with him this long."

"Shut up already!"

"Awkk! Shut up already!"

Noob watched as the man seemed to be slowly losing his patience with Borris.

"Borris, if you don't shut up, I swear I'll bring you back to the item shop, and I won't even ask for a refund of my Robux!"

"Awkk! All right! All right! You win, Cap'n Blunder! I won't keep repeating stuff!"

Cap'n Blunder shrugged his shoulders at Borris' remark. His strange and rather embarrassing name was not lost to Noob.

"Whew! The only way to shut Borris up is to threaten him like that. Believe me, I don't like threatening him, but I've really got no choice. If I don't, he could go on, and on, and on."

"Yeah, I guess that would be kinda annoying if it were left unchecked," Noob said.

"You don't know the half of it! As you've heard, I'm Cap'n Blunder, and this is my faithful custom pet, Borris!"

Cap'n Blunders stretched out a hand to Noob, and they shook hands.

"Nice to meet you, Cap'n. I'm Noob, and I'm new to this here server."

"Yeah. You're in the Roblox Treasure Hunt Simulator. The best server in all of Roblox. I mean, this is the only server where you can get rich overnight. All you got to do is find some treasure, which is pretty common in this giant server."

Noob hesitated before he spoke again. He wanted to ask Cap'n Blunder about his name, but he hesitated. It was really understandable, as Noob didn't want to offend the good captain, right when they first met.

"Uhm…"

"What? You noticed my name, did you? Yeah, I know it's kinda funny. Don't worry. I don't mind you asking about it."

"Wow. How did you know what I was thinking?" Noob asked with surprise.

"I'm a lot more perceptive than most players would give me credit for. In Roblox Treasure Hunt Simulator, you have to really be good at noticing little details or things most dudes wouldn't even give a second look at. It's the only way to somehow get treasure around here."

"Treasure? I like the sound of that!"

"Don't we all? The thing is, not everybody gets the treasure around here. Getting treasure isn't as easy as it sounds."

"Awkk! He should know! Awkk! He's never found any treasure in this place at all!"

"I said shut up, Borris!"

"Hey, I'm not repeating your words anymore, am I? Awkk!"

Noob tried really hard not to LOL on the spot. Borris was clearly a pain in the rear for poor Cap'n Blunder, and he now knew how he probably got his sad name.

"I don't know why I put up with this stupid bird, I tell you! Sending you back to the item store is too good for you! I ought to roast you on the spot for my next meal!"

"Awkk! You wouldn't want to do that. Awkk! I'm too thin. I'm not fat, juicy, or tender. Awkk!"

Noob couldn't help but feel a little sorry for Cap'n Blunder now. Even his pet didn't show him any respect.

"So you haven't gotten any treasure here?" Noob asked with a lot of caution.

"Yeah, it's true. I hate to admit it, but Borris is right. I'm the laughingstock of the entire server. The clown of the entire place, so to speak."

Noob was really starting to feel for poor Cap'n Blunder.

There had to be some way to make him feel better. Noob just wasn't sure what it was.

"Don't worry. I'm sure that you'll find some treasure eventually."

"Oh, I'm sure that I'll get that treasure a lot sooner than you think!"

Cap'n Blunder looked up at Noob and smiled. It was almost as if his mood had changed completely, like a switch was turned on, and he shifted from being depressed to suddenly enthusiastic. The instant change in mood was kinda creepy for poor Noob.

"Oh-kay. That's the spirit! I know that you'll get that treasure, Captain!"

"You don't understand, Noob. I know that I'm going to get that treasure. It's for sure."

"Why do you say that, Captain?"

"You're the key, Noob. You're the key to getting that treasure and making us all very rich."

Chapter Two

Have a Little Faith.

Noob looked at the good captain with more than a little surprise.

"Whoa, whoa. Me? I'm the key to getting some kind of big treasure? I don't understand. How can I be the key to getting any kind of treasure? I mean, I've just arrived here."

"It's simple, Noob. You are the chosen one."

"The chosen one? I'm sorry, Captain, but I don't understand."

"Awkk! There's a legend. A legend! Tell him about the legend, Cap'n! Tell him! Awkk!"

"I would if you would just shut up, Borris."

Borris raised his wings above his head. For a moment, Noob thought that the poor bird had gotten tired of the captain's insults and was going to fly away.

"Legend?"

"Yeah, Noob. There's a great legend here in the server that talks about a new player who will enter it and discover great treasure on his first try. There haven't been any new players here in a while. Not until you came around. I saw you enter the server. This is the starting point of the entire server. I waited patiently and presto! You appeared. I knew that you had to be the legend come true."

It sounded like something from a fairy tale. Noob didn't want to crush the poor captain's feelings, but it seemed almost too good to be true. Still, he had to tell him how he felt.

"Look, Cap'n Blunder. I don't mean to burst your bubble or anything here, but I think that maybe you're putting a little bit too much faith in this legend of yours. I mean, I'm just new here and I don't know the first thing about treasure hunting."

"Don't you see, Noob? You're new to the server. You don't need to know anything about treasure hunting.

You are the legend come true!"

Noob was beginning to doubt if Cap'n Blunder was all there. This whole business about him being a legend and finding lost treasure was a little too much for Noob.

"What do you mean, I'm the legend come true?"

"You still don't get it, do you?"

Cap'n Blunder spoke with a little frustration now. He was getting a little annoyed at Noob's attitude.

"Maybe you don't get it, so I'll be blunt with you. I want you to work with me, Noob. Join me, and we'll find the great treasure that the legends promised you would find. We'll both be rich!"

"I'm sorry, Cap'n, but this is all a little strange for me. I don't mean to shoot your idea down or anything, but I really don't see myself as being a legend that will find some big treasure here. I'm new here. I think it would be best if I just tried to find some treasure on my own."

Noob braced himself. He was worried that Cap'n Blunder would take his words the wrong way, but he had to just be honest about the whole thing now. Noob was quite surprised to find that Cap'n Blunder actually took it all pretty well.

He smiled at Noob before speaking again.

"Okay, Noob. I get it. I really do. You don't believe the legend, eh? You want to try and get treasure for yourself, go ahead."

Noob was more than a little relieved to hear Cap'n Blunder letting him go. He was getting more than a little creepy and he was afraid that Cap'n Blunder would push the 'Legend Thing' on him. Most people like him did that, and Noob was afraid that Cap'n Blunder was no different. To his surprise, the good captain did not force him to join him, and let him on his way.

"Yeah. Yeah, I guess I will be on my way," Noob said.

"Be my guest, Noob."

"Yeah. I'll start treasure hunting now. I can do it, and I can find the treasure. No offense to you or the other treasure hunters on this server, of course."

"None taken, Noob. Like I said, be my guest. Then again, do you know where to start treasure hunting?"

It was a simple question that Cap'n Blunder asked Noob directly. It should have been just as simple to answer it, but Noob suddenly felt quite awkward.

"Uhm, yeah. Yeah, I know!"

"All right. Tell me how to start treasure hunting, then," Cap'n Blunder said.

"I guess I need a boat! Yeah, I need a boat!"

"Where are you going to get your boat, Noob? You can't just go swimming in the ocean there. Do you even know how to swim?"

"I do!"

Noob could see that Cap'n Blunder was taunting him. He was taunting him, and it was really getting to Noob simply because he was right.

"Swimming won't really help you, considering how big the ocean is. So where's your boat? Where do you get a boat? Do you even know where to start looking?"

"Ok! Ok! Ok, I get it! Stop it already, Cap! Can I call you Cap?"

Cap'n Blunder smiled at Noob. This was all going great for him now.

"Of course you can, Noob! Now do you see why it would be better that you join me?"

"I don't think I really have a choice here, Cap. I don't know the first thing about treasure hunting."

"Exactly, Noob. But that's the beauty of it all. You don't need to know! The legend said specifically that a new player will find the biggest treasure of all, and he would be with another captain. I can't believe it, but I'm the captain! You're with me now, and we're going to get that treasure!"

"I still don't know how this is going to work, considering that I have no idea how to start treasure hunting," Noob said.

"Just have faith, Noob. We're going to find that treasure somehow. The important thing is, you're with me now, and that legend will come true!"

"No offense, Cap, but aren't you showing a lot of faith in a new guy like me?"

"It's the legend, Noob. I have faith in you and the legend. It will come true, even if neither of us knows exactly how that will happen."

Noob was very doubtful of everything that Cap'n Blunder had said, but he decided to keep that to himself. There was really no point in popping his bubble like that. If he wanted to believe in the fairy tale, he would simply let him have it. After all, Noob had no idea where or how to start looking for treasure, so it would be a good idea to hang with Cap'n Blunder, no matter how bad his reputation was.

"All right. I believe you, Cap. I'll just tag along with you in your treasure hunting. I'm sure there would be nothing wrong in that, and you're right. I don't know where to start, so this should be good for both of us."

"Wonderful! Come on, Noob! This is going to be the start of a wonderful adventure!"

Borris shook his head and covered his eyes with a wing.

"Awkk! You just made a big mistake hanging with Cap'n Blunder here! Awkk! You're going to regret this, kid."

"Don't listen to this dumb parrot. Come on, Noob. I'll show you to our boat where we can set sail for the treasure."

Noob followed Cap'n Blunder with Borris. He still had his doubts about all of this, but he realized that he really had no choice but to trust the good captain. He was the only chance that Noob had of even getting any kind of treasure. It was time for their adventure to truly begin.

Chapter Three

Fortune and Adventure Await.

"Well here she is, Noob. What do ya think?" Cap'n Blunder said.

Cap'n Blunder showed Noob his ship and he was beaming with pride. Noob stared at the large ship in front of him, and he was actually a bit surprised. With his name and his reputation, Noob expected the good captain to have a substandard ship. The large sailboat in front of him looked anything but. It was quite gorgeous and resembled ships that Noob had seen in pirate movies. It actually looked quite intimidating and artistic.

"It looks, it looks amazing. I confess I didn't expect your ship to look this grand, Cap," Noob said.

"She's my pride and joy, Noob. I worked really hard

scrounging the Robux to acquire her. Ain't she a beauty?"

Noob looked at the ship's side. Painted in intricate script letters was the name 'the Lady Grace.'

"The Lady Grace? That's a fine name for a fine ship," Noob said.

"Awkk! More like the Leaky Tub! Awkk! Don't let appearances fool you kid! Awkk!"

Noob was startled by Borris' words.

"Whoa. What do you mean?"

Cap'n Blunder smiled nervously at Noob.

"Nothing! He meant nothing! The dumb bird has a habit of, well, making me look bad. Even if he doesn't have to!"

The good captain glared at his pet. Borris shook his head.

"Awkk! I'm not lying! Awkk! That ship is barely seaworthy! The cap'n got it at a crazy expensive price, and it can barely sail without springing a leak! Awkk!"

"I am so sick and tired of you making me look bad, Borris! I would have gotten a better ship if I hadn't bought you for an expensive price, so shut up!"

"Awkk! My mouth is shut! I mean my beak. Awkk!"

"Uhm, is Borris telling the truth, Cap? I don't mean to hurt your feelings or anything, but I can't ride in that thing if it's really leaking."

"It's going to be fine, Noob. Borris is just trying to scare you."

Noob nodded and the three of them entered the ship. He tried hard not to think about what Borris had just said.

"It's going to be fine. Let's go! Adventure and treasure await us all!" Cap'n Blunder said.

Noob smiled and nodded. The wind was blowing in his face. It did feel amazing on the ship, and it seemed as if the captain was right. Excitement and adventure was right around the corner, and Noob could hardly wait.

Cap'n Blunder looked anything but blundering as he approached the ship's large steering wheel. If anything, he looked like a man who was ready for anything. He even looked inspirational, and Noob's confidence shot up as he watched Cap'n Blunder take the wheel. Borris still looked as if he had his doubts, but Noob ignored the parrot.

"Anchors away! Release the anchors, Noob!"

"Uh, I don't know where the anchor is, or how to release

it. This is my first time on a ship."

Cap'n Blunder looked annoyed and embarrassed.

"Oh yeah. I forgot about that. Um, I'll do it myself."

Noob nodded. The captain went to the edge of the ship and pressed something. He heard a loud noise, as if something heavy were sliding away, and the ship shook. Noob thought that it would actually turn over, or that there was some kind of earthquake.

"Don't worry. That's just the anchor being released. Hold tight. It's time we set sail for the island of treasures, where our fortunes await!"

"Awkk! The island of treasures! Awkk! Good luck to us all! Awkk!

Borris sounded more worried than excited, but Noob still managed to smile. Cap'n Blunder appeared fully confident as he approached the steering wheel.

The captain moved back to the steering wheel, and the ship finally moved away from the shore. They had started to move away from the island. Whatever happened now, their adventure had truly begun.

Chapter Four

Taking the Wheel.

Cap'n Blunder cut a very inspiring figure as he gripped the ship's steering wheel. He was the picture of total confidence and Noob could not help but feel admiration for the captain. Perhaps he was not the blundering, clumsy man that even the captain himself said he was. Unfortunately, this picture would soon change.

"All right, Noob, set a course for the isle of treasures!"

Noob couldn't believe what he was hearing. How could the captain ask him to set a course on the ship?

"What? Cap, have you forgotten I'm totally new and clueless about this treasure hunting business?! I don't know a thing about this ship or how to get treasure! I'm just here to make the legends come true!"

"Awkk! The kid's right, awkk! He's just our lucky charm! Awkk!"

"Oops! Sorry about that! Guess I got a little too carried away. Borris, you set a course for the isle of treasures!"

Borris slapped his head with a single wing.

"Awkk! I can't do it! Awkk! I don't have hands to operate the controls! Awkk!"

The captain slapped his own forehead with his hand. He was clearly frustrated.

"Do I have to do everything here all by myself? Fine! I'll set the course!"

As he slapped his forehead, he let go of the steering wheel. The ship lurched violently as he let go of the wheel, even slightly. Noob felt himself almost fall to the floor of the ship. He immediately realized that the ship's steering was very sensitive, and letting go of the wheel for even the shortest period of time was potentially a disaster.

"Whoa! Take it easy, Cap! I think it's best that you stay on the wheel!"

The captain was not even paying attention to Noob now. He marched down to the navigation area to set the course. Strangely enough, he did not seem to lose his balance as the ship now began to lurch and tilt even more violently.

"I'll set that course right now!"

"No!"

"Awkk! He's not going to listen! Awkk! The cap'n can be quite stubborn! Awkk! I told you that it was a mistake joining this voyage! Awkk!"

Noob was starting to realize that Borris did have a point here. Now he could see how the captain had earned his name.

The ship began to tilt worse and worse. Noob was now knocked to the floor as the captain disappeared below the decks.

"He's crazy! The ship's out of control!"

Noob took a look at the steering wheel. It began to spin wildly out of control. He had to do something! Noob desperately dived right at the steering wheel. He grabbed the wheel with both hands and struggled to right the ship. It had now lurched to one side so badly that it took all his strength to turn the wheel over and over again to get the ship balanced again.

"Come on, come on!"

The wheel was large and surprisingly heavy. He felt like his arms were on fire and would burst, but he kept at it. He simply had no choice but to keep turning the steering wheel.

"Come on! Come on!"

The ship lurched and swayed but finally, after much struggle, Noob managed to right the ship. It was now floating and travelling in one constant direction. The deck was now steady under Noob's feet, and he knew that the danger had passed.

"Whew! That was a close one!"

Noob's hands were shaking, but he kept them steady at the wheel. He didn't want a repeat of the ship swaying and rocking violently again.

"All right, there! I've finally managed to set a course for the isle of treasures! We should be there in no time now!"

"Awkk! You're crazy, Cap'n! Awkk!"

Noob immediately recognized Cap'n Blunder's voice, and the protests of Borris. Borris was beside himself, but Cap'n Blunder was the complete opposite. He sounded very calm and reserved. He sounded as if he was not even aware of the near disaster that they had barely avoided.

Their voices came from the lower sections of the ship, and they were coming back up. Noob was really beginning to see now that the parrot was actually a lot more sensible than he had first thought.

"Ah, Noob! Nice to see that you can steer the ship. Well, you can rest easy now. I'll take over the steering from here!"

The captain approached Noob and put his hands on the steering wheel. Noob's hands were still shaking as he let go of it.

"Are you crazy? What were you thinking, just letting go of the steering wheel like that? The ship could have turned over and sank! We were on the verge of a complete disaster there!"

"Awkk! I told you the Cap'n was nuts! Awkk!"

"What are you two getting so worked up about? The ship's still sailing and in one piece, right? Everything's fine!"

"Yeah, no thanks to you! If that happens again, not only will the legend not be fulfilled, but we could all end up at the bottom of the ocean!" Noob said.

"You're too much of a worry-wart, Noob! I knew that

you could handle the steering, anyway. Besides, no harm done, right? Now will you both please just calm down and relax? The course has been set, and we'll reach our destination a lot faster than you think."

Noob let go of the wheel. He could not believe what had just happened. He was really beginning to regret joining Cap'n Blunder.

"Yeah, I sure hope so."

Noob let the captain steer, and retreated to another corner of the ship. He tried not to worry too much about any other crazy thing that could happen. He hoped that any treasure they would find would be worth all of this.

Chapter Five

Cast into the Sea.

The ship kept its course and Cap'n Blunder kept his hands on the wheel. The time passed without incident and Noob tried to keep positive. He hoped that whatever happened with Cap'n Blunder earlier was just a temporary thing at best and far behind them.

"I see the isle of treasures dead ahead! We're almost there!"

The captain spoke confidently and with authority. Noob was very pleased to hear this, and he ran over to him at the steering wheel.

"There it is! The isle of treasures! Our destiny awaits, Noob!"

Cap'n Blunder pointed at an island that was visible in front of the ship. There was still some distance between them, but at their present course and speed, it would only be a matter of time before they reached it.

"All right! I can see the island, Cap! It's right ahead of us! I guess once we're there, we can start looking for some treasure!"

"Not just some treasure, Noob! The biggest treasure there is! The legend was very specific that a new player would come along and get the biggest booty that anyone's ever collected!"

"Whoa, whoa! Easy there, Cap! I'm new to this treasure game, remember? Maybe we can hold your horses for now and just focus on stuff one step at a time, right?"

Every time the captain mouthed off about the legend, Noob could not help but feel just a little bit uncomfortable. He didn't know anything about treasure hunting, and it seemed rather intimidating that the captain would place so much responsibility on someone so new like him.

"Haha! You are ever so humble, Noob! Come on, have a little faith. I'm sure the legend will come true and we'll all be rich once we reach that island! Show some spirit!"

Noob nodded and smiled. There was the treasure to look forward to, and the island was just some distance away now. Perhaps the captain was right. Perhaps the legend would come true and they would become very rich with treasure.

"Awkk! We're not moving! Awkk!"

Borris was right. The ship had been moving slower and slower towards the island of treasures, but Noob brushed it aside. He assumed the ship was probably moving slower as it approached to dock. After all, what did he know about sailing? Apparently, this wasn't the case, and it was something a lot more serious. The ship had slowed to a crawl, and now it was not even moving anymore.

"Borris is right, Cap! We've stopped moving. What's going on?"

"Take it easy, you two. It's nothing to worry about, I'm sure!"

The captain tried to start the ship and steer but it would not move. And this was just the beginning of their problems.

"Hey! We're sinking!" Noob said.

He noticed the water that was quickly rising from below. It was filling the ship up rapidly now, and Noob realized it was the water that had stopped their movement.

The water was now almost at the deck. The captain took a bucket and began tossing some of the water out.

"Awkk! A lot of good that'll do! You've gotten us into another fine mess, yes you have! Awkk!"

"You never stop yakking, do you, Borris?" Cap'n Blunder said.

"Awkk! That's because I'm right! You do always blunder into one mess after the other! Awkk!"

"Guys, please! How did this even happen?" Noob said.

"Awkk! Told you before but you didn't listen, kid! Awkk! This ship is leaky and full of holes! Holes that the good captain here didn't bother to ever patch up! Awkk! It's not seaworthy in the least! Now we're going to sink even before we reach the island! Awkk!"

Noob couldn't believe it. The captain couldn't even maintain the boat they were on, a basic task for someone who was sailing in search of treasure.

"Great! This is just great! I hate to agree with the parrot, Cap, but tossing water out by the pail full like that is not going to help us at all!"

"Do you have any better ideas on you, Noob?" the captain said with more than a hint of frustration.

"As a matter of fact, yes I do! I say we simply abandon ship!"

"I'm not going to abandon my ship! I purchased her at a really expensive price and…"

"Cap! Cap! Captain!"

Noob grabbed Cap'n Blunder by the arms and shook him. He didn't want to be so direct, but he didn't know what else to do. The frustration and panic in Noob had built and simply gotten to him. He had to get Cap'n Blunder to listen now.

"Look, I know this ship may have some kind of sentimental value for you. I understand that, but I'm sorry, there is no way we can save it now. It is going to sink whether you like it or not, and if we don't abandon ship, we'll join her! If we sink, the legend is not coming true!"

Noob looked directly into Cap'n Blunder's eyes, and he could see something light up inside, almost like a lightbulb being switched on.

"You're right. We have to get out of here."

The captain sounded very sad, but he had finally realized that there was nothing else to do but abandon the ship to the ocean.

"All right! Come on! Does this ship have any life rafts, emergency boats or anything for this kind of emergency? I'm no sailor, but I do know that ships are supposed to have stuff like that!"

"Awkk! The captain couldn't afford to get any of that! Awkk!"

Noob shook his head and frowned. He sighed, even as the water was now almost all over the boat.

"Why am I not even surprised anymore? Isn't there anything we can use to stay afloat?"

"Awkk! We've got some life preservers! Awkk! You and the captain can put them on yourselves, and we can float to the island. May take a while to get there without a boat, though! Awkk!"

"At least we'll still be alive! Show me where they are, Borris!"

"Awkk! Down below! Awkk!"

Borris pointed with his wing below the decks, where the water was already overflowing.

"Wait a minute! The whole ship's flooded! How am I going to get them there?"

"Awkk! Look! Awkk!"

Noob noticed two yellow shapes come up to the surface of the water. It was almost like the ship was a giant mouth that spat out some food. It was the life preservers. They had finally floated up to the water's surface that was now almost up to Noob and Cap'n Blunder.

"Awkk! Put them on now! Awkk!"

"You don't have to tell me twice, Borris!"

Noob grabbed one and tossed the other one to Cap'n Blunder. Both of them put them on and simply let the water swallow up what remained of the ship. The ship quickly sank under the sea's blue waters. Cap'n Blunder looked on with sadness as his ship disappeared beneath them.

"She's gone! She's gone!" Cap'n Blunder said.

"Just be thankful we're still here! We can still float and swim to the island."

"Awkk! And how long will that take? Awkk! By the time you get there, you'll both probably have white hair! Awkk!"

Borris was spot-on with his observation, as usual. There had to be a faster way to get to the island, and Noob knew instantly how it could be done.

"This is all my fault! It all just is! I'm so miserable! I really mess everything up!" Cap'n Blunder said.

"No time for that now, Cap! Look over there!"

Noob pointed towards the island. There were several small shapes that dotted the island shore.

"Are those boats docked on the island's shores?"

Cap'n Blunder nodded.

"Yeah, but what about them? They're just treasure hunters like us. Treasure hunters that are now going to get a whole lot more treasure than we will. And all because I blundered it all again."

"Cap! Get it together! Borris, can you fly to the island?"

"Awkk! Sure, no problem, but what about you guys? Awkk!"

"That's just it. You fly there and get some help. Tell those treasure hunters that we're floating out here, and guide them to where we are! We can get help and get to that island!"

"They're treasure hunters too, Noob! Are they going to help us?"

Noob shrugged his shoulders.

"Come on. They can't all be so bad that they won't help someone in need. Besides, it's our best chance now."

Cap'n Blunder sighed. The seas were all around them, and the island was still quite far away. He began to realize just how awful he was at this. Noob was right. It was a desperate plan, but it was all they had.

"I guess you're right," he said.

"Awkk! I'm flying there now! You two hang in there! Awkk!"

Cap'n Blunder and Noob were left floating together in the vast sea as they watched Borris fly away to the isle of treasure.

"Well, there he goes. All we can do now is wait," Noob said.

Noob and Cap'n Blunder held on to their precious life preservers. The blue sky and sea stretched as far as they could see. The island of treasure was so far yet so close to them, but they were still both cast adrift. They had never felt so helpless. It was all up to Borris now.

Chapter Six

Paying Back the Debt.

"This is all my fault, Noob. It's all my fault. I should have checked the ship thoroughly so it wouldn't leak. I really do deserve my name."

"Look, Cap. There's no point in moping about the situation now. We're here now, and all we can do is just wait and stay strong."

There was comfort and wisdom in Noob's words. The captain smiled at him and held onto his yellow life preserver.

"You know something, Noob? I may be all clumsy and careless in this treasure hunting business, but I have been at it for quite some time. In all that time, I do know how to spot someone who's a genuine nice guy. I also know how to spot someone who's not as dumb as I am. You're both of those, Noob."

Noob shook his head and smiled.

"Hey, you're not dumb, Cap, but thanks for the compliment."

"Don't try to sweet talk me or hide the truth, Noob. I know I'm not the smartest guy around. I know it was all on me. We lost the ship because of me. I've never found any treasure here on the server, no matter how hard I try."

Cap'n Blunder looked really pitiful now. Noob couldn't help but feel sorry for him as they drifted on the vast sea. He didn't deserve this, and self-pity would not get either of them anywhere.

"Look Cap. I know you don't really feel too good about yourself now, but moping around isn't going to help. Let's just wait for Borris to fly back to us with some help."

"I guess we really don't have much of a choice about that, do we?"

"Exactly. So stay strong. You're the captain of our little group. You're the leader and we'll get that treasure!"

Noob's words actually managed to stir the captain a little

bit. He could see that there was a lot of strength in Noob. Strength that wasn't obvious at first, but was quick to show when some kind of trial or trouble came up.

"I guess you're right, Noob. We'll make it, and we'll find that treasure! I won't be Captain Blunder anymore! I'll be the man that made the legend come true! Uhm, with your help, of course."

"There ya go! That's a lot better than moping now, isn't it?"

The captain nodded. He was really feeling good now, despite their problem. Noob was great with the pep talk.

"Yeah! Oh yeah! We're going to do this, Noob!"

The captain was all pumped up and inspired now, but that did not change the fact that they were still floating in the middle of the vast sea. The island was still several miles away from them, and all they could do was wait. It was really easy for them to get discouraged, but they both tried to keep their spirits up.

"So what got you started with treasure hunting?"

Noob decided to ask the captain just to keep them both from getting too down or depressed with their situation. Perhaps small talk could keep the captain and even his spirits up.

"My father used to be a treasure hunter. Did you know that?"

"Really? If that's the case, I guess it kinda runs in the family then."

Cap'n Blunder nodded.

"Yeah it does, but sometimes I wish it didn't."

"What do you mean?"

"My dad was one of the greatest treasure hunters on the server ever, Noob. He found a lot of treasure and easily made a name for himself. You're still pretty new to all of this, so I won't go into detail about the stuff he discovered or any of his other achievements. Just trust me when I say that he was a legend."

Noob looked up at the blue sky. A bird flew high above them. For a moment, Noob thought that the bird was Borris, but it was flying too high to be him. They only had each other in the vast sea.

"So, what's so bad about that? I mean, he's a legend and all. Isn't that a good thing?"

"It would be a good thing, yeah, if I was a better treasure

hunter. Okay, I get what you said earlier. I really did. There's no point in me feeling bad about how bad I am at treasure hunting, but let's face it, Noob. I really do suck at this stuff. I'm not saying it to mope or feel sorry for myself. I'm just saying it as it is. It's the truth. And because I have such a legendary treasure hunter for a dad, I kinda get measured up to him. So I end up sucking even more because of that high standard. You feel me?"

"I definitely feel you, Cap. It must be tough trying to just be your own treasure hunter because of your dad's big rep. Yeah, I can see how tough that must be."

"Hey, that's exactly why I asked your help in the first place, Noob. I really want to get this treasure really bad. Really bad. I want it not just for the treasure itself, but so that I can get a little respect for something I've done."

Noob understood perfectly where Cap'n Blunder was coming from. It wasn't easy always failing and even having a father who was a legend. It must have appeared as if Cap'n Blunder was shaming their name because of his failures, and his dad's rep. It could really play on him, and Noob felt sorry for him. He wanted to help him, but there was nothing he could do there. That was Cap'n Blunder's own personal battle.

"Don't worry about it, Cap. We're not done yet. Once Borris returns with some help, we'll get to the island and find your treasure! Once we do, you're not going to be Cap'n Blunder anymore. You're going to get some real respect, and you're going to find that treasure."

"Thanks, Noob. You're an inspiration, you know that?"

Noob smiled at Cap'n Blunder. He may not have been the smartest guy around, but Noob could see that the captain could be a great friend. That was definitely worth something.

They both continued to drift in the water for some time. Neither Noob nor Cap'n Blunder knew how much time had passed, or how long they had been floating in the water. They were both starting to feel some panic creeping in. What was taking Borris so long? Would someone ever come for them? It was natural, but they both resisted thinking about such things. There was no point in panicking like that.

"Noob, I'm sorry that I dragged you into this," Cap'n Blunder said.

"What are you talking about, Cap?"

"You know very well what I'm talking about. If I had not gotten you to join me in this little treasure hunting quest, then you wouldn't be floating out at sea with me."

Noob smiled at Cap'n Blunder.

"Forget it, Cap. I agreed to it. Besides, I love excitement and adventure."

"I know you do. I'm just afraid that this adventure may get you killed with me."

Noob shook his head and smiled at Cap'n Blunder. His smile was a lot wider and more enthusiastic than usual.

"Maybe not, Cap! Look up ahead!"

Noob pointed up ahead. He saw something in the distance. Something that got his hopes up.

"Look! There's something coming towards us! It's coming in real fast!"

Cap'n Blunder looked to the horizon, and he saw it too. The object was large and headed right towards them. The way it was moving, along with its speed, made it seem to be a boat of some kind. Noob and Cap'n Blunder both cheered and raised their hands up in the air to get noticed. They splashed around and kept waving at the object that was now closing in on them.

"Hey, over here! We're here!"

The two of them made more than enough noise and ruckus to get noticed. The craft approached them and got closer. Noob and Cap'n Blunder could now see that it was definitely a ship.

"Awkk! I came back for you guys with help! Awkk!"

Noob and Cap'n Blunder heard the familiar cackling voice of Borris. He had flown ahead of the ship, and perched himself upon the captain's shoulder, as he usually did.

"All right! I knew he would come through!"

"Great work, Borris! I swear I will never, ever threaten to cook you again!"

"Awkk! I'll hold you to that! Awkk!"

"Come inside the ship! Hurry! You both must be exhausted!"

The voice came from inside the ship, which now right in front of Noob and Cap'n Blunder. It was a much more modern vehicle than theirs, and it looked a lot more efficient. Both of them were very relieved to see the ship floating beside them.

"Come on in! I'm dropping a ladder for you both. Can you guys climb aboard?"

"I think so. Cap, can you make it up?"

"I can do it, although I admit I probably would not have lasted much longer."

It was Cap'n Blunder who went up the ladder first, followed by Noob. They climbed up and into the ship in no time. It was now time to meet their rescuer.

"Hi guys. Your parrot flew over to the island and introduced himself. He told me about your trouble, and I rushed here to help. He's a pretty talkative little bird."

Cap'n Blunder and Noob stood in front of the ship's operator. He stood in front of the ship's large steering wheel, just as Cap'n Blunder once had done. There was no doubt or fear in him, and Cap'n Blunder suddenly felt sad. He remembered how he once piloted his own ship before, and now seeing this man do it, he began to miss doing so.

"Yeah, well, that's Borris for you. He may be talkative but he's actually pretty reliable," Cap'n Blunder said.

"Awkk! A compliment from you! I can't believe it! Awkk!"

Borris hovered over the three of them and Cap'n Blunder decided to call him down. He looked so energetic that he was afraid Borris would suddenly collapse from exhaustion or something.

"Get down here, Borris! You've flown long enough, I imagine!"

Borris perched himself on the captain's shoulder, as he always did.

"We're very grateful for your help, sir," Noob said.

The man brushed it off and smiled. He appeared quite friendly.

"Oh, it was nothing. I just did what anyone would do. I couldn't just ignore a plea for help."

"Believe me, I've seen and known people who would do exactly that. What's your name?" Cap'n Blunder said.

"I'm Tobias Joe. I was looking for some treasure on the island of treasure until Boris alerted me about your situation."

"I'm Cap'n Blunder and this is my friend Noob."

"I'm pleased to meet you, Cap'n. Noob."

Tobias nodded and smiled at them and then shook their hands. Noob and Cap'n Blunder could see that he was a very polite and friendly young man.

"Likewise. We're forever in your debt, so I'll let you in on a little secret, Tobias."

"Really? What is that?"

"Ever hear of The Legend of the Noob?"

"That's the name of the legend?" Noob asked Cap'n Blunder.

He nodded at Noob.

"Yep. That's the name, Noob. Now can you see why I believe in you? How about you, Tobias? Have you heard of it?"

Tobias smiled as he turned the steering wheel of his ship hard. Noob could see the effort he put into simply turning the wheel. He immediately remembered when he had to turn the steering wheel of Cap'n Blunder's ship earlier. It was agonizing, but somehow he managed. Noob thought about how difficult it was to do the things these guys did. It took a lot of effort and hard work, and he had to respect them for that.

"Heard of it? Heh, I think everyone searching for treasure on the server knows about it. What about it?"

Cap'n Blunder smiled at Tobias.

"This is your lucky day. You're standing in front of the legend himself."

"Oh no. Not again."

Noob sighed. He knew what was coming next, but he couldn't do anything to stop it. The good captain really believed in the legend, and he was about to explain his little theory involving Noob to Tobias.

"Yes, again. Come on, Noob."

"Wait a second. Are you saying that Noob over there is the legend? The legendary new treasure hunter who'll uncover the biggest treasure on the whole server?" Tobias said.

Cap'n Blunder smiled and beamed with pride. Noob was beginning to feel like more of a pet to Cap'n Blunder than Borris was.

"Yeah, he believes it's me all right. Let me just caution you about it right now, though. There's just no evidence that I really am the legendary character, or that the story will even come true at all," Noob said.

"Come on. You're a new treasure hunter, aren't you? And the name, Noob? It's just as the legend says. That's all the proof you will ever need," Cap'n Blunder said.

"For real? Is it really true? I mean, it's a cool legend and all, but well, I'm not sure that it could really happen," Tobias said.

"Awkk! Forget it, Tobias! There's no way you can convince Cap'n Blunder otherwise! Believe me, we've tried! Awkk!"

"Borris is right, Tobias. Cap is a great guy and all, but you're not going to convince him that the legend isn't true. He's convinced I'll lead him to the treasure on that island."

"The biggest treasure on that island, mind you. And not just me now. You too, Borris. If, no, *when* we do find that treasure, I think it's only fair that we split it with you. I mean, you did save us back there. It would only be fair."

Tobias paused at Cap'n Blunder's words. He considered what he was trying to offer him.

"Whoa, you mean that, Cap? Can I call you Cap?"

Cap'n Blunder smiled.

"Why not? Noob already calls me that, and it sounds a lot better than Cap'n Blunder, if you know what I mean."

"I feel you, Cap. Well anyway, that's a very generous gesture if the legend is even true. When we land on that island, you do know that there'll be a lot of treasure hunters out there looking for, well, treasure."

Cap'n Blunder laughed so loud that Tobias' boat shook.

"Me knowing about other treasure hunters? Believe me son, I know about them all too well. I'm just the kind of guy that repays my debts. I know that they call me Cap'n Blunder, but I'm not Cap'n Ungrateful."

Tobias grinned at the captain. It was quite the generous offer, and he appreciated a man with honor.

"Nice to hear that. Well, if that's the case, I guess it's time we started looking for some treasure!"

Chapter Seven

The First Riddle.

"The island of treasure is right in front of us!"

Tobias Joe spoke with excitement. His hands were shaking as he steadied the wheel. Everyone in his boat was very excited to get onto the island. The promise of great treasure and adventure awaited them all.

"Yeah, let's do this!" Noob said.

"Awkk! Treasure! Treasure! Awkk!"

Cap'n Blunder was strangely silent. He did not react with as much enthusiasm as the others on the ship. If anything, he appeared quite serious and lost in his thoughts.

"Hey, you okay there, Cap?" Noob said.

Noob immediately noticed that his new friend was

strangely silent, and he had to ask him about it. He wasn't the only one who noticed.

"Awkk! You're pretty quiet. Awkk!" Borris said.

"Sorry, guys. I guess it's hard to be my normal self right now."

"Tell me about it. I've only been with you for some time here on the server, but you're never this quiet," Noob said.

"Awkk! I've had to deal with him for most of my life and I've never seen him this glum. Awkk!"

Cap'n Blunder smiled at his two friends.

"Thanks for the concern, you two. I appreciate it. I really do. I'm just feeling a bit serious because we're right in front of the island of treasure. I mean, we're so close to getting the treasure now. I guess I can't believe we actually got here, considering how my blundering almost cost us the entire journey. I'm always used to messing things up."

Noob smiled at Cap'n Blunder.

"There we go again, Cap! Come on, smile! I told you not to feel so glum and down, didn't I? You've got to hang tough here. We're right in front of the island of treasure now, and about to land. We're so close to getting that treasure, Cap!"

Cap'n Blunder shook his head.

"That's just it, Noob. I've failed so many times in this treasure hunting thing. I've made so many mistakes. I've more than earned my name of Cap'n Blunder. I guess I'm just afraid that I'll mess everything up again."

Noob smiled at Cap'n Blunder and put a hand on his shoulder.

"You won't, Cap'n. I believe in you," he said.

"Awkk! I believe in you too, Cap'n! Awkk!"

Cap'n Blunder was touched at his friends' show of support. This was the first time he had ever heard Borris encourage him like this. He couldn't believe that Noob was still behind him, even after he had sunk their ship with his carelessness. It was something unbelievable and touching to him. Despite all his many setbacks, he felt very grateful to have friends like these.

"I'm really lucky to have friends like you by my side. I don't deserve such support, but I'll make sure that I earn your respect," he said.

"Hey guys. I don't mean to break the touching moment

back there, but we've made landfall! We're officially at the island of treasure!" Tobias said.

The ship shook and lurched just a little as he dropped the anchor, and Tobias' ship docked beside the other ships. They were all empty and it was a little creepy to be on such a quiet shore.

"Where are the others? The ships are empty," Noob said.

"They're all probably looking for the ancient treasure as we speak, Noob. There's not a moment to waste. We had better get on land now."

"Agreed."

The four of them set foot on the island. Noob noticed that the beach was just as beautiful as the first island he had landed on in the server. The island had thick woods ahead of them. It was dark in the forest and they couldn't make anything out in the woods. The silence seemed to stretch out for the entire island.

"Is it me, or is the entire island quiet? It's a little creepy, guys," Noob said.

"Awkk! Too quiet! Awkk!"

"I know what you mean, guys. It seems a little too quiet," Cap'n Blunder said.

"Come on. Everybody's probably searching for treasure in the woods. The boats are empty for that reason, and they've all already gotten a head start on us. Legend or no legend, you can't beat an early bird, and we're already late as it is. Come on!" Tobias said.

Tobias Joe was a tough treasure hunter who would not be swayed by intimidation or fear. He felt neither and was very excited to get his hands on the treasures that the island promised. His spirit and energy was enough to win over and inspire the others, and they all headed into the woods.

"Sorry guys, but I still can't shake the feeling that something's not right here," Noob said.

"Agreed. It's too quiet."

"Awkk! Too quiet! Awkk!"

"Aww come on, you three! We're already here! Don't tell me you'll all chickens now? No offense to you, Borris."

"Awkk! None taken! Too scared to get angry! Awkk!"

Tobias could understand why the three of his companions were all suspicious and scared. He had his own fears and wasn't sure about any of this, either. Still, they had all gone too far to back out now, and he was going to let them know it.

"Come on guys, we have to keep moving. We didn't come all this way to get scared by a little quiet, did we?"

"A little quiet in the middle of the woods? Not creepy and not scary, Tobias," Noob said.

"No. He's right. We have to keep moving. We can't just quit now. We've simply come too far," Cap'n Blunder said.

Cap'n Blunder himself was surprised at his own words. He didn't know where he was getting the courage to move on, but he was glad he had it, and nothing could turn him back.

"All right then, let's go."

"Awkk! You're the cap'n! Awkk!"

They all pressed on despite their fears, inspired by Cap'n Blunder's firm resolve. They had to cut through some thick weeds and greens, but they managed to move forward.

"All right. We've been moving forward for quite some time now. Any idea where the treasure of this island might be, Tobias?" Noob said.

"Noob's right. I planned on coming here without any kind of map, but that's because my name is Cap'n Blunder! Rushing towards any kind of danger and uncertainty without a plan is something I'm known for, but I'm betting that's just not your style, eh, Tobias? So where are we headed, and where's the treasure in this place?"

"Don't worry guys! I'm way ahead of you. Before I even landed here on the isle of treasure, I did my homework and studied the area thoroughly. According to my calculations, we should be standing right in front of the great temple of Roy!"

"The great temple of Roy, here? Impossible, no one's ever found the great temple of Roy! I don't even see anything but a bunch of trees!"

"Whoa, whoa, whoa!"

Noob had to pause and ask Cap'n Blunder and Tobias about this legendary temple. Judging by its name, it sounded anything but legendary or great.

"What's all this talk about the great temple of Roy? And what kind of a name is that for a great temple?" Noob asked.

"Watch what you say, Noob! The great temple of Roy is one of the greatest mysteries of the server. It's an ancient temple that was built by the greatest leader of the ancients, Roy!" Cap'n Blunder said.

Noob shrugged his shoulders.

"I guess it figures that it would be called the great temple of Roy."

"Exactly! The legends say that Roy hid all of the great treasures of the ancients in the temple, and only the worthiest of the worthy could solve the riddles that would lead to the treasure. The legends were also very specific that someone new would discover the treasure. That's got to be you, Noob!"

"You're putting too much faith in me, Cap! I suck at solving riddles! This isn't going to go well."

Tobias shook his head. He was getting tired of their constant bickering, and simply wanted to get into the temple that was seemingly not even there.

"All right, ladies. Stop arguing! There's no point in debating like that, and there's no turning back now. It's time to enter the great temple of Roy!"

Cap'n Blunder and Noob looked around. They could only see trees all around them, and there was no sign of any temple at all. They were beginning to think that perhaps

Tobias wasn't as sharp as they thought.

"Where is it? There's nothing but trees and plants here!" Noob said.

Tobias shook his head and smiled.

"It just looks that way. The trees and plants have grown so thick that they've completely grown over this sign!"

Tobias cut some bushes with his large knife, revealing an old sign that was hidden before. There was no way to spot it with all the shrubs and bushes, but now it was clear as day.

"Whoa! How did you even know it was there?" Cap'n Blunder said.

Tobias beamed with pride.

"I told you, I do my homework! Look!"

"Awkk! It's a riddle! Awkk! It says what has to be broken before you can use it? Awkk!"

"It goes on to say, 'use this item on the spot marked below the sign, but be warned; if you've gotten this far, others have already activated the island's traps and have vanished into eternity. If you somehow manage to figure out the riddle, you may enter the temple, but you're screwed for sure.'"

"Well, that was very specific and unnerving," Noob said.

"It doesn't matter. I already know the answer to the riddle! I heard that the riddles all use common items, so I brought some stuff that could potentially be used. Here!"

Tobias took out the item and tossed it onto the marker below the sign. Just as predicted, it was instantly broken apart. Right as it broke, the ground shook underneath them. They all thought that an earthquake was occurring.

"What have you done? It's an earthquake!" Cap'n Blunder said.

"I just solved the riddle, that's what! Hold on!"

The three of them struggled to stay standing, even as Borris fluttered about. The ground shook, and the trees in front of them parted. Suddenly the road was clear, and right in front of them was the large temple of Roy! It was a giant stone structure that was very imposing. A large statue of Roy stood and towered over them. There was also a stone staircase that led to the front of the temple.

1The three of them looked in awe at the temple before them. Tobias stood with pride, like a student who had gotten a perfect score on a test. In a sense, it was exactly what had happened.

"Amazing! You did it! You're a genius!"

"Awkk! A genius! Awkk!"

"I never would have thought that was all that was needed to find the temple!"

The three of them climbed the stone steps into the temple. The pieces of the object lay scattered under the sign. What do you think the object was?

Answer: An Egg.

Chapter Eight

The Second Riddle.

"Okey-dokey, we're in the temple of Roy!" Cap'n Blunder said.

The four of them walked around and were treated to an amazing sight. They walked down a long stone corridor. The long and large corridor had a ceiling that stretched as far as they could see, and it was lined with several stone statues of the ancients. They were all in fighting poses and were clearly great warriors of a lost era.

"How did you even manage to solve that riddle?" Noob said.

"Hey, I always had a thing for riddles in my time, Noob. I don't know. They just came naturally, so I guess this should be a piece of cake, eh? The legends say that you need to solve two more riddles to get to the treasure that's buried here in the temple. I say, bring 'em on!"

Noob couldn't understand any of it. He was just awful at solving riddles. He was never really good at puzzles or any brain-benders like it. It was simply something that didn't come naturally to poor Noob. Puzzles and riddles were simply off limits for him, like water for fire or ice cream left to dry out in the sun. He simply detested them, and he had no idea how he could possibly be the key to finding the treasure. If anything, Tobias was already proving far more useful than he was.

"This temple is actually pretty simple. It's really this long corridor that leads to an end. I'm betting that it's where we'll get the treasure. I just hope you're as good at the riddles as you say you are, Tobias,"

Cap'n Blunder said.

"Relax. Like I said earlier, bring 'em on!"

Right as Tobias spoke, a huge cage fell upon the four treasure hunters. The cage came from above them, and it appeared that they had activated some kind of mechanism on the floor. The bars were made of solid metal, and it was impossible to bend or crack them in any way. The spaces between the bars were also quite small, and even Borris could not fly away through them.

"Great to hear that, 'cause I think we're about to get our next riddle soon," Noob said.

"We're trapped! Now what?" Cap'n Blunder said.

"Awkk! Look! Down at the floor! Awkk!"

It was a note that apparently came with the cage. It was Noob who picked up the note and read the riddle that was scrawled on the paper.

"'What has a neck but no head? Simply stick the object's neck through the cage's spaces, and the cage will fall apart.' Great. I have no idea! Anyone have any ideas?"

"Haha! Come on! They should make the riddles a little more difficult, please! That is just too simple, it's a giveaway!"

Noob shook his head. Cap'n Blunder looked at Borris and they all looked equally puzzled. The riddle was a real stumper, and they had no idea what the note was describing.

"So what is the answer, Tobias?" Cap'n Blunder said.

"It's simple! Here!"

It did not faze Tobias in the least, as he took another

common object from his backpack. Tobias whipped out the object to the amazement of the others. It was a perfect description of the riddle, and they suddenly wondered how they could have missed it.

"There you go!"

Tobias placed the neck of the object in question between two of the bars. It fit through the space perfectly, and the bars all dropped down like a pile of sticks. They made a loud noise that almost split everyone's ears, but the sound passed. The important thing was that they were free.

"I can't believe you solved that riddle, Tobias! You're a natural at this!" Noob said.

Tobias smiled at them and kept walking. He really liked being complimented, and Cap'n Blunder began to notice that Tobias did have something of a big ego. He was still grateful for his saving them, but the man did have a little too much pride in himself.

"Stick to me boys, and we'll get that treasure in no time. If my research is correct, which I'm sure it is, we only have one last riddle to go before we get to the treasure!"

"Awkk! He's a genius! Awkk!"

Borris flapped around and flew in circles. He was just as impressed as Noob and Cap'n Blunder were with Tobias. The man definitely had brains.

The three of them moved forward toward the last riddle. They all still couldn't believe how Tobias solved it. The answer was a very common object like the last one, and seemed to be right under their noses. There was a certain genius as to how the riddles were designed. Simple objects that were common, but seemed totally unrelated, were the key to solving the riddles. How about you? What do you think the object was that dismantled the cage?

Answer: A bottle.

Chapter Nine

The Final Riddle.

The four treasure hunters were now almost at the end of the long hall that was the temple of Roy. Roy had constructed his ancient temple with care, combining magic and his own love of riddles to create a temple that was simple yet nearly impossible to truly penetrate. Despite this, they were all near the end of the single long hall.

"We've gotten through every single obstacle that this temple has to offer!" Noob said.

"Don't worry, guys. My research and my planning have gotten us this far. I'm sure we'll reach the treasure now. If said planning is correct, we should encounter one last riddle, the toughest one yet.

I also hear that it's a riddle related to that legend of a new player getting the treasure!" Tobias said.

"Any idea what it could be?"

Tobias shook his head. He was still confident, even if he didn't know exactly what the riddle would be.

"Not really sure, Cap, but I'm more than confident that I can figure it out when it does come."

They did not have long to wait for that to happen. The last stone statue at the end of the hall suddenly moved towards them. Its large stone feet freed themselves from their foundations, and the very temple shook as the stone giant approached them.

"Awkk! Stone giant! Awkk! We're done for now! Awkk!"

Borris, like the others, was absolutely terrified of the large and grim giant as it approached them. Who wouldn't be? It was a freaking stone giant come to life!

"All right. Nobody move."

The giant sounded a lot sleepier than it should have. Noob was surprised at this rather unusual development.

"Don't tell me. You're not going to let us pass," he said.

The giant nodded.

"Of course I won't let you guys pass. It's my sacred duty to guard this place. Blah, blah, and blah. I'm actually surprised you guys made it this far. Most guys never even find the place."

"Of course we're going to find the place. I'm a riddle-solving machine!" Tobias said.

The giant sighed. He seemed to be acting more out of duty than anything else.

"Yeah, the boss man Roy was crazy about riddles just like you. He made three riddles along with the traps and myself to keep anyone out. Look, I think you all know how it goes. I'll tell you the last riddle, and if you can solve it, well, the treasure is right behind me in that stone chest."

The giant pointed at the chest. It was located right at the center of the end of the hall. Everyone gasped. They were so close to their goal now.

"Of course, if you don't solve the riddle, well, I'll have to smash you with my fist. Nothing personal, okay? I mean, my spirit's trapped in this stone form and I really don't have much of a choice in the matter. You'll have thirty seconds to solve the riddle. Comprende?"

"Fire away! I ain't scared! I can figure out any riddle you toss at us!"

Tobias was his usual confident self, but the other three treasure hunters were not as confident. Who could blame them?

"All right. The riddle is, what is millions of years old, but only as old as a few months? Time starts now, dude. Good luck."

Upon hearing the riddle, Tobias immediately went pale. The question defied any kind of logic. How could something be millions of years old, yet be as old as a few months? It simply didn't make any kind of sense.

"Whoa. What the heck would that be?"

"Awkk! Don't look at me! Awkk!"

"Or me! I said I suck at this stuff, remember? Tobias, any ideas? That fist of his is right above our heads! We'll be squashed like bugs in a few seconds!"

"Twenty seconds left, guys."

Tobias was silent. His mind thought desperately of some kind of answer, but none came to him. What could it be?

"Ten seconds, dudes. I'm really sorry about this."

"Tobias, please tell us you've got an answer!" Noob said.

Tobias remained silent.

That was when it happened. Cap'n Blunder suddenly realized something. It was a simple thought that was almost insane, but it was the only chance they had now. If he was right, they would have the treasure. If he was wrong, they would be squashed flat. His thought? He was the chosen one of legend all along.

"Five seconds, guys. I'm gonna smash now, sorry."

"No! Please!"

"Wait! I've got it! I've got the answer to the riddle!" Cap'n Blunder said.

"What is it?" the stone giant said.

"The answer is..."

Cap'n Blunder leaned towards the stone giant's ear and whispered. The giant heaved a sigh of relief, because he didn't really want to kill anyone. His spirit had just been trapped in the stone and forced to do Roy's bidding, even after they all had long passed.

"You're right. Go straight ahead. The treasure's yours."

Everyone gasped in amazement. They all couldn't believe what they had seen, but the one who was most surprised was Cap'n Blunder himself. He couldn't believe that he was actually the chosen one of legend.

"Wow! I don't believe it! How did you figure that riddle out?" Tobias said.

"I'm happy for you, Cap. I really am, but I don't understand how you were the one of legend all along. You said it yourself. It had to be someone new, and you're anything but new to the game. No offense of course."

Cap'n Blunder marched towards the treasure with pride.

"None taken, Noob. I didn't understand myself until I considered what the stone giant said carefully. He said it was something that was millions of years old, but only a few months. That was when it struck me. I was born at the same time as the object. It's been a big part of my life. That was when I realized that 'new' in the legend probably didn't refer to someone new at all. Perhaps it was a wordplay reflecting something that was young, like the object. After all, something new can also mean something that is young. Something or someone. Something eternally young, and someone connected with it. I realized then that I was the one."

"Awkk! Amazing! I never thought I had it in you! Awkk!"

"Thanks for the vote of confidence, Borris."

"We're all proud of you, Cap!" Tobias said.

The four of them approached the treasure chest. Cap'n Blunder opened it and they feasted their eyes on a ton of Robux. There was so much money there that splitting it 4 ways was no problem at all. The four of them split the treasure as promised, and they were all better off for it. Tobias continued treasure hunting. Noob was able to buy a ship and start treasure hunting a lot more seriously. As for Cap'n Blunder, he realized that he was not a blundering kind of guy, after all.

But what could that mysterious object in the riddle have been?

Answer: the moon.

ROBLOX HIGH SCHOOL

ROBLOXIA KID

Entry #1

Super Crazy.

All right. This is the worst day of my life. Guaranteed. I kid you not. I knew that I should never have gotten down to writing a diary about my wonderful, colorful merc life. I knew if I ever started writing a diary about everything that goes on in my life, something bad would happen. I just didn't know it would be this bad! All the more reason to start writing a diary. This is just the kind of stuff I live for!

All right, Pool. Calm down and get a grip on yourself. That's me by the way, for all of you uneducated types. Being Deadpool, I'm sure I deserve no introduction. After all, my name says it all, and I'm sure you've already seen me in one form or another. I'm just that bleeding cool!

All right, all right. Get a grip on yourself, Pool. I mean,

it's not good to brag and all, even if you are so totally awesome! Sorry, I kinda get carried away. That's just me. So anyway, let's get down to the nitty gritty of this exciting tale. It's got everything! Action! Adventure! Romance (okay, maybe not much of that. I mean, who cares about romance anyway, right?)! Bromance! Plot twists, aaand... Me!

Well, it all started this morning when I came back home to my apartment. I had just come from a grueling series of battles, taking down some dudes for cash. I mean, that's what I do, right? I'm a mercenary, and this mercenary's got to make a living and pay the bills. Speaking of bills, my rent was waaay overdue, and my landlady was threatening to kick me out. That would be a big bummer considering that she's the only landlady willing to take the Merc with a Mouth for a tenant. So you could just imagine that I really needed the cash from my recent jobs, and then some.

I came back to the apartment and came upon something shiny at my front door. The object instantly caught my eye because it was so shiny. I bent over and examined it.

"Oooh! What do we have here? A piece of candy? Or something better?"

I picked it up and took a closer look. It looked like a ruby or a gem. A shiny stone or whatever. Either way, I wasn't about to pass up this chance.

"What is this? Looks really expensive. I think I could pawn this for a pretty good price down at Mort's pawnshop."

"You have the gall to assume that what you hold in your hands is a mere piece of jewelry? Are you that simple-minded?"

Suddenly, I heard a voice from inside my head. Or was it coming from the gem that I was holding in my hand? Seriously creepy stuff. At first I didn't really think much of it. After all, I am Deadpool and well, my mental issues have been well documented in the past. But as the conversation kept moving, I realized that this was definitely more than just me talking to myself.

"Did you just talk back to me? You, a shiny piece of rock?"

"Yes. I did, you moron. You are holding one of the infinity gems! My power is so great that I can speak to you in this manner!"

One of the infinity gems! Whoa! I had always heard of those gems. Five gems all from some super-god whatchama-call-it who croaked. Once super-god kicked the bucket, the five gems were scattered all over the universe. I heard from my other sources in the super hero world that anyone who possessed all five of the gems would gain infinite power. I guess that's pretty logical considering that they came from a deceased super-god.

Five gems of infinite power scattered all over the universe, and I had one in my apartment! Whoa, the whole idea just blew me away right then and there!

"For whatever reason, the fates have decided that our paths cross. What will you do, now that you have one of the infinity gems? One of the most powerful items in all of creation?"

"You're an infinity gem, eh? Cool! If that's the case, then there's only one thing I can think of doing with you!"

Just think about that for a moment, dear reader. What would you do if you had an object of incredible power? An object that could probably grant any wish of yours, or at least make you super-powerful! What would you do? I don't know, but I know what I did with the infinity gem right then and there. In the end, I guess there was really only one thing to do with it. After all, I am Deadpool here.

I took my guns out and pointed it at the gem!

"What are you doing?"

"Hey, you're super-powerful right? Super amazing and super everything, eh? Well, I'm super crazy! Let's see what happens if I shoot you!"

"You're crazy! You can't even imagine the terrible consequences of what you're about to…!"

Yeah, I pulled the trigger. There was a big flash of light and…

Kaboom.

Entry #2

Not Much of a Choice.

Okay, so after I pulled the trigger, there was this really big flash of light, right? I was blinded for a few seconds from the flash, and when I opened my eyes, I wasn't in my apartment anymore.

Okay, okay, I know shooting an infinity gem probably wasn't the smartest thing to do, but hey, I'm not the smartest guy around. Craziest? Definitely.

"Okay. What happened? Where am I? And where's the gem?"

I looked around and the gem was nowhere in sight. I guess I probably blew it away, but there were no fragments of the gem anywhere. It was almost like it vanished. Like my guns.

"My guns! My swords! I never leave home without them! Where are they?"

All right. Losing an infinity gem is one thing, but losing my weapons? Totally unacceptable!

I decided to take a walk and see where I was, but with no weapons on me, I felt kinda naked.

"All right. What is this place? It looks like... a school?"

I looked around and saw all sorts of freaky characters. Some of them looked as outrageous as me in my red tights, while others looked downright ordinary. There was a strange trait to all of them though. They were all sort of yellow and kind of bubbly. I am not sure...

Anyway, the ordinary guys and gals and the stranger ones all carried schoolbooks and acted like annoying students during lunchbreak. I looked around and they seemed to be on a campus with long halls, a cafeteria, and other buildings where they could, well, do school stuff. This led me to the only conclusion possible.

"I'm in school! What kind of a bummer is this?"

All right kiddies. Before we go on, let me make one thing clear right now; I hated school. I just hated school in all its forms. I mean, think about it. I was just a plain kid back then, not your friendly neighborhood Merc with a... all right. That didn't seem to sound right there, but you get the point. I hated school! I was just an ordinary kid with zilch for powers, and I couldn't do all the cool stuff that I can do now. It was absolutely the worst part of my life, especially...

"Duhh! Of course you're in school. High school to be exact! What are you complaining about? Cool custom costume, though."

I turned around and saw this cute girl. She looked just a little mean but I didn't see her as the nasty, mean girl type. She looked more like a confident but annoying girl who was more of an in-your-face, type.

"What high school is this?" I asked.

She rolled her eyes up to the sky and shook her head.

"Duhh! What rock did you crawl out of? Like this is so #bornyesterday!"

"Hey! Watch your manners, young lady! That's no way to treat someone who's new here!"

She gave me a confused look now.

"So you're new here? A new student? Well, I guess that does kinda make sense. After all, this is Roblox High School, and a lot of strange stuff happens here. Considering all the strange stuff here, I guess I shouldn't be surprised about you suddenly appearing out of nowhere!"

"Roblox High School? Me appearing out of nowhere?"

The girl nodded.

"Yeah. This is like the most intense high school in all of the Roblox servers! It's high school but with a twist. There are a lot of ordinary students here, and a lot of students with freaky powers!"

"Hmm. Kinda reminds me of another school with gifted students..."

"What?"

I shook my head.

"Never mind. Anyway, you did mention that I kinda popped here from outta nowhere, right? That makes a lot of sense considering that I came from another world."

"Another world? You came from another server in Roblox?"

"Another server? No, I mean another world, literally. I did a pretty dumb thing and I want to find my way back to my world. Somehow."

"So, you're not really a player here in Roblox, eh?"

"This is a video game?"

"Yep. The greatest game in all of Roblox!"

All right. This gal was sounding weirder and weirder with every word. I was really beginning to regret blasting that infinity gem. I took a closer look at her, and I noticed that, yeah, she did look kinda weird. Almost blocky-like, and the other students all had different customizations. Yeah, that explained a lot.

"All right. If I'm in a game in this Roblox thing, I need to get out and somehow get back to my own world. You've got to help me, Miss...?"

"Yona. Call me Yona. And you're..?"

"Deadpool! The Merc with a Mouth!"

"All right, Deadpool. You said you came from another world, right? Well, it does make sense considering you came out of a stone earlier."

"A stone? Did you say a stone? Like a shiny stone? Or gem?"

Things were really picking up now. If Yona had seen me come out of a shiny stone, then that meant the infinity gem was still intact. That also kinda made sense considering that it was a gem of power. Surely, something like that couldn't have been destroyed if I just shot bullets at it. If it was still intact, then maybe I could use it to get back home! Okay, considering that I shot at it for absolutely no reason, well, maybe I should apologize first. After all, I probably did hurt its feelings, shooting at it like that, and the infinity gem looked pretty sensitive. Yeah, I guess I should have thought first before shooting at the gem, but that just wouldn't be Deadpool, right?

"Yeah. I was just on my way back to class when I saw this shiny gem on the ground. I wanted to pick it up, but there was this big flash of light and suddenly, there you were!"

"Whoa! That was the infinity gem, all right!"

"The what?"

"The infinity gem! That was the thing that got me to your world in the first place! Where is it?"

I was so excited that I could barely speak straight. I thought that I could easily get back home now. Unfortunately, it wouldn't be that easy. Nah, nothing's easy when you're Deadpool.

"Hate to burst your bubble or what not, but when you appeared, that infinity gem, as you called it, just vanished."

"It what?"

"It vanished! Poof! Gone! Just like that. It was almost as if you replaced it where you're standing."

This was not good. It was not good at all, but I probably shouldn't have been surprised.

"Great. I'm not surprised considering I shot it, and ended up on your world, er, high school."

Yona gave me a funny look and I thought she would just walk away right then and there. Fortunately, she didn't.

"You shot at this infinity gem? From what you describe, you shot an immensely powerful thing? Why would you do that?"

I really didn't have a good answer for Yona, and I just shrugged my shoulders.

"Okay, you're really starting to creep me out."

Yona was about to walk away, but I stopped her from leaving me there on the spot.

"Yona, wait! Don't go! You can't just leave me here! I mean, you're the only person I know in this whole place, and well, I'm stuck here! You've got to help me! I never even liked high school!"

"Tough luck, Deadpool, because you're stuck in a game where you are in high school! Because of your #reallysmart move, shooting the infinity gem like that, you'll have to go back to high school!"

I bonked myself on the head. Yeah, I must have looked pretty stupid, but I didn't really know what else to do.

"I know, I know. It was a bone-headed move, okay? Don't rub it in. Please help me! Maybe you can just guide me through this Roblox High School, and somehow I can find the infinity gem with your help! Please!"

Yona looked at me, and I didn't know if she was feeling sorry for me or was just creeped out. It was hard to tell considering she was wearing a pair of thick-rimmed glasses.

"Well, this is a tough high school for beginners. And if I left you here all alone, you probably wouldn't have a chance at all to get by."

"No, no! Please! I just want to go home already!"

Yona shook her head, but I was sure now that she felt sorry for me. I can be pretty pitiful or pathetic when I really feel like it.

"All right, all right! Stop whining. I'll help you in high

school. Just follow me and do as I say, and you'll be fine."

I felt so relieved. Finally, there was someone who could help me make something out of this mess that I got myself into.

"All right! Thank you so much, Yona! You'll help me find the infinity gem?"

"I know I'm going to regret this, but yeah, I'll help you. You did mention earlier that you had powers or something back in your world right? Or you were a fighter of some kind?"

"Yeah, I'm Deadpool, Merc with a Mouth!"

"I got that, but you should tone it down. Remember what I said earlier? Roblox High School isn't your average high school. There's lots of strange stuff that goes on here, too. We might even encounter some super-baddies along the way, so stay alert all the time. And follow me all the time, so you can stay out of trouble."

"Stay alert and stay out of trouble! Sounds simple enough! You got it!"

"Great! Come on now, lunch time is almost over! Let me introduce you to my friends and we can get back to class!"

"Introduce me to your friends? And I'm going back to class?"

It was almost as if someone flipped a switch and Yona went from being confused and annoyed at me, to suddenly being excited and all bubbly about showing me around the high school. I started to wonder if I was the only one with a mean streak around here. Maybe being in high school again wouldn't be so bad, as long as I followed Yona's orders to the letter. I didn't really have much of a choice.

Entry #3

A Really Bad Day at School.

Okay, remember the part where I said that maybe this all wouldn't be so bad, as long as I stuck with Yona and stayed out of trouble? That just didn't happen. Everything suddenly started to annoy me around here, and there's not much I can do!

It all started when lunch break ended and Yona brought me back to her class with her. She introduced me to her friends, Angela and Alfred. They looked like nice enough kids, but I was still pretty uptight being back in high school and all. Turns out I had a good enough reason to be uptight.

"You look like a pretty cool dude, Deadpool!" Alfred said.

"Hey, you think I'm cool now, you should have seen me

when I had my guns and katana going on! I was really the bomb back then, Fred! Can I call you Fred?"

"Sure, man."

I was kinda hitting it off a lot better with Fred than with Angela. After all, he was the guy, and it seemed more natural for me to get along with him. See? I told you there was a lot of bromance in this.

"I'm glad to see you and Alfred are getting along, Deadpool, but just remember that you have to stay out of trouble."

"I know, I know, Yona. Believe me, I'm not going to start getting into trouble around here. All I want to do is get home as soon as possible."

The bell rang, and everyone started to walk back to their respective classrooms. That was our cue to get back to class, as well. It was also cue for trouble to start. I just didn't know it yet.

"That's the bell. We better get back to class. Don't worry, Deadpool. You'll fit in just nicely with our classmates. They're nice," Angela said.

"All right. If they're as nice as you three have been, I guess there's really nothing to be afraid of."

I was actually starting to get nervous here. Just imagine! There I was, one of the most fearsome mercenaries the world has ever known! I've gone toe-to-toe with supervillains (and sometimes heroes!) whose powers you could hardly begin to imagine. Yet I was back in high school again, in a strange world called Roblox, and I was nervous to attend class. Yeah, I had good reason to be nervous, all right.

I entered the classroom with Yona, Angela, and Fred. It was a weird mix of different students in class. Like I said earlier, some students looked pretty much normal like my friends. Other students looked downright wacky or intimidating. They had such different costumes and customs that I still pretty much looked normal in my red suit.

"Take it easy, Pool! You're shaking!" Fred said.

"How can I not? I'm nervous! Your classmates all look, well, different!"

It was already bad enough that I was going back to high school. It was worse that a lot of the students looked like they could easily kick my butt. I was really missing my sword and guns now.

My eyes wandered to some students in the front row.

They really looked intimidating, and just a little bit familiar. One of them had long metal arms attached to his back. The other student beside him was large and almost didn't fit in his school chair. He had green skin and looked like he could single-handedly beat everyone up if he ever got angry. The other kid beside him had white face paint and a killer smile. He looked frail, but I could tell that he was really dangerous underneath that clown-like appearance and face paint.

"Those kids in the front row all look dangerous and a little too familiar for me! I think I ought to stay away from them!" I whispered to Yona.

"Those three? What are you talking about? They're the class nerds and smart guys! Don't you remember the first rule of high school? The geeks sit up front while the bullies and jocks sit at the back!" Yona said.

"You've got to be kidding! That green one over there looks so familiar! I just can't place it, but I sure wouldn't want to get him mad!"

"No problem there, Deadpool," Angela said.

"What do you mean?"

"You're talking about Billy, right? He never gets mad. You'll never meet a nicer kid in class. He's never made trouble, ever. They're all pretty nice in the front row, but Billy's the nicest."

"You have got to be kidding me."

"Hey, 'pool! Like, heads up! The teacher's about to call you!" Fred said.

Fred was right. The teacher was about to call me, and I really got nervous now. I realized what was going to happen. She was going to call me up on the stage to introduce myself. That was always how it was in school with new students, and I always hated it.

"Class, it looks like we've got a new student. Would you like to introduce yourself?" the teacher said.

Yep. It was just as I had suspected. This would not be fun at all.

"I've got to stand in front of class! I can't do it! I just can't do it!" I said.

I was literally shaking like a leaf now. Yona and her friends had to push me up to the stage. Yeah, I confess. I have anxiety when it comes to dealing with large crowds of people.

"Come on Deadpool, get it together!" Angela said.

"Yeah, you can do it! You're Deadpool!" Fred said.

"All right, all right! Heh. Hi everyone! I'm from, well, out of town, and I ended up in your school, so I guess I'll be your classmate for a while, till I find my way back. By the way, my name's Deadpool!"

"Deadpool! That's a wonderful name! Nice to meet you. I'm Jerome, by the way."

It was the creepy clown dude. I thought he would squirt me with acid or poison me or something, but he was actually nice, and extended his hand towards me. He was actually one of the first guys to introduce himself in class. I guess I judged him too harshly, or I read too many silly comics back home. Whatever.

"Hey, nice to meet you too, Jerome."

"Deadpool, eh? I like your costume. My name's Billy, by the way."

This time, it was the jolly green giant in front of me who extended his hand. I shook it, or at least tried to shake it. His hand was around five times the size of my own. I tried to hide the fact that I was shaking in my boots, here. After all, Billy looked like the kind of guy who would be really bad if you got him mad. Also, I guess it kinda figured that he liked my costume. After all, all he was wearing was purple pants. I didn't say that to Billy's face, of course, because he was so big. I still couldn't believe that he was as nice as the others said, and I wasn't about to test that theory.

"I'm glad to see that Jerome and Billy have extended their hands in friendship to you, Deadpool. I encourage all of you to make our new student feel very welcome at the school," the teacher said.

I managed to smile behind my red mask. So far, all of my fears and worries about high school were nothing but crazy ideas in my head. It had all actually been quite pleasant so far. I was starting to think that maybe my time here at high school wouldn't be so bad.

Of course, that was not going to happen. This was right about the time when everything started to annoy me.

"Who do you think you are, coming into the school like this? You think you're some bigshot now, eh?"

"Excuse me?"

"You heard me, Deadpool! I'm talking to you!"

It was one of the other kids. He suddenly stood up from his seat at the back row and started shouting at me. I had never seen this dude in my entire life.

"Dude, I don't even know you!"

"Sit down, Snyde!" the teacher said.

"Snyde?" I asked.

"He's one of biggest bullies in class! That kid is always getting on everyone's case!" Yona whispered to me.

The kid who stood up and challenged me looked nothing like a bully. He had a square jawed face and was small, just up to my shoulders. He had a bit of a round tummy and also had this strange logo of what appeared to be a rat on his chest.

"He sure doesn't look like a bully. He looks more smarmy geek than bully."

"What are you talking about? Look!"

Billy pointed towards Snyde, and I saw what was happening. We all did, and it was, well, pretty out of this world, or any world. Snyde spread his arms out, and suddenly there were what appeared to be two giant wings on his back. His ears suddenly became pointed and he began to flap his wings wildly.

"I am vengeance and justice! I am justice in the night, and you are a criminal, Deadpool! It's time to bring you to justice! It's time for the Dark Snyde to take flight!"

"The what? Is he serious?" Yona said.

I know what you're thinking. Snyde sounded like a completely changed person, and I guess that was what happened. Yona did say something about strange things happening in the school, but I didn't really think that the strange stuff would happen so soon.

"He sure looks serious!"

Before I could do anything, Snyde, or Dark Snyde, spread his wings out and glided towards me. The distance was short, and he just rammed through me like some battering ram crashing through a wooden gate. I can tell you right now, I definitely felt it.

It was like being hit by a giant truck. I was knocked across the stage and into the blackboard. The blackboard cracked, and there was a large dent on the wall where I was knocked back.

"Hey! Get off of him!"

It was Yona. She moved towards Dark Snyde and threw a powerful punch at him, sending him flying. He was knocked aside, and I was lying on the floor by myself.

"Whoa, I didn't know you could throw a punch like that!" I said.

I could see Yona's eyes grow wide behind her glasses. She was clearly just as surprised as I was.

"Neither did I," she said.

Something was shining on the ground where Yona knocked Dark Snyde aside. I looked to the floor and saw it. My heart skipped a beat when I saw what it was. I couldn't believe it, but it was undeniable! The shape and color were just exactly as I remembered. It was a small and shiny piece of the infinity gem!

"One of the pieces of the infinity gem! I can't believe this!"

I scooped it off of the floor and placed it in my pocket. The discovery of the fragment changed everything! I immediately realized that the gem must have fragmented when I shot it, and when it transported me here. The fact that it was right on the spot where Snyde was must have meant that Yona knocked it off of him when she punched him. It must have been the fragment of the infinity gem that caused his transformation.

"Whoa, what happened?"

It was Snyde. He was stunned and confused as he lay across from me. Yeah, you read that right. It was really Snyde again. He had reverted back to normal, which only confirmed my suspicions. Without the shard of the infinity gem on him, he must have lost any power that it gave him.

"He's back to normal! I can't believe this!" Jerome said.

"Yeah! When Yona decked him, he suddenly turned human again. That was simply amazing! Amazing and unbelievable!" Billy said.

"That was just awesome!" Angela said.

"Totally out of this world!" Fred said.

Everyone seemed pretty amazed except for Yona herself, who was more confused about what had just happened. She just didn't know that she had that much strength in her.

"I can't believe I just socked Snyde and he went flying! Is he all right?"

"I think he's fine. Besides, if you didn't sock him, he might have eaten me alive or something! I'm just grateful that you socked him when you did!"

"But I'm no super hero! I'm just an average kid in Roblox High School!"

"All right, everyone! Settle down! We've had more than

enough excitement for one day! Everyone get settled, and let's get back to class!"

For once I actually agreed with an authority figure. The teacher was right. I had had enough excitement for one day in high school. My back was aching from being slammed against the wall, and I could barely get up. And to think, this was just my first day. I guess things are just going to get a lot better from here. Oh well. I might as well look on the bright side. At least I managed to get a piece of the infinity gem. Now, I know that I have to find all the pieces to make the gem whole again, and maybe I can somehow get back home. This is all getting too crazy for me. Note to self: never shoot an all-powerful object like that again. Even a Merc with a Mouth has to think first before pulling the trigger sometimes.

Entry #4

Late For School.

I was happy that the rest of the day passed without much incident. Yona was still pretty shaken up by what happened, and I promised to talk to her about it the next day. I was really relieved to get back to the dormitory near the school. Conveniently, I was able to stay in one of their rooms without much hassle. I quickly fell asleep, and that was when I had the freakiest dream.

"Deadpool! Oh, Deadpool!"

"What?!"

I looked up and saw the infinity gem standing right in front of me, only this time it was around like 100 times bigger than its original size. It also had a giant smiley face on it. The infinity gem was much bigger than me now, and it was looking down, smiling at me. How creepy was that?

"Gahh! What on Earth is going on?" I asked.

"What's going on is that I'm talking to you! Yeah, that's right! Me, the infinity gem that you so callously shot into several pieces!"

All right, that smiley face I was talking about earlier? It was now frowning at me. Super creepy stuff.

"How is that even possible? You're just supposed to be a shiny piece of rock, for crying out loud!"

"I was an infinity gem, duh! I was one of the most powerful objects and you just shot me to pieces! That was just not nice!"

I shrugged my shoulders at the giant, shiny and angry rock in front of me.

"Look, Mr. Infinity Gem. I'm sorry, ok? I'm really sorry that I shot you to pieces. Now, I'm stuck in this Roblox world for it, so it's not like you're the only one suffering."

"Exactly, Deadpool. When you so callously gunned me down, I was shattered into several pieces! Once that happened, the shock of breaking apart, and the power inside me, teleported you and my pieces here to Roblox

High School!"

"Wait a second. If you're really shattered, how are you talking to me now, and in giant form?"

My question seemed to really annoy the already ticked off infinity gem. It approached me, and seemed to even get bigger than it already was.

"It's a dream, stupid!"

The gem shouted at me so bad, I thought my eardrums would crack. Yeah, word of advice, dear reader: never tick off an infinity gem.

"Ok, ok, I get it. It's a dream. I get it, so I'm waking up now, and just chilling. It was nice talking to you and..."

"You're not getting off that easy! You're only going to wake up when I tell you to! There's more that I've got to say."

"So this is like, the infinity lecture?"

"Something like that."

I rolled my eyes and braced myself. I guess I did kinda deserve this. After all, if I hadn't shot the gem, I would never have gotten involved in any of this.

"All right, Mr. Infinity Gem. Go on. What else do you want

to say?"

"Since you shot me and started this whole thing, I think it's only right that you look for the remaining pieces. They're scattered all over the school, and some of them were transported to some students."

"Like Snyde?"

"Exactly like Snyde. Those may just be fragments, but they contain, well, infinite powers! It allowed a doofus like Snyde to actually make his fantasies a reality, creating Dark Snyde!"

"Oh, I get it! So these pieces of you, they trigger latent powers in the students."

"That depends."

I pulled at my mask with my hands. I didn't like how this infinity lecture was going, and I didn't like the sound of that.

"What do you mean 'that depends'? That's pretty vague, and well, intimidating-like."

"Yeah, you've got every right to be afraid. You see, when you shot me, I didn't shatter evenly. Some shards were smaller than others, and some were larger. The shard that Snyde had wasn't all that big, but it allowed him to make his fantasy a reality. There are some big shards lying out there, and some students might already have them. Some might be in the school just waiting to be discovered."

I immediately remembered Yona, and how she knocked the snot out of Dark Snyde. She was as freaked out with that power punch just as I was. Unless she was practicing karate in her spare time, she must have had one of the shards!

"Yona. She socked Dark Snyde. Does she have one of the shards?"

The Infinity Gem didn't answer and merely smiled at me. His smile was pretty strange. I didn't really know what to make of it.

"What are you smiling at me like that for? Answer the question already!"

"I think it's time you woke up already, Pool. I've already said too much. Time for you to start doing something productive for once in your life, and get searching!"

"Productive in my life? What do you mean?"

"You know what I mean. Start looking already! I forgot to mention, you're not just looking around for the shards to save the kids in high school from potential trouble. You're doing it so you can recreate me, and maybe, just maybe, if you put me back together, I can get you back home."

Now, the Infinity Gem was talking! Putting him back together like Humpty Dumpty suddenly took on a whole new level of importance. After all, getting back home was the most important thing on my mind.

"So you'll get me back home if I find all the shards and put you back together?"

The Infinity Gem flashed that mischievous smile of his again. He made it even worse when he winked at me. Do you know how creepy an all-powerful gem looks like when it winks? Brr! It already sends shivers down my spine just remembering it. What he said next got to me even more.

"Maybe."

"Maybe? What do you mean, maybe? You mean if I put you together there's even a chance that you WON'T get me back home?"

The Infinity Gem just kept smiling and winked at me again.

"Just don't get on my bad side, and we'll see what we can do. Now get to those shards already!"

"Wait. What do you...?"

"See you around!"

The Infinity Gem raised one of its arms and waved at me, like a kid waving good-bye to his parent as he rode the school bus. I didn't even notice that the gem had arms and hands until then.

"Hey, wait! You don't have the right to wake me up! This is my dream!"

That was when I heard a long and piercing screech. It was my alarm clock. I opened my eyes and looked up at the ceiling of my crappy dormitory room.

"What a crazy dream. What was that all about?"

I moved to turn off the alarm clock, and I was shocked to see the time.

"Whoa! I'm an hour late for class! I've got to get going!"

I dashed out of bed and started to dress up. Dressing up didn't take too long, considering that I still had my full costume on, of course, but I was already late! It was time to get back to school and start the daunting task of gathering all the shards of the infinity gem.

Entry #5

Everything Gets Really Crazy.

It was not fun being late and getting a mild lecture from Miss Morrison. Miss Morrison, by the way, was the teacher of our class. She was the one who had to endure Snyde's transformation into Dark Snyde. Speaking of Snyde, when I entered the classroom, I saw him glaring at me. He really gave me a mean stare like he was still going to eat me alive, even if he wasn't Dark Snyde anymore. Okay, he was a lot less intimidating with his small frame and square face, but you could see the pure rage in those eyes, and believe me, that was no fun.

Worse, the other kids sitting beside Snyde were glaring at me as well. I was sure that those must have been Snyde's gang. I guess they didn't like what happened yesterday either. Great, not only would I have to probably deal with

Snyde in the near future, but with his entire gang, as well. This was just getting better and better.

I saw Billy and Jerome as I entered the class, and they greeted me with smiles.

"Tough luck, Deadpool. It's not a good idea being late like that," Billy said.

Jerome smiled and was about to say something, but Miss Morrison interrupted him. She was really angry.

"Mr. Deadpool! You're an hour late! I won't tolerate truancy like this! Go get a late slip from the principal's office!"

"Yes, ma'am. Sorry. I was just..."

"Enough with the excuses. Go get it already!"

"Yes ma'am!"

I looked around at the class and saw Yona, Angela, and Fred. Yona looked quite worried. It was clear that she didn't get much sleep after what happened with Dark Snyde. I would have to talk with her later to get that shard she had.

I raced to the principal's office to claim my truancy slip. The principal was a large and grumpy sort who sat beside a large desk. The moment I entered, he was already glaring at me.

"Deadpool, is it?"

"Yes sir."

"That's Principal Geist to you! You're here to claim your truancy slip, aren't you?"

"Yes sir. I mean, Principal Geist!"

"Let me tell you a little thing about these truancy slips, Deadpool. You accumulate enough of these slips and you're headed for the slammer!"

"The slammer? What's that?"

The principal leaned over towards me. He looked a lot larger and meaner as he moved closer.

"Believe me, you don't want to know!"

"Yikes!"

He handed me the truancy slip, and I took it with a trembling hand. I gathered all of my courage to ask Principal Geist something that was on my mind.

"Just how many slips does it take to get to the slammer?"

"I'll be the judge of that," he said with a sinister grin.

"Wait, what do you mean you'll be the judge of that? Pardon me, but that could mean that I could get sent to the slammer if I am late again, right? Or maybe never, depending on your mood. Pardon me for saying this, Principal Geist, but that doesn't seem fair."

Principal Geist slammed his fist on the desk, and I could have sworn that the entire office shook.

"You know, the moment I saw you in this school, I knew that you were trouble. I know the troublesome type, and it fits you to a T."

"I'm—I'm trouble?"

"Don't deny it! You know that you're bad news! A lot of strange stuff has been happening at the school, but yesterday was the first time I had to deal with one of the students turning into a flying rodent! Right when you arrived at the school to boot! I would have kicked you out if I could, but this is Roblox High School. No one gets kicked out in a school like this. That does not mean, however, that you can take it easy here. And I can definitely send you to the slammer! So don't make me!"

I could feel the principal's hot breath on me. He was still growling at me, like some giant attack dog kept only in check by some flimsy chain. Principal Geist had no powers, but he didn't need any. He was probably the most intimidating person that I've ever met, in Roblox or otherwise.

"I'll be watching you, Deadpool," he said.

"Y-yes sir. I mean, Principal Geist."

I couldn't wait to get out of that stuffy office. Even after I left the principal's office, I could still feel his eyes on me, and I remembered every word he said. I couldn't believe this. First Snyde and his gang, and now Principal Geist. I was fast making a lot of enemies in Roblox High School. Something told me that this would probably be even worse than my original high school.

After the hair-raising incident with Principal Geist, half of the day seemed to breeze by without much incident. There were subjects about math, literature and history, or at least I thought there was. Most of my head wasn't on the subjects, and I barely listened to what the teachers said. I was too caught up in the day's events and what I had to do to get out of here. So I had to find all the shards to recreate the infinity gem and get back home. I refused to entertain the "maybe" stuff that the gem said in my dream. All that, while trying to avoid getting my butt kicked or being late again. Yeah, a piece of cake.

Before I knew it, lunchtime arrived and I was at the cafeteria with my new friends. There I was with Yona, Angela, Fred, and even Jerome and Billy. I was sitting with Billy and Fred while Jerome, Angela, and Yona were sitting across from us. As usual, Billy hogged most of the bench because of his huge size. Fred and I barely had any room left to sit down.

"Oops. Sorry guys. I know I'm pretty fat. I didn't mean to take up the whole bench. I can stand up if you want so you can sit down better."

Fred and I shook our heads.

"That's all right, big guy. We can manage, right, Pool?" Fred said.

"Yeah, no problem at all."

My butt was almost squeezed off the bench, but I tried not to complain. After all, it wasn't really Billy's fault that he was so big.

"Hey Yona, what happened with Snyde yesterday?" I asked.

It was time to get to the bottom of her powers. After all, I needed all the shards of the gem that I could get my hands on.

"I don't know, you tell me. You're the one that came from another world. I mean, I've never socked anyone that hard before," Yona said.

She was clearly distressed and still affected by what happened. A part of me didn't want to ask her about all that stuff seeing as how affected she was, but I had to do it. After all, it was the only way to get a piece of the shard. After all, it was a piece of the shard that was affecting her.

"Yona, didn't you find anything strange on your person yesterday? You know, like a piece of the shiny stone that I came from?"

"What do you mean?"

"I mean something like this."

I pulled out the shiny shard that fell from Snyde the other day. It glowed so much that everyone's eyes fell on it.

"That was the shard that fell from Snyde yesterday, right? You picked it up!" Billy said.

"Ah, you saw that eh, Billy? Well, I know for a fact that it's the reason why Snyde got his powers in the first place. There are several of these shards scattered all over the school, and some of the kids already have them. It's the only reason why you would have been able to punch Snyde like that, Yona," I said.

"Is that so? Well, I'm afraid you're going to be disappointed then."

"Disappointed? What do you mean?"

"I mean, I don't have a shard like that at all on me."

"What?"

I couldn't believe what I was hearing.

"Are you kidding? Those shards were from the infinity gem that brought me here! They're the only ones that can give anyone in the school powers! You've got to have a piece of it on you."

Yona shook her head firmly.

"I don't. I didn't have any then, and I don't have any now. Maybe that really was what gave Snyde his powers, but that wasn't the case with me."

"Are you sure?"

Yona nodded and gave me a really firm look.

"Positive."

Yona didn't look like she was lying, but I just couldn't

believe her. The infinity gem told me in that freaky dream. The gem shards were scattered everywhere in the school, and they could bring out powers in everyone. It was the only way that someone like Yona would suddenly have the strength to sock the pants out of Snyde. There was no other explanation!

"Look Yona, look again. There's got to be one somewhere with you and…"

"I don't have one at all, Deadpool."

This was really getting sticky. With the way she was denying it, I started to think that maybe Yona was keeping the shard somewhere! Yeah, maybe she'd gotten used to the feeling of so much power and now wanted the shard for herself! Yeah, that had to be the only explanation! I didn't want to be so suspicious of Yona. After all, she was my first friend when I arrived here, but I couldn't let that cloud my judgment. I simply had to find all those shards and get back home!

"Yona, please, you've got to give me that shard. It's the only way I can get home."

"I said I don't have one!"

That was when the real mayhem began. Yona slammed her fist on the table in frustration, and the whole table shook, throwing off all of our food. Yeah, it was another display of super strength from Yona and another sign that she had that shard somewhere.

The food scraps fell everywhere and right where I didn't want them to fall. I watched and saw Billy's sandwich fall right onto Snyde's face, who was sitting at the opposite table. The salami struck his face and it stuck like crazy on his glasses. The juice from Fred's lunch spilled all over one of Snyde's friend's t-shirt, and I saw his face grow red with anger.

"What?! You morons just don't stop getting on our case, do you?"

"You just couldn't stop with Snyde, could you? Now, you want to embarrass all of us as well!"

It was Snyde. He was really angry now, and he was gathering his entire gang towards us. They all had food and stuff all over themselves and they did not look pleased.

Snyde and his gang looked pretty intimidating. Snyde was the smallest member, but he was flanked by three pretty large dudes, and two other guys. One of the dudes was shaved bald with nothing but his spandex shorts on. Another was dressed in his undies, boots, and a killer mohawk. The third one caught my attention. He was dressed in all red and had a very good looking mask. Now that I think about it, he kinda looked familiar, with the killer red suit and the great looking mask. I mean if I had to wear a mask, I would wear that mask. Wait a minute... Anyway, the one thing in common with these guys? They were all super big and super muscular. All of them were so packed with muscles that they were hunched at the back, and their bodies could barely carry the excess muscle mass and density. They all looked like they could whoop our butts pretty good.

"I'm coming after you morons, and I'm bringing my friends with me too!"

Snyde sounded really serious, and the three bouncers with him looked like they all meant business. The other two guys kinda blended in the background, but who cares about them? It was the three guys that I was worried about, and I was really starting to miss my guns and sword right about now.

"Take them out, boys!"

The three big guys were quickly moving towards us. This little drama caught the attention of the other kids in the cafeteria, and they all started cheering as they anticipated a big slug fest.

"They're coming at us, and they don't look happy," Fred said.

"Billy, you're the only one who can match them size for size. Come on! Take them out!" I said.

"What are you talking about? I've never been in a fight before! I'm not a violent sort of person!"

Billy was shaking like a leaf. He looked ridiculous as he was the biggest one among us, but he was the one who was the most afraid.

"Yona, we sure could use one of those power fists of yours right about now!" Angela said.

"I don't know what came over me then! I can't take on three bruisers like this!"

This was all starting to look very bad. No one was ready to stand up and take on those three bruisers, and everyone else in the cafeteria was starting to cheer. There would be a big lunch fight, one way or the other.

"Okay everyone. There's no need to get all excited. Maybe we can just work this out," I said.

"There ain't nothing to work out. We're just here to kick

your butts for all the trouble you've caused Snyde," the bald guy said.

The one in red crunched his fists together while mohawk guy smiled, revealing some missing front teeth under his moustache.

"This going to be one good butt whooping," the mohawk guy said.

He had a foreign sounding accent, and there was again something familiar about this guy.

"You don't happen to wrestle Siberian bears for fun, do you?" I asked.

"Ivan know not what you're talking about."

"Ah, so you're Ivan? And how about you? And you? You know, I especially like that outfit you're wearing. It kinda reminds me of this really cool Merc with a Mouth that I know. Only if he stuffed himself full with 10 Big Macs all at once."

Okay, I confess that I always love to crack jokes and run my mouth when I get tense. I know, I know. It's probably not the best habit to practice, considering how often I get myself into trouble. Well, I simply couldn't help myself. There I was, running my mouth as those giants approached us. I couldn't help but get tense.

The big red guy that resembled my favorite Merc with a Mouth did not take kindly to my taunts. He threw me a solid left hook that hit me right on the face. It was a direct hit, and I went flying across the canteen. I slammed into a nearby lunch table to the delight of some kids in the canteen. I thought I heard Yona and Angela shrieking in the distance, but I couldn't tell. I was so beat up and sore from the punch that I saw stars for a few moments.

I could hear the kids in the canteen cheering wildly as I tried to pick myself up.

"Direct hit! Direct hit!"

"He got him good!"

"Come on, get up! Lunch fight! Lunch fight!"

I wiped the snot from my mask as I tried to get back up. I was covered in all sorts of food and drink now, and believe me, a lot more hurt than just my pride. The big red guy could hit, and hit hard.

"Okay. I'm going to let you get away with that for now, on account of your really good looks. We don't really need to resort to violence and such. We can..."

Before I could complete the sentence, Ivan picked me up

by the mask and raised me up in the air. He threw me down to the ground while still clutching my head. Ouch. 'Nuff said.

"Ivan going to enjoy this!" he said.

"Leave some for me!"

It was the bald guy. He picked me up by the waist and threw me German suplex style to the ground while still holding onto my waist. Double ouch.

The kids were wild with excitement now. There was a big fight unfolding in front of them, and it was all they could do to keep it together.

"Come on! More! More!"

"Yona! Billy, do something! They're kicking poor Deadpool's butt!" Angela said.

"Why are you all looking at me? I just punched Snyde yesterday and slammed the table now. That doesn't make me some kind of badass warrior-girl all of a sudden!"

"And I've always been a peace-loving guy! I'm not one who resorts to violence!" Billy said.

In all the confusion, I didn't notice Snyde and the two other guys behind him move towards Yona and the others. The shard that I had pulled from Snyde was lying on the floor. Apparently I had dropped it in all of the confusion and excitement.

"Give me that shard."

I saw Snyde approach the others and demand for the shard. He spoke in a strange, flat voice, almost as if someone else was inside of him. He sounded like he would do anything to get the shard, and it showed. He was drawn to it, like some metal to a magnet, or a moth to a flame. To make matters worse, he wasn't the only one drawn to the shard.

"What a pretty shard."

"That looks like a pretty stone. I want it."

The two of them sounded as entranced as Snyde was now, and they all wanted a piece of the shard. Not good at all. Not good, and about to get even worse.

"That shard is mine!"

It was Snyde. Suddenly, his voice grew even louder and I saw his ears point upwards. I thought I saw fangs replace his teeth, and his wings grow from his arms again. Apparently, exposure to the shard was triggering his rat powers again.

"Yona! Do something! Snyde's going all Dark Snyde again!" Billy said.

"You do something! I don't have the super strength I had before! I just don't feel it in me anymore!"

"How can you say that?" Jerome asked.

"It's not there! I can just feel it. It's…"

Before Yona could finish, Snyde flapped his wings really hard. The wings generated a powerful whirling effect, tossing everyone aside. The winds from his wings were so powerful that everyone was blown back, even the crowd of kids around us. Strangely enough, the single shard of the infinity gem remained lying on the floor. It wasn't moved at all, and something told me that it was almost calling to Snyde for him to get it again.

"Come to Poppa!" Snyde said.

He moved towards the shard on the floor with full confidence. He was almost on top of the shard now, and all he had to do was pick it up. Snyde was almost full Dark Snyde all over again now. Everyone was knocked to the floor, including me and my opponents. The kids all around us weren't chanting like madmen anymore. Something in the way Snyde had turned and flapped his wings made them realize that there was a genuine threat here. There was real trouble now, and no one could do anything to stop it.

Just as he was about to grab the shard, there was the sound of someone kicking the cafeteria door open.

"Stop this madness, right now!"

I looked up from the floor and instantly recognized Principal Geist. He was standing above all of us now, and I just realized how big he really was. Geist, Billy, Snyde's friends, yeah. This was a high school of pretty big giants.

Snyde turned towards Principal Geist and smiled at him.

"Principal Geist. I'm so glad that you could make it here today. Now you will witness my full transformation into…"

Principal Geist moved towards Snyde and threw the most powerful right cross I've ever seen. The punch was solid, and it sent Snyde flying. He landed on several kids, and he was knocked out instantly. I also noticed that his transformation stopped abruptly.

"Stupid kid. If you stopped yapping and simply picked up that shard, maybe I would have been in trouble. Well, you didn't, and now it's time that I keep the shard for safekeeping."

Principal Geist approached the shard and took it for himself. There was nothing any of us could do.

"Principal Geist! No! You don't know how powerful that shard is!" I said.

He turned toward me and smiled.

"Oh I know how powerful this thing is for sure, Deadpool! Don't even try to lecture me about stuff like this. Remember, I am the principal of this school, and you're just a troublesome student!"

The shard seemed to grow brighter and pulse in the principal's hand. He didn't turn into a giant rat like Snyde did, but there was no way I could tell how the shard was already affecting him.

"Principal Geist, you don't know what you've done! You can't take that shard!" I said.

"And you can? There's no way I'm giving you this shard, Deadpool. And as for you and everyone involved in this little free-for-all, it's detention!"

Detention. I didn't like the sound of that, but there was nothing I could do. Principal Geist was already a strong and powerful dude, and now he had the shard. There was no telling just how powerful he would get. Add to that the fact that there were several shards still out there, and my work was really cut out for me. Plus, I was going to detention with all my friends and enemies. Yeah, everything really gets crazy now.

If you enjoyed this book, please leave a review on Amazon! It would really help me with the series.

Best,

Robloxia Kid

Printed in Great Britain
by Amazon

59738552R00286